Seven Theories of Human Nature

LESLIE STEVENSON

Seven Theories of
Human Nature

NEW YORK AND OXFORD
OXFORD UNIVERSITY PRESS

OXFORD UNIVERSITY PRESS
Oxford   London   Glasgow
New York   Toronto   Melbourne   Wellington
Nairobi   Dar es Salaam   Cape Town
Kuala Lumpur   Singapore   Jakarta   Hong Kong   Tokyo
Delhi   Bombay   Calcutta   Madras   Karachi

Preface

THIS is an introductory book, intended simply as a rapid tour of a fascinating intellectual landscape. If it whets the reader's appetite for more detailed exploration, and helps him to start doing it for himself, then I shall have fulfilled my purpose. I assume no previous knowledge of the topics covered.

Librarians will find it hard to classify this book. Though written by a philosopher, it treats some writers and subjects not counted as philosophical in the academic sense. And though it considers some psychological theories, it could hardly count as a general introduction to psychology. It even strays into questions of biology, sociology, politics, and theology, thus overstepping the conventional faculty boundaries between arts, sciences, social science, and divinity. To use the word which is presently fashionable, it is 'interdisciplinary'. Perhaps it is best described as an extended exercise in what I have called 'applied philosophy' (in *Metaphilosophy* I: 3, July 1970, 258–67), that is, the application of conceptual analysis to questions of belief and ideology which affect what we think we ought to do, individually and socially. Inevitably, questions of pure philosophy are raised and not answered; I hope that some readers will be led into pursuing them further.

My thanks are due to my colleagues Keith Ward, Bob Grieve, and Roger Squires for their critical comments on parts of the manuscript, to my father Patric Stevenson for suggestions about style, to my students at the University of St. Andrews for their testing of my ideas and exposition, to Ena Robertson and Irene Freeman for efficient typing, and to my wife Pat for everything.

St. Andrews,   LESLIE STEVENSON
October 1973

TO MY PARENTS

Contents

PART ONE   Introduction

CHAPTER 1

Rival Theories

WHAT is man? This is surely one of the most important questions of all. For so much else depends on our view of human nature. The meaning and purpose of human life, what we ought to do, and what we can hope to achieve—all these are fundamentally affected by whatever we think is the 'real' or 'true' nature of man. But there are many conflicting views about what human nature really is. 'What is man that Thou art mindful of him ... Thou hast made him a little lower than the angels, and hast crowned him with glory and honour', said the author of Psalm 8 in the Old Testament. The Bible sees man as created by a transcendent God who has a definite purpose for our life. 'The real nature of man is the totality of social relations', said Marx (in his theses on Feuerbach in 1845). Marx denied the existence of God and held that each individual is a product of the human society he lives in. 'Man is condemned to be free', said Sartre, writing in France in the 1940s. Sartre denied the existence of God, but also denied that we are determined by our society or by anything else. He held that every human individual is completely free to decide for himself what he wants to be and do.

Different views about human nature lead naturally to different conclusions about what we ought to do and how we can do it. If God made us, then it is His purpose that defines what we ought to be, and we must look to Him for help. If we are made by our society, and if we find that our life is somehow unsatisfactory, then there can be no real cure until society is transformed. If we are fundamentally free and can never escape the necessity for individual choice, then the only realistic attitude is to accept our situation and make our choices with full awareness of what we are doing.

Conflicting beliefs about the nature and purpose of human life are often embodied in different ways of life, in political and economic systems, and in educational theory and practice. The official version of Marxist theory so dominates life in the communist countries that nobody can publicly question it without endangering his job or his freedom. And children there have it so firmly drummed into them that it may seem to them ever afterwards to be obviously the truth. In the so-called 'free' or 'democratic' countries we easily forget that it is only three centuries or less since Christianity occupied a similar position here. People who publicly dissented from the orthodox version of Christianity could suffer discrimination, persecution, or even death. In some countries Roman Catholicism is still the belief that is taught in all schools, and accepted by the Government as limiting legislation on social matters such as divorce and contraception. Even in a so-called 'secular' society such as contemporary Britain, Christianity retains an official place in the educational system, and the Church of England is the established church. 'Existentialist' views, like Sartre's, are not thus embodied in institutions, for it would be foreign to a theory which emphasizes human freedom to make it an orthodox system to be imposed and taught. Yet such a theory naturally suggests that we should allow as much individual freedom as possible, so it does have implications for social and educational policy.

Let us look a bit more closely at Christianity and Marxism as two rival theories of human nature. Although they are radically different in content, there are some remarkable similarities in structure, in the way the parts of each doctrine fit together and give rise to ways of life. Firstly, they each make claims about the nature of the universe as a whole. Christianity is of course committed to belief in God, a personal being who is omnipotent, omniscient, and perfectly good, who created and controls everything that exists. Marx denied all this, and condemned religion as 'the opium of the people' which distracts them from their real social problems. He held that the universe exists without anybody behind or beyond it, and is fundamentally material in nature, with everything determined by the scientific laws of matter.

As part of their conception of the universe, both Christianity and Marxism have beliefs about the nature of history. For the Christian, the meaning of history is given by its relation to the eternal. God uses the events of history to work out His purposes, revealing himself above all in the life and death of Jesus. Marx claimed to find a pattern of progress in human history which is entirely internal to it. He thought that there is an inevitable development from one economic stage to another, so that just as feudalism had given way to capitalism, capitalism would give way to communism. Thus both views see history as moving in a certain direction, though they differ about the nature of the moving force and the direction.

Secondly, following from the conflicting claims about the universe, there are different descriptions of the essential nature of the individual human being. According to Christianity, he is made in the image of God, and his fate depends on his relationship to God. For each man is free to accept or reject God's purpose, and will be judged according to how he exercises this freedom. This judgement goes beyond anything in this life, for somehow each individual person survives the physical death that we know. Marxism denies any such survival of death and any such judgement. It must also deny the importance of that individual moral freedom which is crucial to Christianity, for according to Marx our moral ideas and attitudes are determined by the kind of society we live in.

Thirdly, there are different diagnoses of what is basically wrong with mankind. Christianity says that the world is not in accordance with God's purposes, that man's relationship to God is disrupted. He misuses his freedom, he rejects God, and is thus infected with sin. Marx replaces the notion of sin by that of 'alienation', which conveys a similar idea of some ideal standard which actual human life does not meet. But Marx's idea is of alienation from oneself, from one's own true nature, since men have potential that the conditions of capitalist society do not allow them to develop.

The prescription for a problem depends on the diagnosis of the basic cause. So, fourthly, Christianity and Marxism offer completely different answers to the ills of human life. The Christian believes that only the power of God Himself can save us from our state of sin. The startling claim is that in the life and death of the particular historical person Jesus, God has acted to redeem the world and restore men's ruptured relationship with Himself. Each individual needs to accept this divine forgiveness, and can then begin to live a new regenerate life in the Christian church. Human society will not be truly redeemed until individuals are thus transformed. Marxism says the opposite, that there can be no real change in individual life until there is a radical change in society. The socio-economic system of capitalism must be replaced by that of communism. This revolutionary change is inevitable, because of the laws of historical development; what the individual should do is to join the revolutionary party and help shorten the birth pangs of the new age.

Implicit in these rival prescriptions are somewhat differing visions of a future in which man is totally regenerated. The Christian vision is of man restored to the state that God intends for him, freely loving and obeying his Maker. The new life begins as soon as the individual accepts God's salvation and joins the Church, the community of the redeemed. But the process is only completed beyond this life, for both individual and community will still be imperfect and infected with the sin of the world. The Marxist vision is of a future in this world, of a perfect society in which men can become their real selves, no longer alienated by economic conditions, but freely active in co-operation with each other. Such is the goal of history, although it should not be expected immediately after the revolution, since a transitional stage will be needed before the higher phase of communist society can come into being.

We have here two systems of belief which are total in their scope. Both Christians and Marxists claim to have the essential truth about the whole of human life; they assert something about the nature of all men, at any time and in any place. And these world views claim not only assent but also action; if one really believes in either theory, one must accept that it has implications for one's way of life.

As a last point of comparison, note that for each belief-system there is a human organization which claims the allegiance of believers and asserts a certain authority on both doctrine and practice. For Christianity there is the Church, and for Marxism the Communist Party. Or to be more accurate, there are now many Christian Churches and many Marxist parties, making competing claims to follow the true doctrine of their founder, defining various versions of the belief as orthodox, and following different practical policies. Such sect-formation is typical of both beliefs.

Many people have noted this similarity in structure between Christianity and Marxism, and some have suggested that the latter is as much a religion as the former. There is food for thought here for believers of both kinds, and for the uncommitted person too. Why should such very different accounts of the nature and destiny of man have such similar structures? Perhaps the differences can be reconciled to some extent, for there are those who claim to be Christian Marxists. But in the traditional interpretations of each belief, there are very basic disagreements about the existence of God and the nature of man.

But, as I have already suggested by quoting Sartre, there are many more views of man. The theories of the ancient Greeks, especially of their great philosophers Plato and Aristotle, still influence us today. More recently, Darwin's theory of evolution and Freud's psycho-analytic speculations have permanently changed our understanding of ourselves. And modern philosophy, psychology, and sociology continue to offer further theories about human nature. Outside the Western intellectual tradition, there are the ancient Chinese and Indian concepts of man, among many others.

Some of these views are embodied in human societies and institutions and ways of life, as Christianity and Marxism are. If so, they are not just theories, but ways of life, subject to change and to growth and decay. A system of belief about the nature of man which is thus held by some group of people as giving rise to their way of life is standardly called an 'ideology'. Christianity and Marxism are certainly ideologies in this sense, but existentialism does not seem to be, since there is no obvious social group for whom it defines a way of life.

An ideology, then, is more than a theory, but is based on a theory of human nature which somehow suggests a course of action. What I want to do in this book is to examine certain influential theories which thus prescribe action as well as claim belief. Not all of them are ideologies, since not all have a corresponding group of people who hold the theory as giving rise to their way of life. But the theories I have selected to discuss all exhibit the main elements of that common structure we have seen in Christianity and Marxism: (1) a background theory of the nature of the universe; (2) a basic theory of the nature of man; (3) a diagnosis of what is wrong with man; and (4) a prescription for putting it right.

Only theories that combine such constituents offer us hope of solutions to the problems of mankind. For instance, the single assertion that all men are selfish is a diagnosis, albeit a brief one, but it offers no understanding of why we are selfish and no suggestion as to how we can overcome it. Similarly, the prescription that we should all love one another gives no explanation of why we find it difficult. The theory of evolution, although it has a lot to say about man and his place in the universe, does not in itself give any diagnosis or prescription.

The theories I am going to examine include those of Christianity, Marx, and Sartre. To them I add those of Plato's *Republic* (one of the most influential books of all time and one of the most readable works of Greek philosophy), of Freud (whose psycho-analytical theories have affected so much of the thought of this century), of B. F. Skinner (the American professor of psychology who claims to have the key to the problems of human behaviour), and of Konrad Lorenz (the Austrian Nobel Prize-winner who has given new direction to the study of animal behaviour, and has led a recent fashion of explaining human nature by analogy with apes and other animals). In each case I cannot hope to trace the many antecedents of each view, although I shall try to sketch the essential background briefly. Nor can I survey the many varieties of Christian, Marxist, existentialist, and psycho-analytic theory. I shall simply try to introduce the key ideas of each, interpreting it through the four-part structure outlined above. In each case I shall take one readily available book as my basic text, and shall make references to it so that the reader can check my assertions and find out more for himself. I shall also suggest further reading relevant to each theory. Some readers will be disappointed that I do not discuss any Eastern views. To them I plead ignorance and shortness of time, and recommend a book described below.

But as well as expounding the basic ideas, I want to suggest some of the main difficulties in them. So for each theory there will be some critical discussion which will, I hope, encourage the reader to think further for himself. Before we begin our main task let us take another preliminary look at the cases of Christianity and Marxism, in order to see what may happen when we begin to criticize theories of human nature.

FOR FURTHER READING

Christianity and Marxism will be discussed in more detail later in this book, and further reading on each will be suggested. But for the comparison between them as belief-systems, the following can be recommended: *Philosophy and Myth in Karl Marx*, by Robert C. Tucker (Cambridge University Press, Cambridge, 1st edn. 1961, 2nd edn. 1973) (see especially the introduction), and *Marxism and Christianity*, by Alasdair MacIntyre (Penguin Books, Harmondsworth, 1971; Schocken Books, New York, 1969).

For more on the notion of ideology see *Ideology*, by John Plamenatz (Macmillan, London, 1971; Praeger, New York, 1970).

For introductions to Jewish, Chinese, Indian, and Islamic theories of human nature see *The Concept of Man*, edited by S. Radhakrishnan and P. T. Raju (George Allen & Unwin, London, 2nd edn. 1966; Johnsen Publishing Co., Lincoln, Nebr., 1966).

CHAPTER 2

The Criticism of
Theories

THE basic Christian assertion about the universe, that God
exists, is of course faced with many sceptical objections. To
take one of them, the existence of evil in the world seems to
count against the existence of God. For if He is omniscient He
must know of the evil, and if He is omnipotent He must be
able to remove it, so if He is perfectly benevolent why does He
not do so? In particular, why does God not answer the prayers
of believers for the relief of the manifold sufferings all over the
world? The basic Marxist assertion about the universe, that
there is an inevitable progress in human history through stages
of economic development, is just as open to scepticism. Is it
really at all plausible that such progress is inevitable, does it
not depend on many non-economic factors which are not predetermined? In particular, communist revolutions have not
occurred in the industrialized countries of Western Europe, so
is this not direct evidence against Marx's theory?

Christian and Marxist claims about the nature of the individual man immediately raise large metaphysical problems. Is
the individual really free, and responsible for his actions? Or is
everything about him determined by his heredity, upbringing,
and environment? Does the individual person continue to
exist after death or not? In the face of the universal and obvious fact of human mortality, the alleged evidence for survival is slim and highly controversial. But can the materialist
view that men are made of nothing but matter really be
true?

Doubts also arise about the respective prescriptions for
man's problem. The Christian claim that a particular historical figure is divine, and is the means of God's reconciliation
with the world, defies all human rationality. The Marxist belief that communist revolution is the answer to the problems of
humanity attaches almost as great a cosmic significance to a
particular historical event. In neither case is the cosmic claim
supported by the subsequent history of those individuals, insti-

tutions, or nations in which the regeneration is supposed to be taking effect. For the history of the Christian Church down the ages, and of Russia since 1917, show a mixture of good and evil like all other human history. The practice of Christian or communist life has not eliminated muddle, disagreement, selfishness, persecution, tyranny, torture, and murder.

These common objections to each ideology are pretty well worn by now. What is interesting is that neither belief has disappeared in the face of them. Admittedly, Christianity has suffered a steady erosion of influence over the last few centuries; and perhaps only a small proportion of the population of the communist countries could count as convinced believers in Marxist theory. But both theories are still very much alive, for there are many Christian believers and many Marxist believers, each on both sides of the iron curtain. They have not vanished from the industrialized countries, in the way that witchcraft and astrology have vanished, except from the inside pages of Sunday newspapers!

How and why is it that a significant number of non-lunatics continue to believe in Christianity or Marxism? Firstly, the believers usually find some way of explaining away the standard objections. The Christian says that God does not always remove evil, or answer our prayers, for what may seem bad to us may ultimately be for the best. The Marxist may say that revolution has not occurred in the West because the workers have been 'bought off' by the concession of higher standards of living, and have not realized that their true interest is in the overthrow of capitalism. Disputes about the great metaphysical questions of determinism or free will, materialism or immortality, seem able to go on for ever without dislodging any side from its position. To the doubts about the respective prescriptions, the believers can reply that the full regeneration of man is still to come, and that the terrible things in the history of Christianity or communism are due to perfection being not yet achieved. By thus explaining away difficulties in his theory and appealing to the future for vindication, the believer can maintain his belief with some show of plausibility. The theorists of Church and Party become well practised at such justification of the ways of God, or of the Party.

Secondly, the believer can take the offensive against criticism, by attacking the motivations of the critic. The Christian can say that those who persist in raising intellectual objections to Christianity are being blinded by sin, that it is their own pride and unwillingness to receive the grace of God that prevents them from seeing the light. The Marxist can similarly say that those who will not recognize the truth of Marx's analysis of history and society are being deluded by their 'false consciousness', the ideas and attitudes which are due to their economic position in society. Capitalist society will naturally produce a 'bourgeois class-consciousness' among those who benefit from it, which will prevent them from acknowledging the truth about their society. So in each case, a critic's motivations can be analysed in terms of the theory he is criticizing, and the believer can dismiss the criticism as based on illusion.

These are two of the main ways in which a belief can be maintained in the face of intellectual difficulties. If a theory of human nature is maintained by the two devices: (1) of not allowing any conceivable evidence to count against the theory; (2) of disposing of criticism by analysing the motivations of the critic in terms of the theory itself, then I shall say that the theory is being held as a 'closed system'. It appears from the above that Christianity and Marxism can be held as closed systems—but this is not to say that all Christians or Marxists hold their belief in that way.

Why should people maintain a belief in the face of difficulties? Inertia, and unwillingness to admit that one is wrong, must play some part here. If one has been brought up in a certain belief and way of life, or if one has been converted to it and then followed it, it takes courage to abandon one's past. When a belief is an ideology, giving rise to the way of life of a social group, it will always be difficult for the members of the group to consider it objectively. There will be strong social pressures to continue to acknowledge the belief, and it will be natural for believers to maintain it as a closed system. People will feel that their belief, even if open to objections, contains some vital insight, some vision of essential truths. To abandon it may be to abandon what gives meaning, purpose, and hope to one's life.

Is it possible then to discuss various theories of human nature rationally and objectively, as I am setting out to do in this book? For when such theories are embodied in ways of life, belief in them seems to go beyond mere reasoning. Indeed, it can make itself apparently impregnable to criticism by the above devices of the closed system. The ultimate appeal may be to faith or authority, and there may be no answer to the questions 'Why should I believe this?' or 'Why should I accept this authority?' which will satisfy someone who is not already inclined to believe. The project of this book may therefore seem to be doomed from the start, if we jump to the conclusion that there can be no objective discussion of rival ideologies.

However I believe that such despair would be premature. For one thing, not all the theories I am going to discuss are ideologies at all, and when they are not there is much less likelihood of their being held as closed systems. But more importantly, even when a belief becomes an ideology and is perhaps held as a closed system by some believers, I think we can see that rational discussion is still possible for those who are prepared to try it. For we can always distinguish what someone says from his motivation for saying it. The motivation may be important in various ways, for instance if we wish to understand the personality of the speaker and the nature of his society. But if we are primarily concerned with the truth or falsity of what is said, and with whether there are any good reasons for believing it, then motivation is irrelevant. The reasons that the speaker may offer are not necessarily the best reasons. There is nothing to stop us discussing what he says purely on its own merits.

This is why the second feature of closed systems noted above, the technique of meeting criticism by attacking the motivation of the critic, is fundamentally irrational. For if what is being discussed is whether the theory is true, or whether there are good reasons for believing it, then the objections that anyone produces against it must be replied to on their own merits, regardless of their possible motivations. Someone's motivation may be peculiar or objectionable in some way, and yet what he actually says may be true, and justifiable by good reasons. Even if motivation *is* to be considered, to analyse it in terms of the theory under discussion is to assume the truth of the theory, and therefore to beg the question. An objection to a theory cannot be defeated just by reasserting the theory.

The first feature of closed systems, the explaining away of all evidence against the theory, must also be looked at with some suspicion. We often feel that such 'explaining away' is not really very convincing, except to someone who is already disposed to believe in the theory. (Consider how Christians may answer the problem of evil, and Marxists the problem of why no revolutions have occurred in the West.) We must try to see when such explaining away is rationally justifiable, and when it is not. To do this, we must decide what *sort* of statement is being made, before we can discuss the relevance of alleged evidence for or against it.

Firstly, a statement may turn out to be a value judgement, saying what *ought* to be the case, rather than a statement of fact, about what *is* the case. For example, suppose someone says that homosexuality is unnatural. It might be objected to him that in almost every known human society there is a certain amount of homosexuality. Suppose he replies that this does not disprove what he says, since it involves only a minority in each society. Perhaps the objector will suggest that it is possible that a majority of a society might indulge in homosexual as well as heterosexual activity (and that this seems to have been the case in ancient Greece). The reply may be 'I would *still* say it is unnatural'. Such a reply suggests that the speaker is not after all asserting anything about what people actually do, but is expressing an opinion about what they ought to do (or ought *not* to do!). This impression would be confirmed if we find that the speaker reacts with horror against anyone described as homosexual. If what is being asserted is thus really 'evaluative' and not factual, then evidence of what actually happens does not disprove it, for it is perfectly consistent to say that what does happen should not happen. But in order for the statement to be rightly allowed to be thus impervious to evidence, it must be recognized as a value judgement, as not even *attempting* to say what *is* the case. And if so, then it cannot be *supported* by evidence either, for what actually happens is not necessarily what should happen.

Statements about human nature are especially subject to this kind of ambiguity. Indeed, the words 'nature' and 'natural' should be regarded as danger signals, indicating possible confusion. If someone says 'Human beings are naturally X', we should immediately ask him 'Do you mean that all or most human beings *are* actually X, or that we *should* all be X, or what?'. In thus distinguishing value judgements from statements of fact, we need not imply that they are merely expressions of individual taste, that they cannot be given objectively valid reasons (whether for or against). The nature of value judgements—whether they can be 'objective', whether they are ultimately distinct from factual statements—is one of the central questions of moral philosophy, and I am not prejudging it here. I am just pointing out that the above kind of clarifying question is often essential when discussing theories of human nature.

There is a second, quite different, way in which a statement may correctly be held to be impregnable to contrary evidence, and that is if it is matter of definition. For instance, if someone says that all men are animals, it is not clear how any conceivable evidence could count against him. Suppose that the theory of evolution were not true, that it were found that we do not after all have a common ancestry with any other species. Would we not still count as animals, albeit a special kind of animal, since we live, feed, breed, and die like all other animals? Suppose robots were made to walk and talk like men, but not of course to feed and breed like us. Clearly they would not be animals, but could they count as men either? It looks as if nothing could be *called* a man unless he could also be called an animal. If so, the statement that all men are animals does not really make any assertion about the facts about men, but only reveals part of what we mean by the word 'man'. It is true by definition, true in virtue of meaning alone. In philosophers' terminology, it is 'analytic' (it can be shown to be true by analysis of the meaning of its terms). If a statement is thus analytically true, it is quite correct to say it cannot be refuted by any conceivable evidence, but neither of course can it be proved by evidence, for it does not *attempt* to say anything about the state of the world.

The example of 'All men are animals' shows that a statement which appears to be saying something about the facts of human nature may really be only a concealed definition. Not all matters of definition are trivial, however. If a word is already used with a standard meaning in the language, it will be extremely misleading for anyone to use it with a different meaning, unless they give us explicit warning. Sometimes theories introduce new terms, or use old words in new ways, and it will then be very necessary for definitions to be given, and for it to be made clear that they are definitions, not claims about any sort of fact. And definitions may have consequences which are not immediately obvious, for instance if it is analytic that all men are animals and that all animals feed, then it is analytic that all men feed. Analytic statements, then, can have their uses, but only if they are clearly distinguished from 'synthetic statements' which make genuine assertions about the facts. There has been a debate among philosophers about whether this distinction is as clear as it seems at first, and even about whether there ultimately is any such distinction. But without entering into that difficult theoretical question here, I think we can see that if someone maintains that all men are X and dismisses without investigation any suggestion that some men might not be X, then we must ask him 'Is it part of your definition of a man that he must be X, or would you allow the conceivability of some man being discovered not to be X?'. Only if he admits it to be a matter of definition can he be allowed to dismiss evidence without further investigation.

Value judgements and analytic statements, then, are not the sort of statements which can be proved or disproved merely by investigating the evidence. If a statement *can* thus be proved or disproved by evidence—and that must mean ultimately by what someone can observe using his senses of sight, touch, sound, smell, and taste—it is called by philosophers an 'empirical' statement. By use of the above clarifying questions it should usually be possible to elucidate whether a statement is evaluative or analytic rather than empirical. The really difficult cases are when a statement does not seem to fall into any of these three categories. Consider again the Christian assertion of the existence of God and the Marxist assertion of an inevitable progress in history. It is pretty clear that these assertions are trying to say something about what is the case, to assert some fundamental truth about the nature of the universe. Their proponents will hardly admit them to be value judgements or mere matters of definition. Yet it is not clear that these assertions are genuinely empirical either, for as we have seen above, although there would seem to be a very great deal of evidence which might well be thought to count against each one, their proponents often do not accept this as contrary evidence but find ways of explaining it away. Now if a believer in a theory seems ready to explain away *all possible* evidence against it (making additions to his theory if necessary) we begin to feel that he is winning too easily, that he is somehow breaking the rules of the game. How can a statement really assert something about the facts unless it is in principle open to testing by observation of some kind?

This is why many philosophers have felt attracted to what has been called 'the verification principle', which states that no non-analytic statement can be meaningful unless it is verifiable by observation (value judgements were dismissed as not really statements at all, only expressions of emotion). If one accepts this principle, one will dismiss any so-called 'metaphysical' statement, which is neither analytic nor empirical, as not just false but meaningless. The questions of the existence of God, and of an inevitable progress in history, and many others (including ones more directly about human nature, such as the existence of an immortal soul) were indeed dismissed as meaningless by the 'logical positivists' (as the proponents of the verification principle were called). Yet many others have thought that this is too short a way with such big questions, and so one of the major philosophical debates in this century has been about whether the verification principle should be accepted.

In so far as any conclusion can be drawn from that debate, it is that although it is very important to distinguish between statements that are analytic or empirical and those that are neither, we cannot dismiss all the latter as meaningless. They are too mixed a bag, and many deserve individual attention. There is fairly general agreement that testability by observation is a criterion not of meaningfulness, but of a statement's being *scientific*. And the emphasis has come to be put on falsification rather than verification, because the essence of scientific method is that hypotheses can be disproved by observation and experiment. No theory can count as scientific unless one can conceive of some observation which would tell *against* the theory, *if* that observation were made. So if a believer in God or in progress in history, or in immortal souls, will not admit that any conceivable evidence could count against his claim, then we can say that his theory is unfalsifiable and therefore not a scientific one.

To call a theory unscientific is not necessarily to condemn it. But it does mean that it cannot claim what well-established scientific theories can claim—that the evidence of our senses makes it irrational not to accept it. Many theories of human nature which have been claimed to be scientific may turn out not to be, because not falsifiable. And if so, this is a very important fact to establish about them, for it removes one of the standard reasons for accepting a theory. There may perhaps be other reasons which might be offered for accepting a non-scientific theory, but we ought to examine them very carefully. Now that we are armed with these distinctions between the evaluative, the analytic, and the empirical (i.e. scientific) we can begin our critical examination of particular theories of human nature.

FOR FURTHER READING

My use of the notion of a 'closed system' is derived from that of Arthur Koestler, in *The Ghost in the Machine* (London, 1967; Pan paper back, 1970; Regnery Gateway paperback, Chicago, Ill.), p. 300. (This book contains many interesting but highly controversial assertions about human nature on topics discussed in Chapters 8 and 9 of this book.)

For the classic statement in English of the verification principle, and of the meaninglessness of ethical and theological statements, see A. J. Ayer, *Language, Truth, and Logic* (first published in 1936, now in Penguins; Dover paperback, New York).

The falsifiability criterion of a theory's being scientific is due to Karl Popper. See his book *The Logic of Scientific Discovery* (first published in 1934, now available in paperback from Hutchinson—London, 1959, revised edn. 1968; Harper & Row Torchbook paperback, New York), especially Chapters I–V. (Later parts of the book become highly technical.)

For an easy introduction to moral philosophy, see J. D. Mabbott, *An Introduction to Ethics* (Hutchinson, London, 1966).

For philosophical doubts about the analytic–synthetic distinction, see the essay 'Two Dogmas of Empiricism', by W. V. O. Quine, in his *From a Logical Point of View* (Harper & Row Torchbook paperback, New York, 2nd edn. 1961). But the reader must be warned that this is philosophers' philosophy, which really presupposes some acquaintance both with philosophical discussions of the past, and with elementary modern logic. This comment also applies to the readings from Ayer and Popper recommended above. Bryan Magee's book on Popper (Modern Masters Series, Fontana, London, 1973; Viking, New York, 1973) gives an easier introduction to some of these questions.

PART TWO   Seven Theories

CHAPTER 3

Plato: The Rule of
          the Wise

LET us start our examination of rival theories of man by considering that of Plato (427–347 B.C.) as an example of the four-fold pattern of claim about the universe, claim about human nature, diagnosis, and prescription. Although so old, it is still of contemporary relevance, for, whenever anyone asserts that the cure for our problems is that we should be ruled by those who really know what's best, then he is asserting the essence of Plato's theory.

A short sketch of Plato's background will help us to understand the origin of his ideas. He was born in the Greek city state of Athens, which had for some time enjoyed economic prosperity through its trade, democratic government in the time of Pericles, and unprecedented advances in intellectual inquiry culminating in the great ethical philosopher Socrates. But Plato grew up in a period of war, which ended in defeat for Athens and a brief period of tyranny. When democracy was restored Socrates was condemned to death on a charge of impiety and corrupting the youth. Socrates' teaching was akin to that of the Sophists, who claimed to teach the art of rhetoric or persuasion, an art which was particularly useful in Athenian democracy. The Sophists also discussed moral and political theory, and among the opinions commonly expressed was a scepticism about whether any moral or political rules were more than arbitrary conventions, in view of the different practices in different societies (known to the Athenians through trade). Socrates' main concern was with how we can know the right way to live, and in this he much influenced Plato, who was deeply shocked at the execution of his teacher for his allegedly subversive questioning of conventional opinions. Disillusioned with contemporary politics and philosophy, Plato sought both knowledge of the truth about the universe, and the cure to the ills of society. The conclusions he reached are put into the mouth of Socrates in the many philosophical dialogues which Plato wrote, and were taught in the

Academy he founded, which was in effect the world's first university.

Deservedly the most famous of Plato's dialogues is the *Republic*, in which he outlines his conception of the ideal human society. In the course of the book, he gives his view on many topics, including philosophy, morals, politics, education, and art. It is mainly this dialogue that I will consider here, and I will use the traditional numbering system (reproduced in nearly all editions and translations) for references to the text. I will first expound the main doctrines, and then criticize them in turn.

THEORY OF THE UNIVERSE

Although Plato mentions God, or the gods, at various places, it is not clear how seriously he takes them, whether singular or plural. When he does talk of God in the singular, it is pretty clear that he does not mean anything like the personal God of Christianity, and even this impersonal notion of God does not play much of a role in the argument of the *Republic*.

What is really central to Plato's concept of the universe is his theory of Forms. This can be summarized under four aspects—logical, metaphysical (to do with what is ultimately real), epistemological (to do with what can be known), and moral. How is it that one word, e.g. 'cat', can truly apply to many different individual things? Plato's answer is that corresponding to each such general word there is one Form, e.g. the Form Cat, which is something different from all the individual cats (596). What makes these particular animals cats is their resemblance to, or 'participation in', the Form Cat. This is the logical aspect of the theory—an answer to a question about the meaning of general words, the so-called 'problem of universals'.

The metaphysical aspect is that these Forms are held to be more real than material things, for they do not change or decay. The Forms are not in space or time, and they are not perceivable by any of the senses (485, 507, 526–7). Plato's vision was that beyond the world of changeable and destructible things there is another world of unchanging eternal Forms. The things we can see and touch are only very distantly related to these ultimate realities, as he suggested by his famous comparison of the human condition with that of prisoners chained facing the inner wall of a cave, so that all they can see are mere shadows of objects in the cave, knowing nothing of the world outside (515).

However Plato thought that by a process of education it is possible for human minds to attain knowledge of the Forms. The epistemological aspect of the theory is that only this intellectual acquaintance with the Forms can really count as knowledge, since only what fully exists can be fully known. Perception of impermanent material things is only belief or opinion, not knowledge (476–80).

The most convincing illustration of these three aspects of the theory of Forms comes from the Euclidean geometry with which Plato was familiar. Consider how it deals with lines, circles, and squares, although no physical object is perfectly straight, circular, or square but may always have some irregularity. Theorems concerning these ideal objects—straight lines without thickness, perfect circles, etc.—are proved with absolute certainty by logical arguments. So here we have indubitable knowledge of timeless objects which are the patterns that material objects imperfectly resemble.

It is the moral aspect of the theory of Forms that plays the most important role in Plato's theory of human nature and society. Consider moral words such as 'courage' and 'justice': as for all general terms, Plato will distinguish the many particular actions which are courageous or just, and the many different individual people who might be said to be courageous or just, from the Forms Courage and Justice. The general word is true of just those actions or people who in some way exemplify the corresponding Form. And rather as in the geometrical examples, no action or person is an absolutely perfect example of courage or justice, because of the truism that nobody is morally perfect. So the moral Forms set the objective moral standards by which human conduct and character should be judged. The word 'good' is the most general moral word, so the Form Good is pre-eminent among the Forms, and plays an almost God-like role, being the source of all reality, truth, and goodness (505–9). The absolute standards set for us by the Forms are not just for individuals, but for the whole of social and political life, they define the ideal form of human society (472–3). The theory of Forms, then, is Plato's answer to the intellectual and moral scepticism of his time. It is one of the most persuasive statements of the power of the human intellect to attain genuine knowledge about the universe and about the goals of human life and society. It can be seen as the culmination of Greek confidence in the intellect and Socratic concern with ethics.

THEORY OF HUMAN NATURE

Plato is one of the main sources for the 'dualist' view of man, according to which the soul or mind is a non-material entity which can exist apart from the body. He maintained that the human soul is indestructible, that it has existed eternally before birth and will exist eternally after death. These doctrines are stated in the *Republic* (608-11), but Plato's main arguments for them are stated in other dialogues, especially the *Meno* and the *Phaedo*. The doctrine of the immateriality and immortality of the soul is not central in the *Republic*, but it goes naturally with Plato's contrast of the world of Forms with the world of perceivable things. For he held that it is the soul, not the body, which attains knowledge of the Forms, and which is the concern of ethics.

More central to the argument of the *Republic* is the doctrine of the three parts of the soul (435-41). Consider cases of mental conflict, such as when someone is very thirsty but does not drink the available water because he knows it is poisoned. Plato argues that there must be one element in the person's mind which is bidding him drink, and a second which forbids him; the first is called desire or Appetite (by which is intended all the physical desires, such as hunger, thirst, and sexual desire), and the second is called Reason. The existence of the third element in the mind is proved, Plato thinks, by other cases of mental conflict where a person feels angry or indignant with himself, for instance in the story he tells of the man who felt a fascinated desire to look at a pile of corpses and yet was disgusted with himself for wanting to. Plato maintains that what is in conflict with his Appetite here is not Reason but a third element which he variously calls indignation, anger, or Spirit. He thinks that children show Spirit long before they display reasoning; it is something like self-assertion or self-interest, and is usually on the side of Reason when inner conflict occurs. Reason, Spirit, and Appetite are present in every person, but according to which element is dominant we get three kinds of men, whose main desire is, respectively, knowledge, success, or gain (581).

Plato has clear views about which of these three elements ought to be the dominant one. As one would expect from his view of the Forms as the ultimate realities knowable only by intellect, it is Reason that Plato thinks ought to control both Spirit and Appetite. But each part of the soul has its proper role to play; the ideal for man is a harmonious agreement between the three elements of his soul, with Reason in control (441-2). This ideal condition Plato describes by the Greek word *dikaiosune*, which is standardly translated as 'justice'; there can be no exact English translation, but as applied to the individual person, perhaps 'well-being' or even 'mental health' convey better the sort of concept Plato uses. Like Socrates before him and much Greek philosophy after him, Plato's emphasis is on the intellect, on knowledge. But this emphasis is simultaneously on the moral, because of his view that virtue, how to live well, is a matter for human *knowledge* rather than just conflicting opinion. There is such a thing as the truth about how we ought to live, and this truth can be known by the human intellect when we achieve knowledge of the perfect unchanging immaterial Forms.

The chief remaining feature of Plato's theory of the nature of man is that we are ineradicably social. The individual person is not self-sufficient, for he has many needs which he cannot supply for himself. Even on the level of the material needs for food, shelter, and clothing, one person can hardly supply all these things for himself with absolutely no reliance on others. Such a person would be spending most of his time in the struggle for survival, he would have little left for distinctively human activities such as friendship, play, art, and learning. Again, there is the manifest fact that different individuals have different aptitudes and interests; there are farmers, craftsmen, soldiers, administrators, etc., each fitted by nature, training, and experience to specialize in one kind of task. Such division of labour is vastly more efficient than the somewhat unrealistic alternative (369-70). According to Plato, and again this is a typical Greek view, to live in society is natural to man; anything else is less than human.

DIAGNOSIS

The Forms define Plato's ideals for man and human society, and when he looks at the facts he finds that they are very far from these ideals. Most individual people do not manifest that harmony of the three parts of the soul which Plato calls 'justice'. Nor do human societies manifest that harmony and stability which he also calls 'justice'. Plato devotes a section of the *Republic* (543–76) to a diagnosis of the various types of imperfect society and the corresponding types of imperfect individual. In a 'timarchic' society such as that of Sparta it is the ambitious, competitive, soldierly kind of person who succeeds, and intelligence is not valued. In an 'oligarchy', political power is in the hands of the rich, and the successful individual is the grasping money-maker. Plato took a very jaundiced view of democracy as he understood it, influenced no doubt by his experience of Athenian politics. He thought it absurd to give every person an equal say, since not everyone is equally knowledgeable about what is best for society. He criticizes the typical individual in a democratic society as lacking in discipline, living only for the pleasures of the moment. Tyranny, Plato thinks, is the typical sequel to the anarchy and chaos resulting from the unbridled liberty of democracy; one leader gains absolute power and maintains it by such unscrupulous means that the most criminal elements in human nature find their expression in the violent kind of society that results. Plato concludes that each of these types of man and society departs further from the ideal and reaches a further level of unhappiness (576–87).

The defects in human nature which Plato diagnoses are intimately related to the defects he finds in human societies. I doubt if one can attribute to him either of the simple views that individuals are to blame or that society is basically wrong. He would say, rather, that the two are interdependent. An imperfect society produces imperfect individuals, and imperfect individuals make for an imperfect society. One cannot have 'justice' in the state without having it in individuals, nor vice versa. For justice is the same thing in both cases—a harmony between the natural constituents, each doing its own job (435); and, correspondingly, injustice is disharmony. The problem, then, is how to establish harmony in individual and state.

PRESCRIPTION

'There will be no end to the troubles of states, or of humanity itself, till philosophers become kings in this world, or till those we now call kings and rulers really and truly become philosophers, and political power and philosophy thus come into the same hands' (473). This is the essence of Plato's prescription, as he states it himself. He is aware that it sounds absurd, but given his theory of Forms and his theory of human nature we can see the rationale for it. If there is such a thing as the truth about how we ought to live, and if this truth can be known by those who are able and willing to learn, then those who have this knowledge are the only people who are properly qualified to direct the running of human society. Philosophers are those who have attained this knowledge by coming to know the Forms, so if society is governed by philosophers, the problems of human nature can be solved. The perfect state is that which is ruled by perfect men, and the notion of perfection here contains the intellectual and the moral and political rolled into one. So the *Republic* is at one and the same time a blueprint for the perfect state, and an analysis of the nature of philosophy—that moral and intellectual knowledge which, Plato thinks, makes a perfect man.

In order to produce such perfect individuals, an elaborate system of education is necessary (376–412 and 521–41). Plato is thus the first of those who see education as the key to constructing a better society. And like many after him, he envisages various stages of education, the higher stages being open only to those qualified to undertake them, the élite who will be the future rulers of society. For these latter, the emphasis is on mathematics and philosophy, those disciplines which lead the mind to knowledge of the Forms and to a love of the truth for its own sake. The élite thus produced will prefer to do philosophy rather than anything else, but they will respond to the call of duty and will apply their knowledge to the running of society. After experience in subordinate offices, they will be ready for supreme power. Only such lovers of truth will be impervious to temptations to misuse their power for personal gain, for they will value the happiness of a right and rational life more than any material riches (521).

What then of the rest of society—the non-élite? There are

various functions which have to be performed, and a division of labour is the natural and efficient way of organizing this. Plato makes a basically threefold division of his ideal society (412–27). Besides the philosopher rulers, there is to be a class traditionally called the Auxiliaries, who perform the functions of soldiers, police, and civil servants. It is they who will put the directions of the Rulers into effect. The third class has no special name, but will contain the workers of all kinds— farmers, craftsmen, traders, etc., all those who produce the material necessities of life. The division between these three classes will be strict; in fact, Plato says that the 'justice' or well-being of the society depends on each person performing his own proper function and not interfering with others (432–4). Like the well-being of the individual, which Plato treats of immediately afterwards in analogous fashion, the health of society consists in a harmonious working together of its three main constituents. He says that his purpose in founding the state is not to promote the happiness of any one class, but, so far as possible, of the whole community (420). He thinks that the state will be harmonious and stable only if the strict three-fold class-division is maintained, so each class must be persuaded that it is their business only to perfect themselves in their own job, and they must be content with such degree of happiness that their place in society permits (421).

CRITICAL DISCUSSION OF PLATO'S THEORY

The *Republic* is one of the most influential books of all times. The above sketch can only give a sample of the richness and diversity of the ideas it contains, and can be no substitute for a reading of the book itself. But I now want to go on to outline some of the main points of doubt about Plato's theory, diagnosis, and prescription, in order to start the reader thinking about them critically.

We need not enter into the many logical, epistemological, and metaphysical problems of the theory of Forms—these are still the subject of technical discussion by professional philosophers. But the moral aspect of the Forms is central to our purpose here, for we have seen that the theory that there is such a thing as the truth about how men ought to live is fundamental to Plato's treatment of the problems of human nature. Now it hardly needs saying that this assumption is a controversial one. Many people down the ages to the present day maintain that many, if not all, of the questions in morals and politics have no universally 'true' answers. It may be said that what is right varies from society to society, or that there is no one right answer even within a given society. So that if two people give different answers to moral questions then there is no truth and falsity of the matter, only a difference in taste, like one person liking beer and another preferring cider. This whole question of the objectivity of value judgements is of course fundamental in moral philosophy, and is the subject of continuing dispute. So we must ask whether Plato has given us any adequate reason to believe that there are objective standards in morals and politics. Since he gives no direct argument for this conclusion, this must be one of the most fundamental points of doubt about his theory.

Even if there are such objective standards, Plato's theory requires also that there are rational methods to find out what they are (the education of the philosopher-rulers is supposed to teach such methods). But what if educated men sincerely disagree about fundamental questions of morals and politics—as we know very well that they often do. Is there any rational way of showing which is the right view? Plato has hardly shown that there is such a method of settling disagreements. He himself seems almost to pass beyond rationality in some places, when he talks of philosophers eventually attaining a vision of the Form of the Good itself, which will illuminate them like the blinding light of the sun (508–9). But what if in such 'vision' different philosophers claim to see different things—is there any way of determining which is right, or can there be only a conflict of opposing claims? When someone thinks he knows the ultimate truth about some important question, it is easy for him to be intolerant of anyone who disagrees, and even to feel justified in forcing his view on those who disagree (as the history of religious controversies bears witness). Plato thinks that philosophers are capable of knowing the absolute truth about how to rule society, and are therefore justified in wielding absolute power. Such a view is in striking contrast to that of Socrates, who was always conscious of how much he did *not* know, and claimed superiority to unthinking men only in that he was aware of his own ignorance where they were not.

There is much that can be questioned in Plato's theory of individual human nature. Is the soul a non-material thing? Is it immortal and indestructible? In what sense, if any, can the soul be said to have parts? And is the threefold division into Reason, Spirit, and Appetite adequate? Only about the latter question shall I say anything more here. Threefold divisions have been popular in several theories of human nature, and perhaps Plato's will do as a first approximation, distinguishing some elements in human nature which can conflict with each other. But it is hardly a rigorous or exhaustive division, even if one relabels the parts in modern terms as intellect, personality, and body. Emotion is something that involves all three, for instance.

There are, I think, two main criticisms to be made of Plato's blueprint for his ideal society. The first concerns his requirement that perfect men—philosopher-kings—should have absolute political power. But is there really any guarantee that any process of education, however well designed and well executed, can produce absolutely perfect men? Plato's view that philosophers will be such lovers of truth that they will never misuse their power seems naïvely optimistic. Do we not need to set up a political system which will guard against the possibility of the misuse of power? Given that all men are imperfect in some way, is it not unrealistic to base a blueprint on the idea that there could be perfect men? Any realistic political system must deal with men as they are, not men as we would like them to be. Plato seems to ask himself the question 'Who is qualified to wield absolute power?' but should we not rather ask the question 'How can we ensure that nobody has absolute power?'. Plato dismisses democracy rather quickly and unfairly; admittedly he is thinking of Athenian-type democracy in which every citizen would have a vote on every decision, which would indeed be a cumbersome if not impossible system in a state of any size. But the basic idea of modern parliamentary democracies—that a government must submit itself for re-election within a certain fixed period of time—provides the kind of safety mechanism for dismissing rulers which is totally absent from Plato's *Republic*. Democracy of this kind may be inefficient and imperfect in various ways, but is not the alternative of absolute power with no guarantee against its misuse very much worse?

The second criticism is that Plato seems more concerned with the harmony and stability of the whole state than with the well-being of the individuals in it. We have already noted one place where he says something like this (420); at 519–20 he says

The object of our legislation is not the welfare of any particular class, but of the whole community. It uses persuasion or force to unite all citizens and make them share together the benefits which each individually can confer on the community; and its purpose in fostering this attitude is not to enable everyone to please himself, but to make each man a link in the unity of the whole.

These passages can be interpreted in innocuous and in sinister ways. We are usually in favour of 'community spirit', of each person contributing something to the well-being of the whole society, and of certain laws (e.g. against murder and theft) being enforced on all. But Plato's blueprint seems to envisage rather more than this, in his strict threefold class division and his insistence that the harmony and stability of the state requires that each person fulfil his allotted function and that alone. The ruler must rule, even if that is not what he would really like to do, and similarly the auxiliaries must be auxiliaries, and the workers must work. This is what Plato calls 'justice' in the state, and it is not at all what we mean by the term, which implies something like equality before the law, and fair shares for all. If the worker is not content to be a worker and have no share whatsoever in politics, then Plato would, I think, forcibly compel him to remain in his station. And the advantage is not all on the side of the rulers and auxiliaries either, for they are not permitted either private property (416) or family life (457). It does seem then that Plato is prepared to deny many of what are widely thought to be essential requirements for individual happiness, in the interests of setting up a stable state which conforms to his ideals. But what is the point of a stable society unless it serves the interests of the individuals in it? Stability and efficiency are valuable, but they are certainly not the only criteria, or even perhaps the most important, for the well-being of a society.

So Plato's practical political programme of giving unrestricted power to a wise élite must be severely criticized. And his philosophical theory of Forms is subject to many philosophical objections. But his general ideas that human reason can attain knowledge through education, and that such knowledge is not only valuable in itself but can contribute to the wise government and reform of society, are ones with which almost everyone will now agree. Perhaps we do not realize that we owe these conceptions to Plato more than to anyone else.

FOR FURTHER READING

Basic text: *Republic* (many translations and editions). The translation by H. D. P. Lee in the Penguin Classics series (Penguin, London, 1955) helpfully divides up the text by subject matter. Other dialogues of Plato are also available in the same series. In the U.S. see the translation with introduction and notes by F. M. Cornford (Oxford University Press paperback, New York).

For a general introduction to Plato's philosophy, see *The Philosophy of Plato*, by G. C. Field (Oxford University Press, London, 2nd edn. 1969). This also contains further bibliography.

For a hostile attack on Plato's political programme, see *The Open Society and Its Enemies*, Volume 1, by K. R. Popper (Routledge & Kegan Paul, London, 4th revd. edn. 1962; Princeton University Press paperback, Princeton, N.J.). Anyone reading this will recognize the source of many of my criticisms of Plato.

CHAPTER 4   Christianity: God's
            Salvation

In the introductory chapters I suggested that Christianity contains a theory of the universe, a theory of man, a diagnosis, and a prescription; and I have already mentioned some of the standard objections. Christian doctrines have of course changed and developed over the two thousand years of their history, and the present time is perhaps a particularly confusing one, when there is wide disagreement about just what the essential doctrines are. Within the three main divisions (Roman Catholicism, Eastern Orthodoxy, and Protestantism) there are many more subdivisions, and even inside any particular sect one can find differences over doctrine. Although all will acknowledge their derivation from the Old and New Testaments, and to some extent from the early Creeds and statements of the Church, there is disagreement about in what sense these sources are authoritative and definitive. In this chapter I shall not attempt any systematic exposition of Christian doctrine (anyone who wants to learn of this should read the Bible, and the statements of faith of the various churches). What I shall try to do is to disentangle from misinterpretation some of the claims which I take to be essential to any belief which is to deserve the name 'Christian'. And at the same time I will point to some of the main difficulties that those claims face, so in this chapter criticism will be intertwined with exposition.

THEORY OF THE UNIVERSE

First, then, let us consider the basic Christian claim about the nature of the universe, that God exists. What *sort* of God is thus asserted to exist? Not, surely, a God who is literally 'up there', located somewhere in space and time. When the Russian cosmonauts reported that they hadn't met God in their space travels, this was surely no genuine evidence against Christianity. The Christian God is certainly not supposed to be one object among others in the universe; He does not occupy a position in space or last for a certain length of time. Neither is He to be identified with the whole universe, the sum total of everything that exists, as some writers (e.g. Spinoza) have said. This is pantheism, not Christianity. Traditionally, the Christian God is transcendent as well as immanent—although in some sense present everywhere and all the time, He is also beyond or outside the world of things in space and time (Psalm 90:2, Romans 1:20). Some contemporary theologians seem prepared to deny this, and to define God as ultimate reality, the ground of all being, or as that which concerns us ultimately; but such definitions seem to be quite compatible with what was traditionally called atheism! We even hear of people calling themselves 'Christian Atheists'. It does appear that in the effort to accommodate Christianity to the modern mind, such doctrines really deny what they are trying to defend.

The transcendent existence of God is, then, essential to Christianity. But there are genuine philosophical difficulties about the doctrine. It was once widely supposed that there were valid arguments to prove the existence of God, but Hume and Kant destructively criticized those arguments in the eighteenth century. Some Christians (mostly Roman Catholics) have continued to claim to be able to prove the existence of God, but the validity of their arguments is of course hotly disputed by non-believers. Many Christians will now agree that God's existence can be neither proved nor disproved by reason alone, that belief in Him is a matter for faith rather than argument.

But still, *what* is it that one believes when one believes in God? This is where the crucial modern debate about meaningfulness and verifiability begins. If God is transcendent, He is of course not visible or tangible, or observable by any of the methods of science. But He is not a mere abstraction like numbers and the other objects of mathematics, for He is supposed to be a personal Being who loves us. If, then, neither empirical observation nor purely logical reasoning can count for or against His existence, just what is being asserted by the believer in God? In Chapter 2 we noted how the suffering and evil in the world would seem to be evidence against there being an omniscient, omnipotent, and benevolent God, and yet the Christian does not necessarily count this as telling against his belief. He may say that out of suffering greater good may come in the end, or that the possibility of evil must be there if men are to be genuinely free to make moral choices. But the non-believer may still wonder why God could not have made the world such that suffering was not the only way to good, and such that men would freely have chosen rightly. So it does look as if the Christian does not take his belief in God to be falsifiable by evidence about the actual state of the world.

Another vital part of the Christian doctrine of God is that He created the world (Genesis 1:1, Job 38:4). (This presupposes His transcendence, for the world could hardly be created by a part, or even the whole, of itself.) But it is a misinterpretation of this doctrine to say that it implies that the Creation was an event in time. Modern theologians are not necessarily dismayed by cosmological theories which imply that the universe has no beginning in time. And it is now widely accepted that the story of the creation of man in Genesis is myth (symbolic of deep religious truths) rather than history, so there is no incompatibility with the theory of evolution, despite the storm raised on the subject in the nineteenth century. Any Christian who still asserts the historical existence of Adam and Eve is insisting on an over-literal interpretation of the words of Scripture. But the question remains, just what *is* meant by saying that God is the creator of the world, and of man? It seems to imply that if God did not exist, the world would not exist; and that the world is somehow fundamentally in accordance with God's purpose, that there is nothing which exists save by His design or at least by His permission. It was once common to argue that the world, especially the world of living things, is very much as if it had been designed by a very intelligent and powerful Creator. But Hume and Kant effectively destroyed this 'Argument from Design'; and modern biological science has provided convincing alternative explanations of the marvellous adaptation of living systems to their environment. So theologians nowadays are much less inclined to test the doctrine of God's creation of the world by observation of the state of the world. But this raises again the question of what *sort* of statement the Christian doctrine of Creation is.

According to the verification principle, mentioned in Chapter 2, if a statement is neither verifiable by observation nor provable by logic alone then it is not literally meaningful, it cannot assert anything about what is the case, but is at best a poetic use of language, an expression of attitudes or emotions. Now some Christians have been content to say that all they are doing when they say that God exists is to affirm an attitude, perhaps that love is the most important thing in the universe, or that we should behave *as if* the universe were ruled by a loving God. But an atheist might also be willing to hold such attitudes, while still disagreeing about whether God actually does exist. Any belief which is to deserve the name of Christianity must be doing *more* than merely express an attitude, vital though attitudes and actions are.

Other Christians accept the challenge of the verifiability criterion of meaningfulness, and try to meet it by suggesting that in certain human experiences—moral or religious or mystical—there is the possibility of empirical verification of God. But it will inevitably be highly controversial how to describe such experiences, and the non-believer will naturally find great difficulty in interpreting any human experience in terms of a transcendent God. Another suggestion has been that in the life after death we shall be able to verify the existence and nature of God, by something like observation. But this is to meet one verifiability problem by posing another, for how can we *now* verify, or find evidence for, the reality of life after death?

Theologians who are aware of more recent work in philosophy will question the verification principle itself as an adequate criterion of meaningfulness. But they will still have to reckon with the philosophically more acceptable principle that any *factual* or *scientific* statement must be falsifiable. If the assertion of God's existence is such that no conceivable evidence could count against it, then it is hard to see how it can be an assertion of what is the case about the universe. Most believers will agree that their belief is not a scientific one, and many are attracted to the idea of science and religion giving not rival but *complementary* accounts of the universe, describing the same ultimate reality from different sides, as it were. However this still does not explain how religious statements can give any kind of *description* of reality, if they are not in principle falsifiable. This remains as one of the most basic philosophical problems about religion, and this is why so much of the contemporary discussion in the philosophy of religion centres round the question of the nature of religious language. Having thus introduced the problem, we shall have to let it rest there in this book.

THEORY OF MAN

The Christian doctrine of man sees him primarily in relation to God, who has created him to occupy a special position in the universe. Man is made in the image of God, to have dominion over the rest of creation (Genesis 1:26); he is unique in that he has in him something of the self-consciousness and ability to love freely which is characteristic of God Himself. God created man for fellowship with Himself, so man fulfils the purpose of his life only when he loves and serves his creator.

But although man is thus seen as fundamentally distinct from the rest of creation, he is at the same time continuous with it (if this is not a contradiction!). He is made of 'dust from the ground' (Genesis 2:7), i.e. of material stuff. It is a common and recurrent misinterpretation of Christian doctrine that it asserts a dualism between the material body and an immaterial soul or mind. Such dualism is a Greek idea (we have noticed it in Plato in Chapter 3), and is not to be found in the Old or New Testaments. In the early centuries of the Church, Christian theology began to employ ideas of Greek philosophy in its formulations of doctrine, and the theory of the immaterial soul did find its way into Christian thinking and has tended to stay there ever since. Christianity is of course committed to the idea of life after death, but it is heterodox to think of this as the survival of an immaterial soul after the death of the material body. The Creeds explicitly state belief in the resurrection of the *body*, and the scriptural warrant for this is in 1 Corinthians 15:35 ff., where St. Paul says that we die as physical bodies but are raised as spiritual bodies. Of course it is not clear what a spiritual body is, but St. Paul does use the Greek word *soma*, which means 'body'.

This belief in life after death by resurrection of the body is, I think, another of the essential doctrines of Christianity. To interpret the doctrine just as 'the evil that men do lives after them', or to take the promise of eternal life (John 4:14) as only of a new way of life in this world, is to evacuate the doctrine of one of its essential contents. The humanist can join with the Christian in seeking a regeneration of man as we know him, an escape from selfishness and pride; it is the hope of a survival of the individual person into the eternal dimension which is distinctively Christian. But as before, this essential transcendent element in the Christian claim runs into philosophical difficulties. If bodies are resurrected, presumably, being *bodies* of some kind, they have to occupy space and time of some kind. Now it is surely not meant that they exist somewhere in the space in which we are located—no Christian should expect a spaceman to be able to come across the resurrected bodies of St. Paul, Napoleon, or Auntie Agatha! So it seems that what we have to try to make sense of is the idea that there is a space in which resurrected bodies exist which has no spatial relations with the space in which we exist. The question of time is at least as difficult. Presumably it is not necessarily intended that there is some time in the future at which the resurrection will take place (although when Paul says 'we shall all be changed, in a moment, in the twinkling of an eye, at the last trumpet' (1 Corinthians 15:51–2) it does sound rather like this). Is there then a time system which has no temporal relation to us, or are the resurrected bodies timeless, in which case what sense can be made of the idea of resurrected *life*? (For life, as we understand it, is a process in time.)

It is another misinterpretation of the Christian doctrine of man to identify the distinction between good and evil with that between spirit and body, or mind and matter. This view that all matter is basically evil is not a Christian one, even if it had its influence on early Christian thought. St. Paul's distinction between spirit and flesh (Romans 8) is not between mind and matter, but between regenerate and unregenerate man. We shall look at the idea of regeneration in a moment.

The most crucial point in the Christian understanding of human nature is the notion of freedom, the ability to love, which is the image of God Himself. Plato (and Greek philosophy in general) puts the emphasis on the intellect, on the ability of man to attain knowledge of theoretical and moral truth; the true purpose of human life is thought to be attainable only by such as are able to gain such knowledge. Christianity, in contrast, puts the emphasis, not just on morality or virtuous living, but on the foundation in character and personality from which such life proceeds. The attainment of the true purpose of human life—love of God, and life according to His will—is open to all regardless of intellectual ability, (1 Corinthians 1:20). 'If I understand all mysteries and all knowledge ... but have not love, I am nothing' (1 Corinthians 13:2). This love (for which the Greek word was *agape*, formerly translated as 'charity') is not to be identified with merely human affection of any kind, it is ultimately divine in nature, and can be given only by God.

DIAGNOSIS

Given the Christian doctrine of man as made by God, the Christian diagnosis of what is basically wrong with man follows easily. He has sinned, he has misused his God-given free-will, he has chosen evil rather than good, and has therefore disrupted his relationship to God (Isaiah 59:2).

But again this doctrine of the fall of man needs disentangling from misinterpretation. The Fall is not a particular historical event—the Genesis story of Adam and Eve, the snake and the apple, is myth rather than historical narrative. It is a symbol of the fact that all men are subject to sin, that there is a fatal flaw in our very nature. But this doctrine of 'original sin' does not imply that we are totally and utterly depraved, that we can do nothing good. It is that nothing we can do can be perfect by God's standards: 'All have sinned, and fall short of the glory of God' (Romans 3:23). Sin is *not* basically sexual in nature, although ever since St. Augustine there has been a tendency in Christian thought to identify sin with the lusts of the flesh. Sex has its rightful place within Christian marriage; the true nature of sin is nothing essentially bodily, but rather the assertion of man's will against God's and his consequent alienation from God.

The Fall of man somehow involves the whole creation in evil (Romans 8:22); everything is in some way 'short of the glory of God'. But it is not necessary for Christians to postulate some kind of personal Devil to express this idea of cosmic Fall. And it is heresy to believe in twin and equal powers of good and evil; for the Christian, God is creator of all, and is ultimately in control of all. But this belief runs directly into the problem of evil, which we have already noted.

PRESCRIPTION

The Christian prescription for man is based on God, just as much as the theory and diagnosis is. If God has made man for fellowship with Himself, and if man has turned away and broken his relationship to God, then only God can forgive man and restore the relationship. Hence the typically Biblical idea of salvation, of a regeneration of man made possible by the mercy, forgiveness, and love of God. In the Old Testament there is the covenant made between God and His chosen people (Exodus 19: 5), by which God redeems them from their bondage in Egypt and promises that they will be His people if they keep His commandments. When the Jews fail to obey God's laws, there comes the idea of God using the events of history, such as defeat by neighbouring nations, to chastise them for their sin (a theme which recurs throughout the histories and prophets in the Old Testament). And then there is the idea of God's merciful forgiveness, His blotting out of man's transgressions, and His regeneration of man and the whole of creation (Isaiah chapters 43–66).

But it is in the New Testament, in the life and work of Jesus, that we find the distinctively Christian (rather than Jewish) idea of salvation. The central claim is that God was uniquely present in the particular human being Jesus, and that God uses his life, death, and rising again to restore men to a right relationship with Himself. No belief can properly call itself Christian unless it accepts the essential content of these claims. It is not enough to say that Jesus was a great man, a man of genius, or even a man of supreme religious genius above all others before or since. The Christian claim is traditionally expressed in the doctrine that Jesus is the Son of God, both human and divine, the eternal Word made Flesh (John 1: 1–18). The early philosophical versions of this doctrine— two natures in one substance, and so on—are perhaps not essential. But the basic idea of incarnation, that God is *uniquely* present in Jesus, is. And equally essential is the idea of atonement, that the particular historical events of the life, death, and resurrection of Jesus (and their continual representation by the Christian Church) are the means by which God reconciles His creation to Himself. It is not enough to say that Jesus' life and death are an example to us all. It is implied that

the resurrection of Jesus really happened (1 Corinthians
15: 17), however flagrant the contradiction with all the known
laws of nature. (The idea of the Virgin Birth is just as improbable, but perhaps less important.)

These doctrines of incarnation and atonement defy human
rationality, and indeed their formulation has provoked much
disagreement within Christianity. How can a particular person
be a member of the transcendent Godhead? The Christian
doctrine of the Trinity—that there are three persons in one
God (Father, Son, and Holy Spirit)—multiplies the conceptual
problems rather than solves them. The standard thing to say,
of course, is that these are mysteries rather than contradictions,
that human reason cannot expect to be able to understand the
infinite mysteries of God, that we only believe in faith what
God has revealed of Himself to us. But the trouble with this
kind of statement is that it can appeal only to those already
disposed to believe, it can do nothing to answer the genuine
conceptual difficulties of the sceptic. The same applies to atonement: not many Christians will interpret this like the propi-
tiatory sacrifices of the Old Testament, as if God requires
blood to be shed (any blood, even that of the innocent) before
he will forgive sins. But it is still an enormous mystery how the
crucifixion of a Jewish religious teacher at the hands of the
Roman governor Pontius Pilate somewhere around A.D. 30 can
effect a redemption of the whole world from sin.

The Christian prescription is not quite complete, however,
with the saving work of Jesus Christ. It remains for this salvation to be accepted and made effective in each individual person, and to be spread throughout the world by the Christian
Church. Each person must accept the redemption that God has
effected for him in Christ, and become a member of the
Church, the community in which God's grace is active. Different Christian traditions have emphasized individual acceptance and Church membership respectively, but all will agree
that both are necessary. Thus the regeneration of man and
world takes effect: 'if anyone is in Christ, he is a new creation'
(2 Corinthians 5: 17). There is not necessarily a single experience of conversion in each individual, nor does regeneration
take place all at once; it must be a lifelong process, which looks
beyond this life to the resurrection of the body for its comple-
tion and perfection (Philippians 3: 12).

A final conceptual problem (or mystery) arises over the parts played by man and God in the drama of salvation. The fundamental Christian conception is certainly that redemption can only come from God, through His offering of Himself in Christ. If we are saved, we are saved by this free grace of God, not by anything that we can do ourselves (Ephesians 2 : 8). Yet, just as clearly, the Christian doctrine is that man's will is free; it is by his own choice that he sinned in the first place, and it must be by his own choice that he accepts God's salvation and works out its regeneration in his life. The New Testament is full of exhortations to repent and believe (Acts 3 : 19), and to live the life that God makes possible through the regenerating power of the Holy Spirit (Galatians 5 : 16). There is thus a tension, if not a contradiction, between the insistence that all is due to God and the exhortation that salvation depends on man's response. St. Augustine emphasized the former, and Pelagius the latter; in this controversy the problem of the freedom of the will arises as a crucial internal problem for Christian theology. Although Pelagius was condemned as heretical, the doctrine of human free will must still remain as an essential element in Christian belief, difficult as it is to reconcile with the theory of the complete sovereignty of God.

Many thinking Christians would acknowledge that there are all these conceptual problems in the essential Christian doctrines. But they would emphasize that Christianity is more than a theory, it is a way of life; and though it may be called an ideology, it is not a political ideology like Marxism. They remain practising Christians, and accept the basic theory despite its difficulties, because of what they find in the life and worship of the Church: a certain growth in the inner or 'spiritual' life which they do not find elsewhere. There can be no complete assessment of Christianity unless this is considered.

FOR FURTHER READING

Basic text: The Bible (many versions and translations); I have been quoting from the Revised Standard Version. A commentary such as *Peake's Commentary on the Bible* will help to elucidate many difficulties. So will *The New Oxford Annotated Bible with the Apocrypha: Revised Standard Version*. An Ecumenical Study Bible, edited by Herbert G. May and Bruce M. Metzger (Oxford University Press, New York, 1974).

The Existence of God, edited by John Hick (Collier–Macmillan, London, 1964; Macmillan paperback, New York), is a collection of readings from classic authors on the traditional arguments for and against the existence of God, together with some readings from modern authors on the verifiability question.

Philosophy of Religion, by John Hick (Prentice-Hall, Englewood Cliffs, N.J., 2nd edn. 1973, paperback), is an introductory book which concentrates attention on the Judaic–Christian concept of God and admirably surveys the contemporary philosophical discussions of it.

Both these books contain further bibliographies.

CHAPTER 5

Marx: Communist
Revolution

IN comparing Marxism to Christianity in the introductory chapters I have already sketched some of the main ideas of Marxism and some of the hackneyed objections to them. In this chapter I would like to go a little deeper by giving an introduction to Marx's life and work, followed by a critical analysis of his theory of history, theory of man, diagnosis, and prescription. I shall not attempt to define or discuss the many subsequent varieties of Marxism and communism; I concentrate on the ideas of Karl Marx himself. (Although Marx and Engels wrote some works in collaboration, there is no doubt that Engels's contribution was relatively minor.)

LIFE AND WORK

Karl Marx was born in 1818 in the German Rhineland, of a Jewish family who became Christian; he was brought up as a Protestant, but soon abandoned religion. He displayed his intellectual ability early, and in 1836 he entered the University of Berlin as a student in the faculty of Law. The dominant intellectual influence in Germany at that time was the philosophy of Hegel, and Marx very soon became immersed in reading and discussing Hegel's ideas, so much so that he abandoned his legal studies and devoted himself completely to philosophy. The leading idea in Hegel's work was that of historical development. He held that each period in the history of each culture or nation has a character of its own, as a stage in the development from what proceeded it to what will succeed it. Such development, according to Hegel, proceeds by laws which are fundamentally mental or spiritual; a culture or nation has a kind of personality of its own, and its development is to be explained in terms of its own character. Hegel took this personification even further and applied it to the whole world. He identified the whole of reality which what he called 'the Absolute', or world-self, or God (this is of course a pantheist rather than a Christian concept of God), and interpreted the whole of human history as the progressive self-realization of this Absolute Spirit. 'Self-realization' is thus seen as the fundamental spiritual progress behind all history. It is the overcoming of what Hegel called 'alienation', in which the knowing person (the subject) is confronted with something other than or alien to himself (an object); somehow this distinction between subject and object is to be merged in the process of Spirit realizing itself in the world.

The followers of Hegel split into two camps over the question of how his ideas applied to politics. The 'Right' Hegelians held that the process of historical development automatically led to the best possible results. So they saw the contemporary Prussian State as the ideal culmination of preceding history. Accordingly, they held conservative political views, and tended to emphasize the religious elements in Hegel's thought. The 'Left' or 'Young' Hegelians thought that the ideal had yet to be realized, that the nation states of the time were very far from ideal, and that it was the duty of men to help change the old order and assist the development of the next stage of human history. Accordingly, they held radical political views, and tended to identify God with man, thus taking a fundamentally atheist view. One of the most important thinkers in this direction was Feuerbach, whose *Essence of Christianity* was published in 1841. Feuerbach held that Hegel had got everything upside-down, that far from God progressively realizing Himself in history, the situation is really that the ideas of religion are produced by men as a pale reflection of this world, which is the only reality. It is because men are dissatisfied or 'alienated' in their practical life that they need to believe in illusory ideas. Accordingly, metaphysics is just 'esoteric psychology', the expression of feelings within ourselves rather than truths about the universe. Religion is the expression of alienation, from which men must be freed by realizing their purely human destiny in this world. Feuerbach is, then, one of the most important sources of humanist thought.

This was the intellectual atmosphere of Marx's formative years. His reading of Feuerbach broke the spell that Hegel had cast on him, but what remained was the idea that in Hegel's writings the truth about human nature and society was concealed in a kind of inverted form. As we shall see, the notions of historical development and of alienation play a crucial role in Marx's thought. He wrote a critique of Hegel's *Philosophy of Right* in 1842–3, and at the same time became editor of a radical journal of politics and economics called the *Rheinische Zeitung*. This journal was soon suppressed by the Prussian Government, so Marx emigrated to Paris in 1843. In the next two years there he encountered the other great intellectual influences of his life, and began to formulate his own distinctive theories. His wide reading included the British economist Adam Smith and the French socialist Saint-Simon. He met other socialist and communist thinkers such as Proudhon, Bakunin, and Engels. (This was the beginning of his lifelong friendship and collaboration with Engels.) In 1845 he was expelled from Paris, and he moved to Brussels.

In these years in Paris and Brussels Marx formulated his so-called 'Materialist Theory of History'. By inverting Hegel's view as Feuerbach had suggested, Marx came to see the driving force of historical change as not spiritual but material in character. Not in men's *ideas*, and certainly not in any sort of national or cosmic personality, but in the *economic* conditions of men's life, lay the key to all history. Alienation is neither metaphysical nor religious, but really social and economic. Under the capitalist system labour is something external and alien to the labourer; he does not work for himself but for someone else—the capitalist—who owns the product as private property. This diagnosis of alienation is to be found in the 'Economic and Philosophical Manuscripts' which Marx wrote in Paris in 1844, but which did not become generally available in English until the 1950s. The materialist conception of history is to be found in other works of this period—*The Holy Family* of 1845, *The German Ideology* of 1846 (written with Engels), and *The Poverty of Philosophy* of 1847.

In Brussels Marx became involved with the practical organization of the socialist and communist movement, a task which occupied much of the rest of his life. For he saw the main purpose of his work as 'not just to interpret the world, but to change it' (as he put it in his *Theses on Feuerbach* in 1845). Convinced that history was moving towards the revolution by which capitalism would give way to communism, he tried to educate and organize the 'proletariat'—the class of workers to whom he thought victory would go in the imminent struggle.

He was commissioned to write a definitive statement of the aims of the international communist movement, and together with Engels, he produced the famous *Manifesto of the Communist Party*, which was published early in 1848. Soon afterwards in that year (although hardly as a result of the *Manifesto*!) there were abortive revolutions in several of the major European countries. After their failure Marx found himself expelled from Belgium, France, and Germany, so in 1849 he went into exile in London, where he remained for the rest of his life.

In London Marx endured a life of poverty, existing on occasional journalism and gifts from Engels. He began daily research in the British Museum and continued to organize the international communist movement. In 1857–8 he wrote another series of manuscripts called *Grundrisse,* sketching a plan of his total theory of history and society. Not until 1973 has the complete text of these been available in English. In 1859 he published his *Critique of Political Economy*, and in 1867 the first volume of his most substantial work, *Das Kapital*. These last two works contain much detailed economic and social history, reflecting the results of Marx's labours in the British Museum. Although there is less evidence of Hegelian philosophical ideas such as alienation, Marx was still trying to apply his materialist interpretation of history to prove the inevitability of the downfall of capitalism.

It is these later works, from the *Communist Manifesto* onwards, that have been best known and have formed the basis of much communist theory and practice. In them we find German philosophy, French socialism, and British political economy, the three main influences on Marx, integrated into an all-embracing theory of history, economics, and politics. This is what Engels came to call 'scientific socialism'; for Marx and Engels thought they had discovered the correct *scientific* method for the study of history, and hence the truth about the present and future development of the society of their time. But the recent publication of the earlier works, particularly the Paris Manuscripts of 1844, has shown us much about the origin of Marx's thought in Hegelian philosophy, and has revealed the more philosophical nature of his early ideas. So the question has been raised whether there were two distinct periods in his thought—an early phase which has been called humanist or even existentialist, giving way to the later and more austere 'scientific socialism'. I think it is fair to say that the consensus of opinion is that there is a continuity between the two phases, that the theme of alienation is buried but still there in the later work; the contents of the *Grundrisse* of 1857–8 seem to confirm this. My discussion of Marx will therefore be based on the assumption that his thought is not discontinuous. My page references in what follows are to the Pelican book *Karl Marx. Selected Writings in Sociology and Social Philosophy*, which is perhaps the most useful of the many volumes of selected readings from Marx and Engels, containing as it does selections from both the early and late phases. Page references to the American paperback edition are supplied at the end of the chapter.

THEORY OF THE UNIVERSE

Let us now begin our critical analysis of Marx's main theory. He was of course an atheist, but this is not peculiar to him. What is distinctive of his understanding of the world as a whole is his interpretation of history. He claimed to have found the *scientific* method for studying the history of human societies, and looked forward to the day when there would be a single science, including the science of man along with natural science (p. 85). Accordingly, he held that there are universal *laws* behind historical change, and that the future large-scale course of history can be *predicted* from knowledge of these laws (just as astronomy predicts eclipses). In the preface to the first edition of *Capital*, Marx compared his method to that of the physicist and said 'the ultimate aim of this work is to lay bare the economic law of motion of modern society'; he also talked of the natural laws of capitalist production 'working with iron necessity towards inevitable results'. He agreed with Hegel that each period in each culture has a character of its own, so that the only truly universal laws in history could be those concerned with the processes of *development* by which one stage gives rise to the next. He divided history roughly into the Asiatic, the ancient, the feudal, and the 'bourgeois' or capitalist phases, and held that each had to give way to the next when conditions were ripe (p. 68). Capitalism was expected to give way, just as inevitably, to communism (pp. 150–1).

However, there are strong reasons for questioning the concept of laws of history. Certainly, history is an *empirical* study in that its propositions can and must be tested by evidence of what has actually happened. But it does not follow that it has the other main feature of a *science*, that it tries to arrive at *laws*, i.e. generalizations of unrestricted universality. For history is after all the study of what has happened on one particular planet in a finite period of time. The subject matter is wide, but it is one *particular* series of events; we know of no similar series of events elsewhere in the universe, so human history is unique. Now for any particular series of events, even an apparently simple one like the fall of an apple from a tree, there is no clear limit to the number of different scientific laws that may be involved—the laws of gravity and mechanics, of wind pressure, of elasticity of twigs, of decay of wood, etc., etc. If there is no one law governing the fall of an apple, then how much more implausible it is to postulate a general law of development behind the whole of human history.

The idea that the course of history is predetermined, so that one main function of historical study is large-scale prophecy, is at least as questionable. Certainly there may be some long-term and large-scale *trends* to be found, for instance the increase of human population since the Middle Ages. But a trend is not a *law*; its continuation is not inevitable but may depend on conditions which can change. (It is obvious that population cannot increase indefinitely, indeed its growth might be quite suddenly reversed by nuclear war or widespread famine.)

The other main feature of Marx's view of history is what is called his materialist conception of history. This is the theory that the supposed laws of history are *economic* in nature, that 'the mode of production of material life determines the general character of the social, political, and spiritual processes of life' (p. 67, cf. pp. 70, 90, 111–12, etc.). The economic structure is supposed to be the real basis by which everything else about a society is determined. Now it is undeniable that economic factors are hugely important, and that no serious study of history or social science can ignore them. Marx can take some of the credit for the fact that we now recognize this so readily. But he himself is committed to the more dubious assertion that the economic structure of a society *determines* its 'superstructures'. This proposition is difficult to interpret, for it is not clear where the dividing line between basis and superstructure should run. Marx talks of 'the material powers of production' (p. 67) which presumably would cover land and mineral resources, tools and machines, plus perhaps the knowledge and skills of men. But he also talks of the economic structure as including 'relations of production', which presumably means the way in which work is organized (e.g. division of labour and certain hierarchies of authority); yet the description of such organization must surely use concepts like property and money, which seem to be the kind of legal concepts that Marx would wish to put into the superstructure. If the basis includes only the material powers of production, then Marx is committed to a rather implausible 'technological determinism'; but if it includes also the relations of production, then the distinction between basis and superstructure is blurred.

From his general theory of history Marx derived a very specific prediction about the future of capitalism. He confidently expected that it would become more and more unstable economically, that the class struggle between bourgeois and proletariat would increase, with the proletariat getting both poorer and larger in number, until in a major social revolution the workers would take power and institute the new communist phase of history (pp. 79–80, 147–52, 194, 207, 236–8). Now the huge and simple fact is that this has not happened in the main capitalist countries—Britain, France, Germany, the U.S.A. On the contrary, the economic system of capitalism has become more stable, conditions of life for most people have improved vastly on what they were in Marx's time, and class divisions have been blurred rather than intensified (consider the large numbers of 'white-collar' workers—office staff, civil servants, teachers, etc., who are neither industrial labourers nor industrial owners). Where communist revolutions *have* taken place, they were in countries which had little or no capitalist development at the time—Russia in 1917, Yugoslavia in 1945, China in 1949. This must surely constitute the major falsification of Marx's theory. It cannot really be explained away by saying that the proletariat have been 'bought off' by concessions of higher wages—for Marx predicted their lot would get worse. Nor is it plausible to say that colonies have formed the proletariat *vis-à-vis* the industrialized countries—for some, such as Scandinavia, have had no colonies, and even in the colonies conditions did improve, however slightly. To maintain Marx's theory as he stated it, in the face of such counter-evidence, makes it into a matter of blind faith, a closed system, rather than the scientific theory he claimed it to be.

THEORY OF MAN

Except perhaps when he read Hegel's philosophy as a young man, Marx was not interested in questions of 'pure' or academic philosophy, which he would dismiss as mere speculation compared to the vital task of changing the world (p. 82). So when he is called a materialist, this refers to his materialist theory of history and not to a theory about the relation of mind to body. Certainly, he would dismiss belief in life after death as one of the illusory ideas of religion, and would emphasize that everything about the individual person (including his consciousness) is determined by the material conditions of his life (pp. 69, 85). But this could well be an 'epiphenomenalist' view—that consciousness is non-material in itself but entirely determined by material things—rather than a strictly materialist view that consciousness is itself material.

His view on the metaphysical question of determinism is rather ambiguous too. Of course his general view sounds determinist, with his theory of the inevitable progress of history through economic stages and his referring of all change to economic causes. And yet, just as with the Augustinian–Pelagian controversy within Christianity, there seems to be an irreducible element of free will too. For Marxists constantly appeal to their readers and hearers to realize the direction in which history is moving, and to *act* accordingly—to help bring about the communist revolution. Within Marxism there has been controversy between those who emphasize the need to wait for the appropriate stage of historical development before expecting the revolution, and those who emphasize the need to act to bring it about. But perhaps there is no ultimate contradiction here, for Marx can say that although the revolution will inevitably occur sooner or later, it is possible for individuals and groups to assist its coming and ease its birth pangs, acting as the midwives of history. Further inquiry into determinism and free will would probably be condemned as useless speculation.

What is most distinctive of Marx's concept of man is his view of our essentially *social* nature: 'the real nature of man is the totality of social relations' (p. 83). Apart from a few obvious biological facts such as the need to eat, Marx would tend to say that there is no such thing as individual human nature—what is true (and even universally true) of men in one society or period is not necessarily true of them in another place or time. Whatever a person does is an essentially social act, which presupposes the existence of other people standing in certain relations to him (pp. 91–2, 251). Even the ways in which we eat, sleep, copulate, and defecate are socially learned. This is true above all of every activity of production, for the production of our means of subsistence is typically a social activity in that it requires the co-operation of men in some way or other (p. 77). It is not that society is an abstract entity which affects the individual (p. 91), but rather that what kind of individual one is and what kind of things one does are determined by what kind of society one lives in. What seems instinctual in one society— e.g. a certain role for women—may be quite different in another society. In one of Marx's typical aphorisms: 'it is not the consciousness of men that determines their being, but, on the contrary, their social being determines their consciousness' (p. 67). In modern terms, we can summarize this crucial point by saying that sociology is not reducible to psychology, i.e. it is not the case that everything about men can be explained in terms of facts about individuals; the kind of society they live in must be considered too. This methodological point is one of Marx's most distinctive contributions, and one of the most widely accepted. For this reason alone, he must be recognized as one of the founding fathers of sociology. And the *method* can of course be accepted whether or not one agrees with the particular *conclusions* Marx came to about economics and politics.

But there does seem to be at least one universal generalization that Marx is prepared to make about human nature. This is that man is an *active*, productive being, who distinguishes himself from the other animals by the fact that he *produces* his means of subsistence (p. 69). It is natural for men to work for their living. No doubt there is an empirical truth here, but it seems that Marx also draws a value judgement out of this, namely that the kind of life which is *right* for men is one of productive activity. As we shall see, this is implicit in his diagnosis of alienation as a lack of fulfilment in industrial labour (p. 177), and in his prescription for future communist society in which everyone can be free to cultivate their own talents in every direction (p. 253). No doubt it is because of this point, which is clearest in his early writings, that Marx has been called a humanist.

DIAGNOSIS

Marx's theory of what is wrong with man and society involves his concept of alienation, which, as we have seen, is a descendant of the concept used by Hegel and Feuerbach. For Marx, alienation sums up what is wrong with capitalism; the concept rolls up together both a description of certain features of capitalist society and a value judgement that they are fundamentally wrong. But the trouble with the notion of alienation is that it is so vague that we hardly know *which* feature of capitalism Marx is condemning. Logically, alienation is a relation, that is, it must be *from* somebody or something; one cannot just be alienated any more than one can kill without killing something. Marx says that alienation is from man himself and from Nature (p. 177). But this does not help us very much, for it is not clear how one can be alienated from oneself; and the concept of Nature involved here has obscure Hegelian roots in the distinction between subject and supposedly alien object. For Marx, Nature means the man-created world, so we can take him as saying that men are not what they should be because they are alienated from the objects and social relations that they create. The general idea that emerges from this rather mystifying terminology is that capitalist society is in some respects not in accordance with basic human nature. But it still remains to be seen what those respects are.

Sometimes it seems that private property is what Marx primarily blames for alienation, for he says that the abolition of private property is the abolition of alienation (p. 250). But elsewhere he says that 'although private property appears to be the basis and cause of alienated labour, it is rather a consequence of the latter' (p. 176). He describes this alienation of labour as consisting in the fact that the work is not part of the worker's nature, he does not fulfil himself in his work, but feels miserable, physically exhausted and mentally debased. His work is forced on him as a means for satisfying other needs, and at work he does not belong to himself but to another person. Even the objects he produces are alien to him, because they are owned by someone else (pp. 177–8). Sometimes Marx seems to be blaming alienation on the institution of money, as a means of exchange which reduces social relationships to a common commercial denominator (pp. 179–81). Elsewhere he says that the division of labour makes man's work into an alien power opposed to him, preventing him from switching from one activity to another at will (which Marx improbably alleges will be possible in communist society) (pp. 110–11). And in another passage, Marx locates the basis of social evils and the general explanation of them in the principle of the State itself (p. 223).

What then *is* Marx diagnosing as the basic cause of alienation? It may be hard to believe that anyone would seriously advocate the abolition of money (a return to a system of barter?), the disappearance of all specialization in work, or the nationalization of all property (even tooth-brushes, shirts, books, etc.?). It is the private ownership of industry—the means of production and exchange—that is usually taken as the defining feature of capitalism. And the main points in the programme of the *Communist Manifesto* are the nationalization of land, factories, transport, and banks. But it is not at all clear that such institutional changes could cure the alienation of labour which Marx describes in such psychological terms (in the early works referred to in my previous paragraph). And if the State is the basis of social evils, nationalization would make things worse, by increasing the power of the State.

It looks as if we must understand Marx as saying, at least in his early phase, that alienation consists in a lack of *community*, so that people cannot see their work as contributing to a group of which they are members, since the State is not a real community (p. 226). Such a diagnosis would suggest a prescription not of nationalization but of decentralization into genuine communities or 'communes' (in which the abolition of money, specialization, and private property might begin to look more realistic).

If this is contentious, there is a more general diagnosis implicit in Marx, which would perhaps command universal assent. This is that it is always wrong to treat any human being as only a means to an economic end. This is just what did happen in the unrestrained capitalism of the early nineteenth century, when children worked long hours in filthy conditions and died early deaths after miserable lives. Industry is made for man, not man for industry—and 'man' here must mean *all* the human beings involved. But it is of course more difficult to agree on how to give effect to this very general value judgement.

PRESCRIPTION

'If man is formed by circumstances, these circumstances must be humanly formed' (p. 249). If alienation is a social problem caused by the nature of the capitalist economic system, then the solution is to abolish that system and replace it by a better one. And we have already seen that Marx thinks that this is bound to happen anyway, for capitalism will burst asunder because of its inner contradictions, and the communist revolution will usher in the new order of things in which alienation will disappear and man will be regenerated in his true nature. Just as Christianity claims that salvation has already been enacted for us, so Marx claims that the resolution of the problems of capitalism is already on the way in the movement of history.

But Marx holds that only a complete revolution of the economic system will do. There is no point in trying to achieve limited reforms such as higher wages, shorter hours, etc., for these do not alter the evil nature of the basic system, and only distract attention from the real task, which is to overthrow it. Hence the radical difference between the programme of the Communist Party and that of most trade unions and social democratic parties. This doctrine of 'the impotence of politics' follows from Marx's premises in his materialist theory of history—for if all legal and political institutions are really determined by the underlying economic system, then they cannot be used to change the economic system. However this doctrine flies in the face of the facts of the development of capitalism since Marx's time. Legal and other institutions *have* modified the economic system of capitalism very considerably, beginning with the Factory Acts of the nineteenth century which limited the worst excesses of exploitation of workers, continuing with National Insurance, unemployment benefit, National Health Services, and steady progress by trade unions in increasing real wages and decreasing working hours. In fact, many of the specific measures proposed in the *Communist Manifesto* have come into effect in the so-called capitalist countries—graduated income tax, centralization of much economic control in the hands of the state, nationalization of several major industries including transport, free education for all children in state schools. The unrestrained capitalist system as Marx knew it in the nineteenth century has everywhere ceased to exist, and this has happened by step-by-step reform, not by once-for-all revolution. This is not to say that the existing system is perfect—far from it. But it is to suggest that Marx's rejection of any idea of gradual reform is radically mistaken; and reflection on the suffering and violence involved in real revolutions may confirm this.

Like Christianity, Marx envisages a total regeneration of man, but he expects it entirely within this secular world. Communism is 'the solution to the riddle of history' (p. 250), for the abolition of private property is supposed to ensure the disappearance of alienation and the coming of a genuinely classless society. Marx is very vague on how all this will be achieved, but he suggests that there will be an intermediate period during which the transition will take place, and that this will require 'the dictatorship of the proletariat' for its accomplishment (p. 261). But in the higher phase of communist society, the State will wither away, and the true realm of freedom will begin. Then human potentiality can develop for its own sake (p. 260), and the guiding principle can be: 'From each according to his ability, to each according to his needs' (p. 263).

Some of this utopian vision must surely be judged wildly unrealistic. Marx gives us no good reason to believe that communist society will be genuinely classless, that those who exercise the dictatorship of the proletariat will not form a new governing class with many opportunities to abuse their power, as the history of Russia since the revolution obviously suggests. There is no ground for expecting any set of economic changes to eliminate *all* conflicts of interest for ever. The State, far from withering away, has become ever more powerful in communist countries; (perhaps the very nature of modern industry and technology makes this inevitable).

Yet with other elements in Marx's vision, we cannot but agree. The idea of a decentralized society in which men co-operate in communities for the common good, the application of science and technology to produce enough for all, the short-ening of the working day so that men can increasingly choose to spend their leisure time in the free development of their potential, the idea of a society in balance with nature—all these are ideals which almost everyone will share, even though it is not clear that they are compatible. No doubt it is because Marxism offers this kind of hopeful vision of the future that it can still win and retain the allegiance of so many people. For despite the obvious defects of life in the existing communist countries, many of their inhabitants maintain a genuine belief in Marxist theory. And despite the reforms that have already altered the face of capitalism, many people in the West see the need for a further transformation of the existing socio-economic system and look to Marx for inspiration for such a change.

Like Christianity, Marxism is more than a theory, and the disputability of many of its theoretical assertions does not make it lie down and die. It contains a recipe for social salva-tion and offers a critique of any existing society. However, Marx's emphasis on social and economic factors directs our at-tention to one, but only one, of the obstacles in the way of human progress. We must look elsewhere, for instance to Freud, for more about the nature and problems of human *in-dividuals*.

FOR FURTHER READING

Basic text: *Karl Marx: Selected Writings in Sociology and Social Philosophy*, translated by T. B. Bottomore, edited by T. B. Botto-more and M. Rubel (Penguin, London, 1963; McGraw-Hill paper-back, New York, 1964). Perhaps the best selection of readings from all periods of Marx's work. It has a bibliography of Marx's principal works at the end.

Exploration of Marx's writings could continue with the volumes in the Pelican Marx library, which includes the first complete transla-tion of the *Grundrisse*. David McLellan's *The Thought of Karl Marx*

(Macmillan, London, 1971; Harper & Row, New York, 1972) is a useful guide.

For one of the most famous of the many critical studies, see Karl Popper's *The Open Society and Its Enemies*, Volume II (Routledge & Kegan Paul, London, 5th edn. 1966; Princeton University Press paperback, Princeton, N.J.). Readers will recognize in it the source of many of my points.

For a readable biography of Marx, placing most emphasis on the development of his ideas, see Sir Isaiah Berlin's *Karl Marx: His Life and Environment* (Oxford University Press, London, 3rd edn. 1963; Oxford University Press Galaxy Books paperback, New York). This also contains further bibliography.

For an introduction to later forms of Marxism, see C. Wright Mills's *The Marxists* (Penguin, London, 1963; Dell paperback, New York).

Page references in this chapter are to the Penguin edition of *Karl Marx: Selected Writings in Sociology and Social Philosophy*. Readers of the McGraw-Hill paperback edition should use the references below.

Stevenson	*McGraw-Hill paperback*
page 50 refers to pages	70; 52; 141–2
51	51, 54, 75, 98
52	51; 64–5, 138–43, 186, 201, 231–3
53	67; 53, 70–1
54	68; 76–7, 245; 61–2; 77; 51; 53
55	169; 247; 169; 244; 168
56	169–70; 171–2; 97; 217; 220
57	243
58	244; 256; 255; 258

CHAPTER 6

Freud: Psycho-
Analysis

THE next theory of human nature I should like to consider is
that of Freud, for it is commonplace (but still true) to say that
he has revolutionized our understanding of ourselves in this
century. So no adequate discussion of human nature can fail to
grapple with his thought. But this is a peculiarly difficult task
to attempt in a single chapter, even if we concentrate only on
Freud himself and ignore the many later developments in
psycho-analytic theory and practice. For Freud spent nearly
fifty years developing and modifying his theories, writing so
vast an amount of material that the non-specialist cannot hope
to read it all. What I shall attempt to do here is to sketch
briefly his life and work (for this will suggest some of the complexity and richness of the latter), then summarize some of the
most fundamental points of his theory, diagnosis, and prescription, and finally raise some of the main critical questions which
must be asked.

LIFE AND WORK

Sigmund Freud was born in Moravia in 1856, but in 1860 his
family moved to Vienna, where he lived and worked until the
last year of his life. Even in his schooldays his interests extended to the whole of human life, and when he entered the
University of Vienna as a medical student he did not immediately concentrate on medicine. He became interested in biology, however, and spent six years doing research in physiology
in the laboratory of the great German scientist Brücke. In
1882 he became engaged to be married, and therefore needed a
career with a more secure financial reward, so he unwillingly
began work as a doctor in the Vienna General Hospital. In
1886 he was able to marry, and to set up the private practice in
'nervous diseases' which he maintained until the end of his
life.

Freud's working life from then on can be roughly divided

into three phases. In the first of these he made his great discoveries and developed the theory and treatment which has come to be known as psycho-analysis. His interest in psychological problems had been fired by a visit to Paris in 1885–6 to study under Charcot, a French neurologist who was then using hypnotism to treat hysteria. Faced with similar symptoms in his own patients, Freud experimented with both electrotherapy and hypnotic suggestion, but found them unsatisfactory, so he began to try another method which had been used by Breuer, a senior Viennese consultant who was a friend of his. Breuer's approach was based on the assumption that hysteria was caused by some intense emotional experience that the patient had forgotten; the treatment was to induce the recall of the experience, and hence a discharge of the corresponding emotion. This idea that people could suffer from some idea or memory or emotion of which they were not conscious, but from which they could be cured by somehow bringing it into consciousness, is the basis from which Freud's psycho-analysis developed. He went on to introduce the concepts of resistance, repression, and transference, which we shall look at soon. In 1895 he published *Studies on Hysteria* jointly with Breuer, but soon afterwards he broke with his friend and went on his own theoretical way. At the same time he was writing (to Fliess, another friend who influenced him in this period) the *Project for a Scientific Psychology*, a manuscript which was not published until 1950. In this he tried, somewhat abortively, to relate the psychological theory he was then developing to a material basis in the physiology of the brain, which he had already studied in his pre-medical work. In the last few years of the century he undertook the difficult task of analysing his own mind, and arrived at the concepts of infantile sexuality and of interpreting dreams, both of which are central to the mature theory of psycho-analysis.

The second phase of Freud's work, in which the great books expounding this mature theory appeared, can conveniently be dated from the publication in 1900 of *The Interpretation of Dreams*, the work which he himself regarded as his best. There followed in 1901 *The Psychopathology of Everyday Life*, in which he analysed the unconscious causation of everyday errors, and in 1905 *Three Essays on the Theory of Sexuality*. These three works applied psycho-analytic theory to the whole of normal mental life, not just to pathological conditions. The international recognition and spread of psycho-analysis began, and in 1909 Freud was invited to America where he delivered the lectures which formed the first of his expository works, the *Five Lectures on Psycho-Analysis*. In 1913–14 came *Totem and Taboo*, applying his theories to anthropological material, and in 1915–17 he gave the *Introductory Lectures on Psycho-Analysis* in the University of Vienna, in which he expounded at length the complete theory as it had developed up till then.

From after the end of the First World War until his death, the third phase of Freud's work included further developments and changes in theory, together with wide-ranging speculative attempts to apply his theories to social questions. During this period he suffered more and more from the cancer which eventually killed him. In 1920 came *Beyond the Pleasure Principle*, in which he first introduced the concept of a death instinct independent of the erotic or life instinct which he had long before postulated. Another late development was the tripartite structure of the mind—id, ego, and super-ego—given in 1923 in *The Ego and the Id*. Most of Freud's last years were devoted to sociological works. *The Future of an Illusion* of 1927 is about religion, treating it, as the title suggests, as false beliefs whose origin must be explained psychologically. *Civilization and Its Discontents* (1930) discusses the conflict between the demands of civilized society and the instincts implanted in every person, and *Moses and Monotheism* (1939) discusses the history of the Jews from a psycho-analytic point of view. In 1938 Hitler invaded Austria, but Freud was allowed to leave for London, where he spent the last year of his life writing a brief exposition of the latest version of his doctrine—*An Outline of Psycho-Analysis*.

There is no better introduction to Freud's thought than his own *Five Lectures* of 1909. Accordingly, in what follows I shall make my page references to the Pelican book *Two Short Accounts of Psycho-Analysis*, which contains these lectures together with another expository work, *The Question of Lay Analysis* of 1926. In the latter Freud discussed whether non-doctors should be allowed to practise psycho-analysis, and explained his basic theory in terms of the tripartite structure which he had recently formulated. (For American references see the end of the chapter.)

THEORY OF THE UNIVERSE

What is distinctive in Freud's thought comes not under this heading but in his theory of man, but we should take note of his background assumptions and how they differ from those of the theories discussed so far. Freud started his career as a physiologist and claimed to remain a scientist throughout and to treat all phenomena, including those of human nature, scientifically (p. 100). He made no theological assumptions (he was in fact a convinced atheist), nor any metaphysical assumptions like Plato on the Forms, or Marx on the movement of history. What he did assume (no doubt from his training in nineteenth-century science and his research in Brücke's Physiological Laboratory) is that all phenomena are determined by the laws of physics and chemistry, and that even man himself is a product of natural evolution, ultimately subject to the same laws.

THEORY OF MAN

I shall try to summarize Freud's basic concepts under four main heads. The first is a strict application of the principle of determinism—that every event has preceding sufficient causes —within the realm of the mental. Things that had formerly been assumed to be of no significance for understanding a person, such as slips of the tongue, faulty actions, and dreams, Freud took as determined by hidden causes in a person's mind. So they could be highly significant, revealing in disguised form what would otherwise remain unknown (pp. 56, 60, 65–6). Nothing which a person does or says is really haphazard or accidental; everything can in principle be traced to causes which are somehow in the person's mind. This might seem to imply a denial of human free will, for even when we think we are choosing perfectly freely and even arbitrarily, Freud could say that there are uncontrollable causes determining our choice. There is an interesting parallel with Marx here, for both are saying that our consciousness, far from being perfectly 'free' and 'rational', is really determined by causes of which we are not aware; but whereas Marx says that these causes are social and economic in nature, Freud claims that they are individual and mental.

The second main point—the postulation of *unconscious* mental states—thus arises out of the first. But we must be careful to understand this concept of the unconscious correctly. There are lots of mental entities, for instance memories of particular experiences or of particular facts, of which we are (fortunately!) not continually conscious, but which we can call to mind whenever necessary. These Freud would call 'preconscious' (that which can become conscious), reserving the term 'unconscious' for that which *cannot* become conscious at all under normal circumstances. The assertion is, then, that the mind is not co-extensive with what is conscious or can become conscious, but includes items of which the person can have no ordinary knowledge at all (pp. 107, 43, 47). To use a familiar but helpful analogy, the mind is like an ice-berg, with only a small proportion of it visible above the surface, but a vast hidden bulk exerting its influence on the rest. For the unconscious is *dynamic* in nature, that is, it actively exerts pressures and influences on what a person is and does. For instance, there are unconscious desires, which can cause someone to do things that he cannot explain rationally, to others or even to himself.

In asserting the existence of unconscious mental entities, is Freud committed to a dualism between mind and body, or between mental states and physical states? I think this would be a misinterpretation of him. Many philosophers would now agree that in talking of ordinary *conscious* mental states (e.g. thoughts, wishes, emotions) we are not thereby committed to a metaphysical dualism. The question of the ultimate nature of such mental states is a philosophical problem which is left open by our everyday language about them. There is no reason to suppose that the case is any different for unconscious mental states. Freud himself, with his physiological training, would certainly have rejected any suggestion of dualism. After his early attempt to find a physiological basis for his psychological theories (in the *Project* of 1895), he came to the view that such matters are not of psychological interest (p. 103) and was content to leave them to the future development of neurophysiology. But that all the mental entities he postulated had *some* physiological basis, although as yet unknown, he did not doubt. So his theory of man is not a dualist one like Plato's.

There is an interesting parallel with Plato, however, in the theory of the tripartite structure of the mind, which Freud introduced in his later expositions in the 1920s. This is not the same as the distinction between conscious, pre-conscious, and unconscious which he had used until then. He now distinguished three major structural systems within the human mind or personality: the *id*, which contains all the instinctual drives seeking immediate satisfaction; the *ego*, which deals with the real world outside the person, mediating between it and the id (pp. 104–5); and the *super-ego*, a special part of the ego which contains the conscience, the social norms acquired in childhood (p. 137). The super-ego has a connection with the id also, for it can confront the ego with moral rules like a strict father; the ego has to reconcile the conflicting demands of id, super-ego, and external reality. Whatever can become conscious is in the ego, although even in it there may be things which remain unconscious, whereas everything in the id is permanently unconscious (p. 108). So the id corresponds closely to Plato's element of Appetite or desire, but it is not so clear how ego and super-ego correspond to Plato's elements of Reason and Spirit. In its reality-testing function the ego would seem to be akin to the Reason, but Reason for Plato has also a moral function which Freud would give to the super-ego. And yet the spirited element seems to be performing a moralistic function in the situation of self-disgust by which Plato illustrated it.

The third main feature of Freud's concept of man is his theory of the instincts or 'drives'—or rather, his several theories of them, for this is one of the most variable parts of his work. The instincts are the motive forces in the mental apparatus, all the 'energy' in our minds comes from them alone (p. 110). (Freud used this mechanical or electrical language in an almost literal way, influenced no doubt by his scientific training and his *Project* of 1895.) Although he held that one can distinguish an indeterminate number of instincts, he also thought that they could all be derived from a few basic ones, which can combine or even replace each other in multifarious ways. Now he undoubtedly held that one such basic instinct is sexual in nature (p. 69); but it is a vulgar misinterpretation of Freud to say that he traced *all* human behaviour to sexual motivations. What *is* true is that he gave sexuality a much wider scope in human life than had formerly been recognized (p. 76). He claimed that sexual instincts exist in children from birth onwards (pp. 71, 121), and he asserted the crucial importance of sexual energy or 'libido' in adult life (p. 118). But Freud always held that there was at least one other basic instinct or group of instincts. In his early work he talked of the self-preservative instincts such as hunger, and contrasted these with the erotic instincts, one unusual aggressive manifestation of which was sadism. But in his later work from about 1920 onwards he changed the classification, putting erotic and self-preservative instincts into one basic 'Life' instinct (Eros), and referring sadism, aggression, self-destruction, etc., to a basic 'Death' instinct (Thanatos).

The fourth main point is Freud's developmental or historical theory of individual human character. This is not just the rather obvious truism that personality depends on experience as well as on hereditary endowment. Freud started from Breuer's discovery that particular 'traumatic' experiences could, although apparently forgotten, continue to exercise a baneful influence on a person's mental health (p. 39). The fully fledged theory of psycho-analysis generalizes from this and asserts the crucial importance, for adult character, of the experiences of infancy and early childhood (pp. 70, 115). The first five years or so are held to be the time in which the basis of individual personality is laid down. So one cannot fully understand a person until one comes to know the psychologically crucial facts about his early childhood.

Freud produced detailed theories of the stages of development through which every child grows (pp. 73, 121). These particular theories can of course be distinguished from the general developmental approach, and are more easily tested by observation. They are specifically concerned with the development of sexuality; Freud widened the concept of sexuality to include any kind of pleasure obtained from parts of the body. He suggested that infants first obtain such pleasure from the mouth (the oral stage) and then from the other end of the alimentary tract (the anal stage). Both boys and girls then become interested in the male sexual organ (the phallic stage). The little boy is alleged to feel sexual desires for his mother, and to fear castration by his father (the situation of the 'Oedipus complex') (p. 125). Both desire for mother and hostility to father are then normally repressed. Freud supposed that the little girl develops 'penis envy' at the same stage; but he never treated feminine sexuality so thoroughly. From age five until puberty (the 'latency' period) sexuality is much less apparent. It returns in its full 'genital' development at the beginning of adulthood.

DIAGNOSIS

Like Plato, Freud says that individual well-being or mental health depends on a harmonious relationship between the various parts of the mind, and between the person and the real world in which he has to live. The ego has to reconcile id, super-ego, and external world, perceiving and choosing opportunities for satisfying the instinctual demands of the id without transgressing the standards required by the super-ego (pp. 111, 137). If the world is unsuitable and does not give any such opportunities, then of course suffering will result, but even when the environment is reasonably favourable, there will be mental disturbance if there is inner conflict between the parts of the mind. So neurosis results from the frustration of basic instincts, either because of external obstacles or because of internal mental imbalance (p. 80).

There is one particular mental misadaptation which is of crucial importance in the causation of neurotic illnesses, and this is what Freud called repression. In a situation of extreme mental conflict, where a person experiences an instinctual impulse which is sharply incompatible with the standards he feels he must adhere to, it is possible for him to put it out of consciousness (pp. 48-9), to flee from it, to pretend that it does not exist (p. 113). So repression is one of the so-called 'defence mechanisms', by which a person attempts to avoid inner conflicts. But it is essentially an escape, a pretence, a withdrawal from reality (p. 80), and as such is doomed to failure. For what is repressed does not really disappear, but continues to exist in the unconscious portion of the mind. It retains all its instinctual energy, and exerts its influence by sending into consciousness a disguised substitute for itself—a neurotic symptom (pp. 52, 114). Thus the person can find himself behaving in ways which he will admit are irrational, yet which he feels compelled to continue without knowing why. For by repressing something out of his consciousness he has given up effective control over it; he can neither get rid of the symptoms it is causing, nor voluntarily lift the repression and recall it to consciousness.

As we should expect from his developmental approach to the individual, Freud locates the decisive repressions in early childhood (p. 115). And as we might expect from his emphasis on sexuality, he holds them to be basically sexual (p. 71). It is essential for the future mental health of the adult, that the child successfully passes through the normal stages of development of sexuality. But this does not always proceed smoothly, and any hitch in it leaves a predisposition to future neurosis (pp. 75, 122); the various forms of sexual perversion can be traced to such a cause. One typical kind of neurosis consists in what Freud called 'regression' (p. 75), the return to one of the stages at which childish satisfaction was obtained. He even identified certain adult character-types as oral and anal, by reference to the childhood stages from which he thought they originated.

There is much more detail in Freud's theories of the neuroses, into which we cannot enter here, but we have already noted that he can attribute part of the blame for them on the external world, and so we should look a bit more at this social aspect of his diagnosis. For the standards to which a person feels he must conform are one of the crucial factors in mental conflict, but these standards are (in Freud's view) a product of the person's social environment—primarily his parents, but including anyone who has exerted influence and authority on the growing child. It is the instillation of such standards that constitutes the essence of education, and makes a child into a member of civilized society; for civilization requires a certain control of the instincts, a sacrifice of instinctual satisfaction (p. 81) in order to make cultural achievements possible (p. 86). But the standards instilled are not automatically the 'best' or most rational or most conducive to individual happiness. Certainly, individual parents vary widely, and maladjusted parents will be likely to produce maladjusted children. But Freud was prepared to entertain the possibility (most obviously in his late work *Civilization and Its Discontents*, although the beginnings of this line of thought are apparent in much earlier works) that the whole relationship between society and the individual has got out of balance, that our whole civilized life might be neurotic (p. 119). Even as early as the *Five Lectures* of 1909, he asserted that our civilized standards make life too difficult for most people and that we cannot deny a certain amount of satisfaction to our instinctual impulses (pp. 86–7). So there is a basis in the writings of Freud himself for those later Freudians who diagnose the main trouble as lying in society rather than in the individual.

PRESCRIPTION

As usual, prescription follows from diagnosis. Freud's aim was to restore a harmonious balance between the parts of the mind, and between the individual and his world. The latter might well involve programmes of social reform, but Freud never specified these in any detail; his everyday practice was the treatment of neurotic patients by psycho-analysis. The word 'psycho-analysis' refers at least as much to Freud's method of treatment as to the theories on which that treatment is based. It is this method which we must now examine.

The method developed gradually out of Breuer's initial discovery that one particular hysterical patient could be helped by being encouraged to talk about the fantasies which had been filling her mind, and could actually be cured if she could be induced to remember the 'traumatic' experiences that had apparently caused her illness in the first place (pp. 33–9). Freud started using this 'talking cure', and, assuming that the pathogenic memories were always somewhere in the person's mind even if not ordinarily available to consciousness, he asked his patients to talk freely and uninhibitedly, hoping that he could interpret the unconscious forces behind what they said (pp. 58–9). He encouraged them to say *whatever* came into their mind, however absurd (the method of 'free association'). But he often found that the flow of associations would dry up, and the patient would claim to know nothing more, and might even object to further inquiry. When such 'resistance' happened, Freud took it as a sign that he was really getting near the correct interpretation of the repressed complex. He thought that the patient's unconscious mind would somehow realize this and try to prevent the painful truth being brought into consciousness (p. 48). Yet only if the repressed material could be brought back into consciousness could the patient be cured, and his ego given back the power over the id which it had lost in the process of repression (pp. 66, 115).

But to achieve this happy result could take a long process, involving perhaps weekly sessions over a period of years. The analyst must try to arrive at the correct interpretations of his patient's condition, and present them at such a time and in such a way that the patient can accept them (p. 134). The patient's dreams will provide very fruitful material for interpretation, for according to Freud's theory the 'manifest' content of a dream is always the *disguised* fulfilment of repressed wishes, which are its real or 'latent' content (pp. 60–4). Faulty actions can also be interpreted to reveal their unconscious causation (p. 65). As one would expect from the theory we have summarized, the interpretations will very often refer to a person's sexual life, his childhood experiences, his infantile sexuality, and his relationships to his parents. Clearly all this demands a relationship of peculiar confidence between patient and analyst, but Freud found that much more than this happened; in fact, his patients manifested a degree of emotion towards him that could almost be called falling in love. This phenomenon he labelled 'transference', on the assumption that the emotion was somehow transferred to the analyst from the real-life situations in which it was once present, or from the unconscious fantasies of the patient (pp. 82–3, 139–41). The handling of such transference is of crucial importance for the success of the analysis, for it itself can be analysed and traced back to its sources in the patient's unconscious (pp. 141–2).

The goal of psycho-analytic treatment can be summarized as self-knowledge. What the cured neurotic does with his new self-understanding is up to him, and various outcomes are possible. He may replace the unhealthy repression of instincts by a rational, conscious, control of them (*sup*pression rather than *re*pression); or he may be able to divert them into acceptable channels (sublimation); or he may decide that they should be satisfied after all (pp. 85–6). But there is no possibility at all of a result that is sometimes feared by the layman—that primitive instincts when unleashed will take over completely—for their power is actually *reduced* by being brought into consciousness (pp. 84–5).

Freud spent his life treating individual neurotic patients. But he never thought that psycho-analytic treatment is the answer to *every* human problem. When grappling speculatively with the problems of civilization and society he was realistic enough to realize their extreme complexity and to abstain from offering any panacea. But he did hold that psycho-analysis had much wider applications than just the treatment of neurotics (p. 168). He said 'our civilization imposes an almost intolerable pressure on us and it calls for a corrective', and speculated that psycho-analysis might help to prepare such a corrective (pp. 169–70). At the end of *Civilization and Its Discontents* he cautiously proposed an analogy between cultures and individuals, so that cultures too might be 'neurotic'. But he recognized the precariousness of the analogy, and refused to 'rise up before his fellow-men as a prophet'.

CRITICAL DISCUSSION

The position of psycho-analysis on the intellectual map is still a matter of dispute. Psycho-analysts continue to practise, with a variety of Freudian and post-Freudian doctrines. But many academic psychologists and some practising psychiatrists condemn psycho-analysis as almost totally unscientific, as more akin to witchcraft than to respectable scientific medicine. Some critics fasten on the cult-like orthodoxy imposed by the various schools of psycho-analysts, and the 'indoctrination' which every aspirant psycho-analyst is required to go through (by being analysed himself). They therefore classify the theory and practice as that of a quasi-religious faith. It certainly has a method of disparagingly analysing the motivations of its critics (for any questioning of the truth of psycho-analytic theory can be alleged to be based on the unconscious resistance of the critic to its unpleasant implications). So if (as many say) the theory also has a built-in method of explaining away any evidence which appears to falsify it, then it will indeed be a closed system, in the sense defined in Chapter 2. And since belief in the theory is a requirement of membership of psycho-analytic institutes, it might even be said to be the ideology of those social groups. However, we should look more closely at the case against Freud before we pass judgement.

We must first distinguish two independent questions: the truth of Freud's theories, and the effectiveness of the method of treatment based on them. On the status of the theories, the crucial problem is whether they are falsifiable, for we have seen that Freud claimed his theories to be scientific ones, and we have taken empirical falsifiability as a necessary condition for scientific status (in Chapter 2). But for some of the central propositions of Freudian theory it is not clear whether they are falsifiable at all. Let us illustrate this with examples from the four main sections in which we summarized the theory. The postulate of psychic determinism leads to specific propositions such as that all dreams are disguised wish-fulfilments. Can this be tested? Where an interpretation in terms of an independently established wish of the dreamer is proposed and accepted, well and good. But what if no such interpretation is found? A convinced Freudian can still maintain that there is a wish whose disguise has not been seen through. But this would make it impossible to show that a dream is *not* the disguised fulfilment of a wish, and would therefore evacuate the proposition of any genuine empirical content, leaving only the prescription that we should *look* for a wish fulfilled by the dream. The proposition can be empirical only if we can have independent evidence for (a) the existence of the wish and (b) the correct interpretation of its disguise.

Consider next the postulation of unconscious mental states, and in particular the tripartite structure of id, ego, and super-ego. Freud did not of course expect these entities to be visible or tangible, and we have seen that he dismissed the question of what they are made of as of no psychological interest (p. 103). But that was because he had then abandoned any hope of discovering a physiological basis in the brain for such mental factors. It remains logically possible that neurophysiology may progress to a point where we could identify three physical systems in the brain which play the roles ascribed by Freud to id, ego, and super-ego. But as yet there is no sign of such a possibility being realized. In the meantime we must ask ourselves whether the postulation of unconscious mental states offers any genuine explanation of human behaviour. It would be too quick a move to dismiss them just because they are unobservable, for scientific theory often postulates entities which are not directly evident to any of the human senses—e.g. atoms, electrons, magnetic fields, and radio waves. But in these cases there are clear 'correspondence rules' connecting the unobservable entities with observable phenomena, so that, for instance, we can infer the presence or absence of a magnetic field from the visible behaviour of a compass needle. The trouble with many of the Freudian entities is that there are no such unambiguous rules for them. Stamp collecting may be asserted to be a sign of unconscious 'anal retentiveness', but could one show that such an unconscious trait is *not* there in someone?

Freud's theory of instincts is perhaps the part which is least open to empirical testing, as is suggested by his vacillations on the subject. One can describe as instinctive any form of behaviour that is not learned from the experience of the individual (although it may often be difficult to *show* that it has not been learned). But nothing seems to be added by referring instinctive behaviour to *an* instinct as its cause—for what evidence can there be for the existence of an instinct except the occurrence of the corresponding unlearned behaviour? And if it is claimed that there are only a certain number of basic instincts, it is not at all clear how one could decide which are basic, and how they are to be distinguished and counted. Could any evidence of human behaviour settle whether either of Freud's main instinct theories is right, as against, say, an Adlerian theory of a basic instinct of self-assertion or a Jungian theory of an instinctual need for God? Once again, the postulation of unobservables is useless unless falsifiable.

The developmental approach to individual character and the theory of the stages of infantile sexual development are more easily tested by observation. In this area, some of Freud's propositions are clearly supported by the evidence, others are neither supported nor refuted, while others are very difficult to test (see Kline's book recommended below). The *existence* of what Freud called the oral and anal characters has been confirmed by the discovery that certain traits of character (for instance, parsimony, orderliness, and obstinacy—the anal traits) do tend to go together. But the theory that these types of character *arise* from certain kinds of infant-rearing procedure has not been supported by the available studies. However there are practical difficulties in getting the necessary correlations between infantile experience and adult character, so the theory is not yet refuted. For some other parts of Freud's psychosexual theories there are conceptual difficulties about testing. How, for example, could one test whether infants get erotic pleasure from sucking? Some studies suggest that infants who have less opportunity to suck during feeding tend to do more sucking of their thumbs—but can this really be construed as evidence for the *erotic* nature of sucking?

This rather brief treatment of a few examples does at least show that there is serious doubt about the scientific status of some of Freud's key theoretical assertions. Some seem unfalsifiable, while of those that *can* be tested only some have received clear support from the evidence. The testing is subject to a mixture of complex practical and conceptual difficulties.

It has been suggested (by both psycho-analysts and philosophers) that psycho-analysis is not primarily a set of assertions to be tested empirically, but more a way of understanding people, of seeing a *meaning* in their actions, their mistakes, their jokes, and their dreams. It may be said that since human beings are vastly different from the entities studied by physics and chemistry, one should not condemn psycho-analysis for failing to meet criteria for scientific status which have been taken from the established physical sciences. Perhaps the psycho-analytic discussion of a dream is more akin to literary criticism, such as the interpretation of an obscure poem, in which there are reasons (but not conclusive reasons) for a variety of interpretations. Many of Freud's conceptions can be seen as extensions of our ordinary ways of understanding each other in terms of everyday concepts such as love, hate, fear, anxiety, rivalry, etc. And the experienced psycho-analyst can be seen as someone who has acquired a deep understanding of the springs of human motivation and a skill in interpreting the multifarious complexities of how they work out in particular situations, regardless of the theoretical views he may espouse.

Such a view of psycho-analysis has been given philosophical backing by a sharp distinction between *motives* and *causes*, and hence between scientific explanation (in terms of causes) and the explanation of human actions (in terms of motives, purposes, or intentions). And it has been suggested that Freud himself misinterpreted what he was doing, when he theorized in terms of causes rather than motives. However, like other alleged sharp dichotomies, this one is open to philosophical doubts. For after all, both our everyday understanding of people and the psycho-analyst's interpretations must be supported by reasons, and those reasons must surely consist of evidence of how people behave. Is it so clear, then, that there is any ultimate difference in kind between everyday explanations of people's behaviour and scientific explanations of it? Remember that falsifiability is a necessary condition not just of a statement's being scientific but of it being factual. So the discussion of psycho-analysis leads into the continuing philosophical debates about how far the methods of scientific investigation and explanation are applicable to human beings.

Doubts about psycho-analytic theory naturally extend to the treatment based on it. But when that treatment has already been widely applied, we should be able to form some estimate of its effectiveness. This would in principle give a further test of the theory, for if it is really true we would expect the treatment to be effective. However, matters are not easy here either. For one thing, a true theory might be badly applied in practice; and for another, there is doubt about what constitutes 'cure' from neurotic illness. A proportion of two-thirds has been given as the approximate rate of cure for patients who complete psycho-analytic therapy. This may seem favourable, but of course it must be compared with a 'control group' of similar cases who have been treated by other psychiatric methods or not treated at all. The proportion of recovery in such groups is also of the order of two-thirds, so there is no proof yet of any therapeutic effectiveness.

Thus no clear verdict can be passed on Freud's theories as a whole. His genius is undisputed, but however influential a man's thought, we can never be excused the task of critically evaluating what he says. Freud said so much of such great importance that the digesting and testing of it will occupy both philosophers and psychologists for many years to come.

FOR FURTHER READING

Basic text: *Two Short Accounts of Psycho-Analysis*, translated and edited by James Strachey (Penguin, London, 1962). This contains a biographical sketch, and further bibliography.

Most of the first 'short account', *Five Lectures on Psycho-Analysis*, is reprinted in *A General Selection from the Works of Sigmund Freud* edited by John Rickman (Doubleday Anchor Book paperback, New York, 1957). Rickman's selection does not, however, include the second 'short account', *The Question of Lay Analysis*. The 'short accounts' are in vols. XI and XX of Freud's *Complete Psychological Works* (Hogarth Press, London; Macmillan, New York).

Exploration of Freud's own writings could continue with the *Introductory Lectures on Psycho-Analysis* of 1915–17 (see *Complete Psychological Works* vols. XV and XVI).

For a hostile view see H. J. Eysenck, *Uses and Abuses of Psychology* (Penguin, London, 1953; New York, 1964), Chapter 12, and for details of the empirical testing of Freudian theories, see *Fact and Fantasy in Freudian Theory* by Paul Kline (Methuen, London, 1972; Barnes & Noble, New York).

For a philosophical study of Freudian concepts, see *The Unconscious* by Alasdair MacIntyre (Routledge & Kegan Paul, London, 1958; Humanities Press, New York, 1962).

For biography, see the famous *Life and Work of Sigmund Freud* by Ernest Jones, conveniently edited and abridged in one volume by Lionel Trilling and Steven Marcus (Penguin, London, 1964; Basic Books, New York, 1961).

For an introduction to the later developments in psycho-analytic theory, see *Freud and the Post-Freudians* by J. A. C. Brown (Penguin, London, 1964, and New York).

Because the two 'short accounts' to which I give references are not available in one paperback in the U.S., I give below volume and page references to the *Complete Psychological Works*.

Stevenson	Complete Psychological Works
page 64 refers to pages	XX 191; XI 30, 33, 37–8
65	XI 19, 22–3, XX 197; XX 194
66	XX 195–6; XX 223; XX 198; XX 200; XI 40; XI 46
67	XI 41–2, XX 209; XX 207; XI 16; XI 41, XX 204; XI 43–5, XX 210–11; XX 213
68	XI 201, 223; XI 49; XI 24; XX 202–3; XI 49; XI 27, XX 203
69	XX 204; XI 41; XI 45; XX 210; XI 45; XI 50; XI 54; XX 207
70	XI 54–5; XI 12–15; XI 31–3; XI 23–4
71	XI 38; XX 205; XX 220; XI 33–7; XI 37; XI 51–2, XX 225–7; X 226–7; XI 53–4; XI 53
72	XX 248; XX 249–50
73	XX 194

CHAPTER 7

Sartre: Atheistic
                   Existentialism

IN moving from Freud to Sartre we go from the Vienna of the
turn of the century to the Paris of the 1930s and 1940s, from
the psychological side of medicine to a philosophy expressed in
imaginative literature as well as in academic exposition. Yet
there is a common concern with the problems of the human
individual, and in particular with the nature of consciousness.
We shall find that Sartre too has a fourfold theory of human
nature, but we should first put him in the context of existentialism as a whole.

Many writers, philosophers, and theologians have been
called 'existentialist'. In so far as a common core can be discerned there would seem to be three main concerns which are
central to existentialism. The first is with the *individual*
human being, rather than with general theories about him.
Such theories, it is thought, leave out what is most important
about each individual—his uniqueness. Secondly, there is a
concern with the *meaning* or purpose of human lives, rather
than with scientific or metaphysical truths about the universe.
So inner or subjective experience is somehow regarded as more
important than 'objective' truth. Thirdly, the concern is with
the *freedom* of individuals as their most important and distinctively human property. So existentialists believe in the
ability of every person to choose for himself his attitudes, purposes, values, and way of life. And they are concerned not just
to maintain this as a truth, but to persuade everyone to act on
it. For in their view the only 'authentic' and genuine way of
life is that freely chosen by each individual for himself. These
three concerns, then, are really aspects of one basic theme.

But this common core of existentialism can be found in
a wide variety of contexts. It is naturally expressed in descriptions of the concrete detail of particular characters and situations, as in plays and novels. However someone can count as an
existentialist philosopher only if he makes some attempt at
general statement about the human condition (even if that

statement consists in denying the possibility or the importance of other general statements!). Existentialist philosophies come in various forms, the most radical division being between the religious and the atheistic. The Danish Christian thinker Kierkegaard (1813–55) is generally regarded as the first modern existentialist. Like Marx, he reacted against the Hegelian system of philosophy, but in a quite different direction. He rejected the abstract theoretical system as like a vast mansion in which one does not actually live, and maintained instead the supreme importance of the individual and his choices. Distinguishing three main ways of life—the aesthetic, the ethical, and the religious—he required each individual to choose between them. But he also held that the religious way (more specifically, the Christian one) is the highest, although it can be reached only by a free 'leap into the arms of God'. The other great nineteenth-century source of existentialism, the German writer Nietzsche (1844–1900), was aggressively atheist. He held that since 'God is dead' (i.e. the illusions of religion have been seen through) we will have to rethink the whole foundations of our lives, and find their meaning and purpose in human terms alone. In this, he had much in common with his earlier compatriot Feuerbach, whose humanistic atheism I mentioned briefly when introducing Marx. What is more distinctive of Nietzsche is his emphasis on our freedom to change the basis of our values, and his vision of the 'Super-man' of the future, who will reject our present meek religiously based values by more real ones based on the human 'will to power'.

In the twentieth century too, existentialists have included both Christians and atheists. Existentialism has been a major force in theology, both Protestant and Catholic, as well as in philosophy. The philosophical movement has been centred on the mainland of Europe, especially in Germany and France, and has had much less influence in English-speaking countries. Its sources can be traced to Kierkegaard and Nietzsche, but also to the 'phenomenology' of the German-speaking philosopher Husserl (1859–1938). This somewhat obscure philosophical method tried to find an unproblematical starting-point by describing only the 'phenomena' as they seem to be, without making any assumptions about what they really are. So it gave philosophy a subjective, quasi-psychological twist, making it the study of human consciousness. It is this concern with consciousness that we find in twentieth-century existentialist philosophers. In Germany the most important of these is Heidegger (born in 1889), whose major work, the huge and obscure *Being and Time*, appeared in 1927. His central concern is however with human existence, and the possibility of 'authentic' life through facing up to one's real position in the world, and in particular to the inevitability of one's death.

But I do not wish to deal here with existentialism in general; the above has been sketched as background for our consideration of the most famous of the French existentialists, Jean-Paul Sartre (born in 1905). In a brilliant educational career he absorbed, among much else, the thought of the great European philosophers, especially that of Hegel, Husserl, and Heidegger. Many of the obscurities of Sartre's own philosophical style can be traced to the influence of these three writers of ponderous German abstractions. Themes from Husserl's work can be detected in his first books—the novel *Nausea* of 1938, and three philosophical studies of psychological topics: *Imagination* (1936), *Sketch for a Theory of the Emotions* (1939), and *The Psychology of the Imagination* (1940). His central work, expounding at length his philosophy of human existence, is the celebrated *Being and Nothingness*, first published in 1943. He gave a much shorter and clearer account of atheistic existentialism in *Existentialism and Humanism*, a lecture delivered in Paris in 1945, but unfortunately his treatment there is popular and superficial, and should not be relied upon as an exposition of his thought. During the Second World War he was active in the French Resistance to the Nazi occupation, and some of the atmosphere of that time can be found in his work; for instance the choice which confronted all Frenchmen of collaboration, resistance, or quiet self-preservation was a very obvious particular case of what existentialists see as the ever-present necessity for individual choice. Such themes are expressed in Sartre's trilogy of novels *Roads to Freedom*, and in some of his plays. More recently he has amended the individualistic existentialism of his early writings and has espoused a form of Marxism, which he has described as 'the inescapable philosophy of our time' needing however to be refertilized by existentialism. This change of view is expressed in his *Critique of Dialectical Reason* (Volume 1) of 1960. But I will not attempt to deal with this here; I will consider only the existentialist philosophy of *Being and Nothingness*, making my page references to Hazel Barnes's English translation.

THEORY OF THE UNIVERSE

Sartre's most important assertion about the world as a whole is his denial of the existence of God. He does not argue for this negative conclusion, although he does claim that the idea of God is self-contradictory (p. 615). He seems rather to take it as already amply demonstrated by previous thinkers, and is concerned in his own work to consider its consequences. Like Nietzsche, he holds the absence of God to be of the utmost importance for us all; the atheist does not merely differ from the Christian on a point of metaphysics, he must hold a profoundly different view of human existence. If God does not exist, then everything is permitted (as Dostoyevsky once put it). There are no transcendent or objective values set for us, neither laws of God nor Platonic Forms nor anything else. There is no ultimate meaning or purpose inherent in human life; in this sense life is 'absurd'. We are 'forlorn', 'abandoned' in the world to look after ourselves completely. Sartre insists that the only foundation for values is human freedom, and that there can be no external or objective justification for the values anyone chooses to adopt (p. 38).

THEORY OF MAN

In one sense, Sartre would deny that there is any such thing as 'human nature' for there to be true or false theories about. This is a typically existentialist rejection of general statements about man. Sartre has expressed it by saying that man's existence precedes his essence (pp. 438–9); we have not been created for any purpose, neither by God nor evolution nor anything else. We simply find ourselves existing, and then have to *decide* what to make of ourselves. Now he can hardly mean to deny that there may be certain properties which are universal among human beings—for instance, the necessity to eat to survive. That there are some such general facts is obvious, although there may be room for dispute about their number. So presumably what he means is that there are no 'true' general statements about what all men *ought* to be, and this is simply the rejection of any notion of objective values, which we have already noted.

Nevertheless Sartre, as an existentialist philosopher, is bound to make *some* general statements about the human condition. His central assertion is of course that of human freedom. We are, in his view, 'condemned to be free'; there is no limit to our freedom except that we are not free to cease being free (p. 439). But we must examine how he reaches this conclusion via an analysis of the notion of consciousness. He starts with a radical distinction between consciousness (*L'être-pour-soi*, being-for-itself) and non-conscious objects (*L'être-en-soi*, being-in-itself) (p. xxxix). This basic dualism is shown he thinks, by the fact that consciousness necessarily has an object, it is always consciousness *of* something which is not itself (p. xxxvii). The next point to appreciate is the connection Sartre sees between consciousness and the mysterious concept of 'nothingness' which appears in the title of his book. We shall be wise to avoid any attempt to trace the roots of this concept in German philosophy, and just pick out some intelligible points from Sartre. We have noted that consciousness is always of something other than itself; Sartre holds that it is always aware of itself as well (pp. xxix, 74–5), so it necessarily distinguishes between itself and its object. This is connected with our ability to make judgements about such objects. A judgement can be negative as well as positive; we can recognize and assert what is truly *not* the case, as when I scan the café and say 'Pierre is not here' (pp. 9–10). If we ask a question, we must understand the possibility of the reply being 'No' (p. 5). So conscious beings, by their very nature, can conceive of what is *not* the case.

Sartre makes mystifying verbal play with his concept of nothingness, sometimes in absurdities such as 'the objective existence of a non-being' (p. 5) (which, if it means anything, can only mean that there are true negative statements), sometimes in dark sayings like 'Nothingness lies coiled in the heart of being—like a worm' (p. 21). But as far as I can see, the crucial role of nothingness is to make a conceptual connection between consciousness and freedom. For the ability to conceive of what is not the case is the freedom to imagine other possibilities, the freedom to suspend judgement (pp. 24–5). We can never reach a state in which there are no possibilities unfulfilled, for whatever state we are in, we can always conceive of things being otherwise. (Sartre thinks that we are always trying to reach such a state, to become objects rather than conscious beings; hence his description of human life as 'an unhappy consciousness with no possibility of surpassing its unhappy state' (p. 90), 'a useless passion' (p. 615).) The notion of desire involves the recognition of the *lack* of something (p. 87), as does the notion of intentional action (p. 433), for I can only try to achieve a result if I believe that what I intend is not already the case. The power of negation is, then, the same thing as freedom—both freedom of mind (to imagine possibilities) and freedom of action (to try to actualize them). It follows that to be conscious is to be free.

Note how this position of Sartre's directly contradicts two of Freud's. Obviously, it is incompatible with Freud's postulate of complete psychic determinism (p. 459). But it also involves a conflict with the postulate of unconscious mental states, since Sartre holds that consciousness is necessarily transparent to itself. Every aspect of our mental lives is intentional, chosen, and our responsibility. For instance, emotions are often thought to be outside the control of our wills, but Sartre maintains that if I am sad it is only because I choose to make myself sad (p. 61). This view, outlined more fully in his *Sketch for a Theory of the Emotions*, is that emotions are not things which 'come over us', but ways in which we apprehend the world. What distinguishes emotion from other ways of being conscious of objects is that it attempts to transform the world by magic—when we cannot reach the bunch of grapes, we dismiss them as 'too green', attributing this quality to them although we really know quite well that their ripeness does not depend on their reachability. So we are responsible for our emotions, because they are ways in which we choose to react to the world (p. 445). We are equally responsible for longer-lasting features of our character. We cannot just say 'I am shy' as if this were an unchangeable fact about us like 'I am a Negro', for our shyness is the way we behave and we can choose to try to behave differently. Even to say 'I am ugly' or 'I am stupid' is not to assert a fact already in existence, but to anticipate how women or society will react to my behaviour in the future, and this can be discovered only by trying (p. 459).

So even though we are often not aware of it, our freedom and hence our responsibility extends to everything we think and do. There are times, however, when this total freedom is clearly manifested to us. In moments of temptation or indecision—for example, when the man who has resolved not to gamble any more is confronted with the gaming tables once again—we realize that no motive and no past resolution determines what we do *now* (p. 33). Every moment requires a new or renewed choice. Following Kierkegaard, Sartre uses the term 'anguish' to describe this consciousness of one's own freedom (pp. 29, 464). Anguish is not fear of an external object, but the awareness of the ultimate unpredictability of one's own behaviour. The soldier fears injury or death, but feels anguish when he wonders whether he is going to be able to 'hold up' in the coming battle. The person walking on a dangerous cliff-path fears falling, but feels anguish because he knows that there is nothing to stop him throwing himself over (pp. 29–32).

DIAGNOSIS

Anguish, the consciousness of our freedom, is painful, and we typically try to avoid it (p. 40). But such 'escape' is illusory, for it is a necessary truth that we are free. Such is Sartre's diagnosis of man's condition. The crucial concept in his diagnosis is that of self-deception or 'bad faith' (*mauvaise foi*). Bad faith is the attempt to escape anguish by pretending to ourselves that we are not free (p. 44). We try to convince ourselves that our attitudes and actions are determined by our character, our situation, our role in life, or anything other than ourselves. Sartre gives two famous examples of bad faith (pp. 55–60). He pictures a girl sitting with a man who she knows very well would like to seduce her. But when he takes her hand, she tries to avoid the painful necessity of a decision to accept or reject him, by pretending not to notice, leaving her hand in his as if she were not aware of it. She pretends to herself that she is a passive object, a thing, rather than what she really is, a conscious being who is free. The second illustration is of the café waiter who is doing his job just a little too keenly; he is obviously 'acting the part'. The bad faith here is that he is trying to identify himself completely with the role of waiter, to pretend that this particular role determines his every action and attitude. Whereas the truth is of course that he has chosen to take on the job, and is free to give it up at any time. He is not *essentially* a waiter, for no man is essentially anything. Sartre rejects any Freudian explanation of bad faith in terms of unconscious mental states. A follower of Freud might try to describe the above cases as examples of repression—in the case of the girl she is repressing the knowledge that her companion has made a sexual advance to her, in the case of the waiter he is repressing the knowledge that he is a free agent who does not have to continue acting as a waiter a moment longer than he wants to. But Sartre points out what seems to be a self-contradiction in the very idea of repression: we must attribute the repressing to some agency within the mind ('the censor') which makes distinctions between what is to be repressed and what is to be allowed into consciousness, so this censor must be aware of the repressed idea in order not to be aware of it. The censor itself is thus in bad faith, and so we have not gained any explanation of how bad faith is possible by merely localizing it in one agency of the mind rather than in the person as a whole (pp. 52–3).

Sartre goes on to suggest that sincerity, the antithesis of bad faith, presents just as much of a conceptual problem. For as soon as we describe ourselves in some way (e.g. 'I am a waiter'), by that very act a distinction is made between the self doing the describing and the self described. The ideal of complete sincerity seems doomed to failure (p. 62), for we can never be just objects to be observed and accurately described. Sartre is expressing here what others have called 'the systematic elusiveness of the self'. But his account makes it even more paradoxical and perplexing than it really is, for he constantly repeats the formula that 'human reality must be what it is not and not be what it is' (e.g. p. 67). This is of course a self-contradiction, so Sartre cannot mean it literally; I think we must take it as shorthand for 'human reality must not be *necessarily* what it is but must be *able* to be what it is not' (as he puts it on p. 58—my italics). This directs our attention back to Sartre's most basic point, that to be conscious at all is to be free. Consciousness conceals in its being a permanent risk of bad faith, but Sartre maintains that it is *possible* to avoid this and achieve authenticity (p. 70).

PRESCRIPTION

In view of his rejection of any possibility of objective values, Sartre's prescription has to be a curiously empty one. There is no *particular* course of action or way of life that he can recommend to others. All that he can do is to condemn any bad faith, any attempt to pretend that one is not free. And all that he can recommend is authenticity, that we each make our individual choices with full awareness that nothing determines them for us. We must accept our responsibility for everything about ourselves, not just our actions, but our attitudes, our emotions, and even our characters. The 'spirit of seriousness', which is the illusion that values are objectively in the world rather than sustained only by human choice, must be repudiated (pp. 580, 626). There is no escape from the anguish of freedom; to flee responsibility is itself a choice (pp. 479, 555–6).

In *Existentialism and Humanism* Sartre illustrates the impossibility of prescription by the case of a young Frenchman at the time of the Nazi occupation, who was faced with the choice of either going to help the free French forces in England or staying at home to be with his mother who lived only for him. One course of action would be directed to what he saw as the national good, but would probably be of insignificant effect in the total war. The other would be of immediate practical effect, but would be directed to the good of only one individual. Sartre holds that no ethical doctrine, Christian or Kantian or any other, can arbitrate between such incommensurate claims. Nor can strength of feeling in the individual faced with the choice settle the matter, for there is no measure of such feeling except in terms of what he actually does, which is of course precisely what is at stake. To choose an adviser is itself a choice. So when Sartre was consulted by this young man, he said merely 'You are free, therefore choose'.

However Sartre does clearly commit himself to the intrinsic value of authentic choice. His descriptions of particular cases of bad faith are not morally neutral, but implicitly condemn any self-deception, any refusal to face reality and admit one's own choices. He thus offers another perspective on the ancient virtue of self-knowledge prescribed by Socrates, Freud, and many others. But Sartre's understanding of the nature and possibility of self-knowledge differs in crucial ways from Freud's. We have seen that psycho-analysis is based on the hypothesis of unconscious mental states which have causal effects on people's mental life. Freud conceived of these causes as acting in a quasi-mechanical way, like flows of energy, and he thought of his job in psycho-analysis as the uncovering of these hidden causes. Sartre emphatically rejects the idea of unconscious causes of mental events; for him everything mental is already out in the open, available to consciousness (p. 571). The job of what he calls 'existential psycho-analysis' is not to look for *causes* of a person's behaviour, but for the *meaning* of it (pp. 568–9). Some contemporary psychiatrists, such as R. D. Laing, follow Sartre on this point. (In the last chapter I mentioned the suggestion that Freudian psycho-analysis itself is really an interpretation of motives, purposes, and intentions rather than a discovery of causes.) So to understand a person Sartre looks for *choices* (p. 573), and he holds that since a person is essentially a unity, not just a bundle of unrelated desires or habits, there must be for each person a fundamental choice (the 'original project') which gives the meaning of every particular aspect of his behaviour (pp. 561–5). The biographies Sartre has written of Baudelaire, Genet, and Flaubert are particular exercises in interpreting the fundamental meaning of a person's way of life. Existential psycho-analysis is, then, the means by which Sartre hopes that we can achieve genuine self-knowledge. He ends *Being and Nothingness* with a promise to write another work, on the ethical plane, to show how we can live as free beings aware of our freedom.

CRITICAL DISCUSSION

My first complaint against Sartre is one about style rather than content. *Being and Nothingness*, it is only fair to warn the reader, is easily the most unreadable of the texts I refer to in this book. This is a matter not just of length and repetitiousness, but of a word-spinning delight in the abstract noun, the elusive metaphor, and the unresolved paradox. To trace this to the influence of Hegel, Husserl, and Heidegger may explain but can hardly excuse it. One may be thankful that Sartre is not as obscure as they are, but surely he could have said what he has to say more clearly and a lot more briefly. It is all the more tantalizing when one finds passages of relative clarity and great insight buried inside the conglomeration of verbiage. However the effort to understand him does begin to reveal a view of human nature which has a certain compelling fascination.

To turn to matters of content, let us first consider the problem of how bad faith is possible. We have noted that Sartre rejects, for conceptual reasons, any Freudian explanation of this. But it is not clear whether he offers any adequate solution of his own to the conceptual problem of how consciousness can 'be what it is not and not be what it is', despite the extended discussion of being-for-itself in Part Two. He appears to rest too easily in such paradoxical statements and to shirk the difficult philosophical task of explaining in clear unparadoxical terms what it is about consciousness that generates the problem.

There is an apparent contradiction between Sartre's constant insistence on our freedom, and his analysis of the human condition as necessarily determined in certain respects. For he holds that as conscious beings we are always wanting to fill the 'nothingness' which is the essence of our being conscious; we want to become things rather than remain perpetually in the state of having possibilities unfulfilled (p. 90). He also holds that the relationship between two consciousnesses is necessarily one of conflict, for each wants to achieve the impossible ideal of making the other into a mere object (pp. 394, 429). In these two respects, he analyses human life as a perpetual attempt to achieve the logically impossible. But why *must* it be so? Surely there is a direct contradiction between these 'musts' and our supposed freedom? Cannot someone *choose* not to want to become an object, or to make other people into objects? It is hard to see whether Sartre even tries to resolve these contradictions at the heart of his theory.

We have noted that the only positive recommendation that Sartre can make is that one should avoid bad faith and choose authentically. But can self-knowledge or authenticity be the only basis for how to live? If no reasons whatsoever can be given for choosing one way of life rather than another, the choice is arbitrary. It looks as if on his own premises Sartre would have to commend the man who chooses to devote his life to exterminating Jews, provided that he chooses this with full

awareness of what he is doing. Conversely, the man who devotes himself to helping 'down and outs' but is not aware of his
own real motive for doing so (perhaps a reaction against his
parental background) would apparently have to be condemned as inauthentic. Or can it be argued that authenticity
must involve respecting the freedom of other people? Sartre
never wrote his promised book on ethics, and perhaps the
reason is that he realized that no social ethic could be developed
from the individualist premises of *Being and Nothingness*. No doubt this is also why he has come to adopt a Marxist
standpoint, to seek the social conditions which would make it
possible for *all* men to exercise their freedom.

Yet there is something important to learn from Sartre's deep
analysis of how the very notion of consciousness involves that
of freedom. We have seen how he wants to extend the concept
of choice far beyond its normal use, to hold us responsible not
just for our actions, but for our emotions and even for our
characters. If I am angry, it is because I have chosen to be
angry; and if I am the kind of person who is usually passively
resigned to his condition, that too is a disposition that I choose
to adopt. This view does seem to contradict our normal concepts of emotion and character, for emotions are supposed to
'come over one' whether one wills it or not. And our character
is supposed to be a *fact* about us like our weight—something
we can try to change gradually by taking certain steps, admittedly, but not something which we can change at a stroke, like
standing up or sitting down. And yet Sartre's view here is not
just an arbitrary misuse of language. For we do commonly reproach people for their emotions and characters—'How *could*
you feel like that?', '*Must* you be so...?'. And such reproach is
not always useless. For to make someone *aware* that he is feeling or behaving in a certain way does make a difference to him.
The more he is aware of his anger or pride, the more he is not
just angry or proud, and the more capable he is of becoming
something else. Perhaps this is the essence of Sartre's point.
The vast verbiage of his philosophy issues ultimately in a
directly practical and intimate challenge to us all, to become
more truly self-aware and to exercise our power of changing
ourselves.

FOR FURTHER READING

Basic text: *Being and Nothingness*, translated by Hazel Barnes (Methuen, London, 1957; Citadel Press paperback, Secaucus, N.J.). This lengthy and difficult book is best read with the help of an introduction which directs one to the more important and relatively clear passages. I hope that the chapter above may be of some help, but Manser's book described below gives a more comprehensive and detailed guide.

Sartre: A Philosophic Study by Anthony Manser (Athlone Press, London, 1966; Oxford University Press Galaxy Books paperback, New York) is a survey of the whole of Sartre's thought, including his literature and politics but giving most attention to his philosophy.

For an introduction to other existentialists, see *Existentialism* by Mary Warnock (Oxford University Press OPUS paperback, Oxford, 1970; Galaxy Books paperback, New York).

CHAPTER 8

Skinner: The Con-
ditioning of Behaviour

PERHAPS the reader is wondering by now whether it is worth
giving so much attention to the philosophers and speculative
thinkers of the past. In a scientific age, should we not look to
psychology for the truth about human nature? In the last hun-
dred years psychology has established itself as an independent
branch of empirical science clearly separated from its early
philosophical sources, so surely we can now expect some properly scientific answers to our questions about human nature?
The fact is, however, that psychology is an extraordinarily
difficult and complex discipline, which yields clear answers
only to very carefully and precisely defined questions on specific topics. So if an experimental psychologist begins to *generalize* about human nature, his statements are likely to be as
speculative as those of the thinkers we have considered, at least
in the present state of his subject. It is also true that there are
still various schools of thought and methodologies within psychology, so that it is not as free from 'philosophical' questions
as we might like to think. As a sample of what one kind of
psychology has to offer, let us consider the work of B. F. Skinner, Professor of Psychology at Harvard University since 1948,
who has been one of the most influential experimental psychologists in the behaviourist tradition. Since he is also one of
those who is prepared to generalize about human nature and
to offer diagnoses of, and prescriptions for, our problems, we
will find plenty to discuss without necessarily being drawn into
the details of his experimental work, upon which non-psycho-
logists can hardly be qualified to comment.

As background to Skinner's work it will be useful to consider
that of his earlier compatriot J. B. Watson, who is generally
recognized as the founder of psychological behaviourism. In
the last quarter of the nineteenth century the first psychological laboratories had been set up, and psychology began to be
an empirical science, under the leadership of men like Wundt
in Germany and William James in America. They defined it

not as the study of soul or mind (which would suggest some sort of metaphysical dualism) but as the study of consciousness. They thought that since each of us is aware of the contents of his own consciousness, we can simply report them by introspection and thus give the empirical data for psychology. But it was soon found that such reports could not agree on the description and classification of sensations, images, and feelings. So the introspective method ran into an impasse. At the same time Freud's work was suggesting that important aspects of the mind were not accessible to consciousness. In the study of animals introspection is obviously not available, and yet (since Darwin) one would expect the study of animals to be closely related to that of men. And in any case the notion of consciousness poses almost as many philosophical problems as that of soul or mind.

So when Watson proclaimed, in a paper of 1913, that the subject matter of psychology should be *behaviour*, not consciousness, his views found a ready acceptance which reorientated psychology completely. For the behaviour of animals and men is publicly observable, so reports and descriptions of it can form the objective data of psychology; and the concept of behaviour apparently involves no questionable philosophical assumptions. This rejection of the introspective method was the most fundamental point of Watson's new programme. It is of course a purely *methodological* point about what psychology ought to study, and is quite independent of any metaphysical statement that consciousness does not exist, or that it is nothing but the material processes inside a person's skull. It is also independent of the philosophical thesis (called logical or analytical behaviourism) that our words for mental phenomena really refer only to behaviour and dispositions to behaviour. But Watson and his followers were wont to go beyond their merely methodological point and allege that belief in consciousness is a hangover from our superstitious pre-scientific past, akin to belief in witchcraft.

There were two other main points in Watson's creed, however, which are really empirical theories within psychology rather than methodological points. The first was his belief that environment is much more important than heredity in the determination of behaviour. This is a natural concomitant of his methodology, for the external influences on an organism's behaviour are easily observable, and manipulable by experiment, whereas the internal influences (and in particular the genes) are much more difficult to observe and manipulate. But of course this fact alone does not tell us anything about the relative influence of environment and heredity on behaviour. However Watson assumed that the only inherited features of behaviour were simply physiological reflexes; he attributed everything else to learning. Hence his claim (which he admitted went beyond the known facts): 'Give me a dozen healthy infants, well-formed, and my own specified world to bring them up in and I'll guarantee to take any one at random and train him to become any kind of specialist I might select— doctor, lawyer, artist, merchant-chief, and yes even beggar-man and thief, regardless of his talents, penchants, abilities, vocations, and race of his ancestors' (*Behaviourism*, 1924, revd. edn. 1930, p. 104). Watson's other empirical guess was a particular theory of how learning takes place, namely by the conditioning of reflexes. This was suggested by Pavlov's famous experiments in which he trained dogs to salivate at the sound of a bell, by regularly ringing the bell just before feeding them. Watson's programme was to explain all the complex behaviour of animals and men as the result of such conditioning by their environment.

In the work of experimental psychology since Watson's time, doubt has been cast both on his extreme emphasis on environment, and on his particular theory of learning. However, Skinner has carried on with Watson's programme. He sticks to the behaviourist methodology even more rigorously, and eschews all reference to unobservable entities. He shows a similar faith in the programme of explaining all behaviour of animals and men as the effect of the environment upon them, an effect mediated by a few basic conditioning processes. *The Behaviour of Organisms: An Experimental Analysis* (1938) is his fundamental technical work on conditioning. In *Science and Human Behaviour* (1953) he applied his theories to human life and society in general, and in *Verbal Behaviour* (1957) to human language in particular. He has also published a novel, *Walden Two* (1948), in which he describes a Utopian community organized on his principles of behavioural conditioning. And recently he has produced *Beyond Freedom and Dignity* (1971) in which he claims again that a technology of behaviour can solve the problems of human life and society, if only we will give up our illusions about individual freedom, responsibility, and dignity. In what follows I shall make my page references to *Science and Human Behaviour*, which is the most wide-ranging and readable of these works. And I shall incorporate criticism with exposition, because the analysis of what Skinner means leads directly to criticism of it.

THEORY OF THE UNIVERSE

Skinner is the most rigorously 'scientific' of the thinkers I consider in this book. He believes that only science can tell us the truth about nature, including human nature, for science is unique in human activity in showing a cumulative progress (p. 11). What is fundamental to science is neither instruments nor measurement but scientific *method*—the disposition to get at the facts, whether expected or surprising, pleasant or repugnant. All statements must be submitted to the test of observation or experiment, and where there is insufficient evidence we must admit our ignorance. The scientist tries to find uniformities or lawful relations between phenomena, and to construct general theories which will successfully explain all particular cases (pp. 13–14). Furthermore Skinner sees no clear distinction between science and technology; he says that the job of science is not just to predict, but to *control* the world (p. 14).

Most scientists would agree with Skinner in his description of scientific method, except that they might make a clearer distinction between science and technology, between prediction and control. But some scientists are Christians while others are humanists, some are left-wing and others right-wing. Skinner seems to think that there is no basis except in science for answering *any* sort of question. Certainly, he finds no scientific basis for belief in God, and treats religion as merely one of the social institutions for manipulating human behaviour (pp. 350–8). Value judgements are, he thinks, typically the expression of the pressure to conform which is exerted by any social group (pp. 415–18), a kind of concealed command (p. 429). They can be given an objective scientific basis only if they concern means to ends. 'You ought to take an umbrella' might be roughly translated as 'You want to keep dry, umbrellas keep you dry in the rain, and it's going to rain' (though Skinner replaces the ordinary notion of wanting by the supposedly more scientific notion of 'reinforcement') (p. 429). The only objective basis he can see for evaluating cultural practices as a whole is their survival value for the culture (pp. 430–6). But even here he says that we do not really *choose* survival as a basic value, it is just that our past has so conditioned us that we do tend to seek the survival of our culture (p. 433). If we want a label for this attempt to answer *all* questions purely scientifically, perhaps 'scientism' will do.

THEORY OF MAN

Skinner proposes that the empirical study of human *behaviour* is the only way to arrive at a true theory of human nature. So naturally he will reject any kind of metaphysical dualism. But with it he rejects any attempt to explain human behaviour in terms of mental entities, whether they are everyday concepts of desires, intentions, and decisions, or Freudian postulations such as id, ego, and super-ego (pp. 29–30). He rejects such entities not only because they are unobservable, but because he thinks they are of no explanatory value anyway. For instance, to say that a man eats because he is hungry is not to assign a cause to his behaviour but simply to redescribe it (p. 31). It is no more explanatory than saying that opium puts you to sleep *because* it has a 'dormitive power'. Of course, Skinner must admit the possibility of discovering physiological preconditions of behaviour (the literally inner states). But he holds that even when the progress of physiology tells us about these, we shall still have to trace *their* causation back to the environment, so we may as well bypass the physiology and look directly for the environmental causes of behaviour (p. 35). He has to admit that genetic factors are relevant, for it is obvious that different species behave in very different ways. But he dismisses the layman's use of 'heredity' as a purely fictional explanation of behaviour, and holds genetic factors to be of little value in 'experimental analysis' because they cannot be manipulated by the experimenter (p. 26).

This position is a rather confusing mixture of methodological precept and empirical theory, both derived from Watson's behaviourism. We must try to sort out the different components in the mixture. Obviously Skinner defines psychology as the study of behaviour. But this does not settle whether psychology is to be permitted to postulate unobservable entities to explain behaviour. Many psychologists are quite happy to talk in terms of drives, memory, emotions, and other 'mental' entities, provided of course that what is said about them is testable by the observation of behaviour. But it appears that Skinner is adopting a much more austere methodology, and is rejecting all mention of unobservables. In this he is trying to be more 'scientific' than most scientists, for the physical sciences very often postulate unobservable theoretical entities such as magnetic fields, mechanical forces, and subatomic particles. In the heyday of the philosophy of logical positivism it was doubted whether this was really proper procedure, but it is now generally acknowledged that to disallow it would be an impossible restriction on scientific method. Provided that what is said about unobservable theoretical entities is falsifiable by observation, there is no valid objection to them. So if Skinner is rejecting inner mental causes of behaviour *just* because they are unobservable, then I think we must judge this to be a quite unnecessarily restrictive methodology.

But he does offer another reason for rejecting what he calls 'conceptual' inner causes (p. 31), namely that they are of no explanatory value (as noted above). However he has not shown that such conceptual inner causes must be merely redescriptive of what they are supposed to explain; he has only given a few examples in which he thinks this to be true. Certainly, an inner state S can only be a genuine explanation of behaviour B if we can have some evidence for the existence of S other than the occurrence of B, but surely this condition is sometimes satisfied. For instance (in Skinner's own example) we can have good evidence for saying that someone is hungry even though he is not *actually* eating, if we know that he has not eaten for 24 hours (and perhaps he *says* he is hungry!). It is just not true that a single set of facts is described by the two statements: 'He eats' and 'He is hungry'. Obviously, one can be hungry when one is not eating, and (less often) one can eat when one is not hungry. Skinner has not given any adequate reason for the rejection of all conceptual causes of behaviour.

What of his rejection of physiological states as causes? The fact that these are not easily observable or manipulable does nothing to show that they do not play a crucial role in the causation of behaviour (as we noted when discussing Watson's environmentalism). Skinner's assumption is that physiological states inside an organism merely mediate the effect of its environment (past and present) on its behaviour. So he thinks that psychology can confine its attention to the laws connecting environmental influences directly with behaviour. There are two separable assumptions here. Firstly, that human behaviour is governed by scientific laws of *some* kind: 'If we are to use the methods of science in the field of human affairs, we must assume that behaviour is lawful and determined' (pp. 6 and 447). Secondly, that these laws state causal connections between environmental factors and human behaviour: 'Our "independent variables"—the causes of behaviour—are the external conditions of which behaviour is a function' (p. 35).

These two assumptions could be taken in a purely methodological interpretation, as expressing a programme of *looking* for laws governing human behaviour, and specifically for laws connecting environment with behaviour. As such, there can be no objection to them. But it is fairly clear that Skinner also takes them as general assertions of what is the case about human behaviour. As such, we must ask whether there is any good reason to think that they are true, for these are the crucial assumptions on which Skinner's theory of human nature is based. (They are recognizably descended from Watson's environmentalism.) Firstly, do we have to assume that *all* human behaviour is governed by causal laws, if we are to study that behaviour scientifically? There is no more reason to assume this than there is for Marx to maintain that if we are to study history scientifically there must be laws which determine everything which happens. Universal determinism is not a necessary presupposition of science, although the *search* for causal laws is central to science. Admittedly, it would be rather disappointing if psychology could not proceed beyond the mere reporting of particular events and statistical regularities. But whether there are causal laws governing behaviour is something which we must leave psychology to discover. That *all* behaviour is governed by such laws is a 'metaphysical' assumption which ill befits a supposedly strict empiricist such as Skinner.

The more specific assumption that all behaviour is a function of *environmental* variables is even more dubious. What it means, in detail, is that for any piece of behaviour, there is a finite set of environmental conditions (past or present) such that it is a causal law that anyone to whom all those conditions apply will perform that behaviour. This is reminiscent of Watson's claim that he could take any infant at random and make of it anything he liked, given only the appropriate environment. It entails a denial that inherited factors make any difference to the behaviour of human beings. So that, for instance, any healthy infant could be trained to become a four-minute miler, a nuclear physicist, or anything else. In its full generality, this claim seems fairly obviously false. The fact that the differences in ability between identical twins brought up apart are much less than the average range of ability in the whole population is evidence against it. Heredity does play *some* part, though this is not to deny the huge importance of environment. To attribute all to environment is another assumption which Skinner does not submit to empirical test.

We should now pay some brief attention to the specific mechanisms of conditioning by which Skinner thinks the environment controls behaviour. His theory is descended from the ideas of Pavlov and Watson, but this is the area in which Skinner has made his own major contributions to the advancement of psychological knowledge. In the 'classical' conditioning of Pavlov's experiments, the 'reinforcer' (food) was repeatedly presented together with a 'stimulus' (the ringing of a bell), and the 'response' (salivation) would then appear for the bell without the food. The main difference in Skinner's 'operant' conditioning is that what is conditioned is not a reflex response like salivation, but any kind of behaviour which the animal may perform quite spontaneously without any particular stimulus. For instance, rats can be trained to press levers, and pigeons to hold their heads abnormally high, in each case simply by feeding the animal whenever it presses the lever, or raises its head above a certain level. So when the environment is arranged such that the reinforcer follows upon a certain kind of behaviour (called the 'operant', since the animal thus operates on its environment), then that behaviour is performed more frequently (pp. 62–6). (This is of course the general principle on which all animal training works.) In a vast amount of careful experimental work, Skinner and his followers have discovered many new facts about the processes of conditioning, for instance, that intermittent reinforcement tends to produce a greater rate of response—so if we want a rat to do as much lever-pressing as possible, we should feed it irregularly, not after every press.

Skinner's experimental work is impressive and unimpugnable, but what we can and must criticize here is his extrapolation from it to human behaviour in general. In *Science and Human Behaviour* he outlines the understanding of behaviour that he has gained from his animal experiments (mainly with rats and pigeons) and then goes on to apply these conceptions to human individuals and institutions—government, religion, psychotherapy, economics, and education. But it is quite possible that Skinner's discoveries about rats and pigeons apply only to those species (and perhaps related ones), but not to more complex animals and especially not to men. Although he rightly points out that we cannot assume that human behaviour is different in kind from animal behaviour (pp. 38–9), his whole approach seems to make the equally unjustified assumption that what applies to laboratory animals will apply (with only a difference of complexity) to men (pp. 205 ff.).

One very important area in which Skinner has applied his theories to human behaviour is that of language. In *Verbal Behaviour* he attempts to show that all human speech can be attributed to the conditioning of speakers by their environment (which includes of course their social environment, the noises made by surrounding humans). Thus, a baby born in England is subjected to many samples of English conversation, and when its responses are reasonably accurate reproductions of what it has heard they are 'reinforced', and thus the child comes to learn to speak English. Adult speech, too, is analysed by Skinner as a series of responses to stimuli from the environment, including verbal stimuli from other people.

The crucial defects in Skinner's account of language have been pointed out by Chomsky, whose work has given new direction to research in linguistics and psychology in the last decade. Chomsky argues that although Skinner has tried to describe *how* language is learned, his account is of little value because he pays no attention to the question of *what* it is that we learn when we acquire the ability to speak a language as our native tongue. Clearly, we can hardly ask how we learn X unless we first know what X is; we must have a criterion for someone having *succeeded* in learning X. Now human language is a very different sort of phenomenon from rats' pressing of levers. Skinner could hardly deny this, but would suggest that the differences are only a matter of degree of complexity. But Chomsky suggests that the *creative* and *structural* features of human language—the way in which we can all speak and understand sentences we have never heard before, just by our knowledge of the vocabulary and grammar of our language—make it quite different in kind from any known kind of animal behaviour. If so, the attempt to analyse human speech in terms derived from the behaviour of lower animals would seem to be doomed from the start. And the same would apply to other distinctively human forms of behaviour.

Even the suggestions Skinner does make for how linguistic behaviour is learned can be seen to be based on very shaky analogies. For instance, the reinforcement which may encourage correct speech by an infant is very rarely feeding, but more likely some sort of social approval. He suggests that we can be reinforced by being paid attention, or even by merely saying something which is satisfying to ourselves, perhaps just because it is an accurate reproduction of what we have heard. The trouble here is that this is merely speculation. The use of a term like 'reinforcement' which has a strictly defined meaning for certain experiments with animals in no way guarantees scientific objectivity for its use in human situations which are allegedly analogous. So once again, Skinner's supposedly strictly empirical approach turns out to conceal a large element of unempirical speculation.

There is another important respect in which Chomsky argues that Skinner's theories fall down when applied to human language. This is the matter of inherited factors, of the contribution made by the speaker rather than his environment to his learning of language. Obviously, English children learn English, and Chinese children learn Chinese, so the environment does have major effects. But again, all normal human children learn one of the human languages, but no other animal learns anything which resembles human languages in the crucial respect of the formation of indefinitely many complex sentences according to rules of grammar. So it seems that the capacity to learn such a language is peculiar to the human species. Skinner holds that our language-learning must be due just to a complex set of reinforcements from our human environment. Chomsky suggests that the amazing speed with which children learn the grammatical rules of the language they hear from a very limited and imperfect sample of that language can be explained only by the assumption that there is in the human species an *innate* capacity to process language according to such rules. So behind all the apparent variety of human languages there must be a certain basic systematic structure common to all, and we must suppose that we do not *learn* this structure from our environment, but process whatever linguistic stimulation we receive in terms of this structure. This fascinating hypothesis has by no means been proved, but the available evidence does tend to favour it rather than Skinner's extreme environmentalism.

Speech is of course not the only human activity. But it is especially important as a representative of the 'higher' human mental abilities. So if Skinner's theories fail to explain it adequately we must conclude that even if they explain some human behaviour they cannot give a true account of human nature in general. There remains the possibility that other important aspects of human behaviour are not learned from the environment but are genuinely innate.

DIAGNOSIS

Skinner's diagnosis can be seen as the exact opposite of Sartre's. Sartre maintains that we are free, but keep pretending that we are not. Skinner says we are determined, but still like to think that we are free. He analyses our current social practices as based on theoretical confusion. We are increasingly realizing how environment determines behaviour, and hence we exonerate people from blame by pointing to the circumstances of their upbringing. Yet we also maintain that people are often genuinely responsible for their actions (p. 8). We are thus in an unstable transitional stage, and 'the present unhappy condi-

tion of the world may in large measure be traced to our vacil-
lation'; 'we shall almost certainly remain ineffective in solving
these problems until we adopt a consistent point of view' (p. 9).
'A sweeping revision of the concept of responsibility is needed'
(p. 241), for our present practice of punishment is remarkably
inefficient in controlling behaviour (p. 342). We will have to
abandon the illusion that men are free agents, in control of
their own behaviour, for whether we like it or not we are all
'controlled' (p. 438).

This diagnosis of 'the unhappy condition of the world' seems
very dubious. Admittedly there are important practical problems about deciding the extent of responsibility, and these are
closely connected with deep theoretical and philosophical questions about the concept of freedom. But Skinner's dismissal of
the concept is an inadequate and unargued response to these
problems. In his latest book, *Beyond Freedom and Dignity*, he
seems to be saying that just as it was the mistake of animism to
treat inanimate *things* as if they were people and attribute
thoughts and intentions to them, so it is a mistake to treat
people as people and attribute desires and decisions to them!
Of course this is absurd. The first point that needs to be made
to get us out of this confusion is this. The thesis of universal
determinism is that every event (including all human choices)
has a set of sufficient preceding causes. Now even if this thesis is
true (and remember that Skinner has given us no reason to
believe it), we are not precluded from picking out as 'free'
those human actions which include among their causes the
choice of the person. The concept of a free action surely does
not imply that it has no causes at all (that would make it
random), but that it is a result of the agent's choice. We could
still hold people responsible for the actions they choose, even if
those choices themselves have causes. Skinner himself seems to
believe it important to use methods of social control which
depend on individual choice rather than on forms of conditioning of which people are not aware.

PRESCRIPTION

Like Marx, Skinner holds that human circumstances can and
should be humanly formed. If the environment makes us what
we are, then we should change the social environment de-

liberately so that the human product will meet more accept-able specifications' (p. 427). He thinks that psychology has reached the point where it can offer techniques for the manipu-lation and control of human behaviour, hence for changing human society for better or for worse (p. 437). If we will only give up the illusions of individual freedom and dignity, we can create a happier life by conditioning everyone's behaviour in appropriate ways. For instance, we can give up the inefficient practice of punishment, and instead induce people to act leg-ally by making them *want* to conform to the standards of society (p. 345). This can be done by a combination of education and positive inducements, not necessarily by propaganda or any concealed manipulation. Thus science could lead to the design of a government which will really promote the well-being of the governed (p. 443), and perhaps even to a set of 'moral values' (Skinner's quotes!) which may be generally ac-cepted (p. 445). Provided that control is diversified between different individuals and institutions there need be no danger of despotism (pp. 440–6).

This vague programme sounds optimistic and yet rather sin-ister in its jaunty dismissal of individual freedom. What Skin-ner has in mind comes out a little more clearly in his novel *Walden Two*, in which his ideal community combines the cul-ture-vulture atmosphere of an adult education summer school with the political system of Plato's *Republic* (for there is a wise designer of the community who has arranged everything on 'correct' behaviourist principles from the start!). But Skinner's utopia is open to much the same objections as Plato's. On what basis are the designers of a culture to decide what is best for everyone? How can misuse of their power be prevented? Des-pite his mention of safeguards against despotism, Skinner seems politically very naïve. His very terminology of 'designing a culture' and 'the human product' suggests that he makes the highly questionable assumption that it should be the aim of social reform to produce a certain ideal kind of society and individual. An important alternative view is that the aim should be purely negative—to eliminate specific causes of human unhappiness, such as poverty, disease, and injustice—and that to try to condition people according to some blue-print is to trespass upon what should be the area of individual choice. (This is the distinction which Popper makes, in his criticism of Plato noted above in Chapter III, between 'utopian' and 'piecemeal' social engineering.)

So we do not have to accept Skinner's judgement that individual freedom is a myth and therefore not important. There are immediate practical issues involved here, for behaviour therapy based on Skinnerian principles of conditioning is already being applied to neurotics and criminals in some places. But in cases not of physical illness but of behaviour which is 'abnormal' or 'deviant' by some criterion, when (if ever) does anyone have the right to try to condition someone else's behaviour? There are deep problems—factual, conceptual, and ethical—about how the purely scientific approach to a person, as an organism whose behaviour has identifiable and manipulable causes, can be combined with the ordinary assumption by which we treat our fellows as rational beings who are responsible for their intentional actions. Skinner assumes that the two are simply incompatible, and that the latter must give way to the former (p. 449). But this is just the dogmatic and uncritical position taken by one particular psychologist. It would be a great pity if this discouraged us from seeking better understanding of human nature from experimental psychology.

FOR FURTHER READING

Basic text: B. F. Skinner, *Science and Human Behaviour* (Macmillan, New York, 1953; Free Press paperback, New York, 1965).

Skinner's Utopian novel *Walden Two* (Macmillan, New York, 1948) and his *Beyond Freedom and Dignity* (Penguin, London, 1973; Bantam Books paperback, New York, 1972) outline his ideal society and the means by which he thinks we can achieve it.

For a review of the progress of experimental psychology since Watson, see *Behaviour* by D. E. Broadbent (Methuen, London, University Paperbacks 1961). This is written for the layman, and has some critical discussion of Skinner's work in Chapter 5.

For Chomsky's criticisms of Skinner's theory of language, see his review in *Language*, 35, 1 (1959), reprinted in *The Structure of Language*, edited by Fodor and Katz (Prentice-Hall, Englewood Cliffs, 1964). But this is rather difficult reading; for a better introduction to

Chomsky's views see his *Language and Mind*, enlarged edition, (Harcourt Brace Jovanovich Inc., New York, 1972), or the book on Chomsky by J. Lyons in the Modern Masters Series (Fontana, London, 1970; Viking, New York, 1970).

CHAPTER 9

Lorenz: Innate
Aggression

WE have criticized Skinner for neglecting the possibility that certain important features of human behaviour are innate rather than learned from experience. So let us now turn to Lorenz, who bases his diagnosis of human ills on precisely this possibility. Lorenz is one of the founding fathers of the branch of the life sciences called ethology. Etymologically, the term 'ethology' means the study of character, but it is now used to mean the scientific study of animal behaviour. However this does not make clear how an ethologist differs from a psychologist, who would also claim to study animal behaviour scientifically. Perhaps ultimately there is no difference, but there certainly have been two different approaches which are only now achieving some *rapprochement*. We have seen that behaviourists such as Watson and Skinner have been committed not only to the methodology of studying behaviour rather than consciousness, but also to certain wide-ranging empirical theories—that behaviour is caused almost entirely by environmental influences mediated through conditioning mechanisms. Consequently, their experiments have studied the details of how environment can *change* behaviour. In the twenties and thirties of this century, the early ethologists realized that very many of the behaviour patterns of animals (those which have traditionally been called 'instinctual') could not be explained in the behaviourists' way. What was distinctive of such behaviour was that it was *fixed*, it could not be eliminated or altered by the environment, however much that environment was experimentally manipulated. So the ethologists concentrated on these fixed 'instinctual' behaviour patterns, and observed the 'natural' behaviour of the animal in the wild before intervening to perform experiments.

So the distinctive emphasis of ethology arises out of the anti-behaviourist assumption that some of the most important aspects of animal behaviour are innate. To explain such behaviour ethologists appeal not to the past experience of the *individual* animal, but to the process of evolution which has given rise to that *species* of animal. To account for the existence of an instinctive behaviour pattern in a species we must say what survival value it has for the species. So ethology is based, more directly than psychology in general, on the theory of evolution. And contemporary ethological theories of human nature appeal to the evolutionary past of man in order to explain his present condition. This therefore seems the appropriate place to sketch briefly the essentials of the theory of evolution, which is in any case something that no adequate theory of human nature can afford to neglect.

Darwin was not the only person to arrive at a theory of the evolution of species by gradual divergence from common ancestors, but his *Origin of Species* (1859) is the classic work which convinced both scientific and popular opinion of the truth of the theory. Its full title is 'The origin of species by means of natural selection: or the preservation of favoured races in the struggle of life', which effectively summarizes its key idea. It was written for the general educated public, and documents the argument with an immense wealth of evidence which Darwin had accumulated from his research during the previous twenty years. In this book he does not explicitly state what it clearly implied—that man too was descended from animal ancestors—but this obvious implication caused a famous controversy with some of the theologians of the time. In later books Darwin did explicitly apply his theories to man, in *The Descent of Man* (1871) and *The Expression of the Emotions in Man and Animals* (1872) (note how the title of the latter suggests an ethological theme).

Darwin's theory is a logical deduction from four true empirical propositions. The first two concern matters of genetics —that traits of parents tend in general to be passed on to their offspring, but there is nevertheless considerable variation between individuals of a given species. These two truths emerge clearly from a wide variety of observations, and they are utilized in the deliberate breeding of different varieties of domestic animals. But their theoretical explanation was not discovered until after Darwin's time, in Mendel's theory of genes. (The facts of 'mutation' (occasional changes in genes), the number of genes available, and their patterns of interaction, explain the variation stated in the second proposition.) The

third and fourth premisses of Darwin's argument are the facts
that species are capable of a geometric rate of increase, whereas
the resources of the environment cannot support such a rate. It
follows from these last two facts that a very small proportion of
seeds, eggs, and young reach maturity; in short, there is a
struggle for existence, primarily between members of the same
species. Now from this struggle and from the fact of variation
within a species, we can deduce that there will be certain individuals (those whose characteristics are most 'advantageous'
in the given environment) which will live longest. They will
have the best chance of leaving offspring, therefore, given the
first fact of inheritance, their traits will tend to be passed on,
whereas disadvantageous traits will tend to die out. Thus over
a period of time the typical characteristics of a population of
animals can change. And given the immense periods of geo-
logical time, and the wide variety of environments, different
species can slowly evolve from common ancestors. All that is
needed to produce such evolution is the constant pressure of
natural selection acting on the variations caused by random
mutations. There is no need to postulate the biologically implausible inheritance of 'acquired' (individually learned) characteristics, as Lamarck did, and as Darwin himself did at some
stages of his work.

Apart from this very general argument for the mechanism of
evolution, there is much direct empirical evidence for man's
common ancestry with other animals. Comparative anatomy
shows the human body to have the same general plan as other
vertebrates—four limbs with five digits on each, etc. The
human embryo goes through stages of development in which it
resembles those of the various lower forms of life. In the adult
human body there are 'remnants' of such lower forms—e.g. a
vestigial tail. The basic chemistry of our bodies—e.g. digestion,
blood, genes—is similar to those of other mammals. Finally
there are the fossil remains of creatures which were ape-like
but resembled humans more than any existing apes. So our
animal ancestry is overwhelmingly confirmed by the evidence.
Some questions may remain about the detailed mechanism of
evolution, but that we have evolved is now an established fact,
which no true theory of human nature can contradict.

But exactly what implications the fact of evolution has is a
matter of dispute which cannot be settled by the theory itself.

Some nineteenth-century churchmen thought it contradicted the Christian doctrine of creation, but most present-day theologians find no real conflict (Teilhard de Chardin has even constructed a peculiarly evolutionary theology). Marx welcomed the theory as a confirmation of his view of the progressive development of human history (he even wanted to dedicate the English edition of *Das Kapital* to Darwin, but the latter politely declined the honour!). Yet right-wing politicians claimed that evolution showed unrestrained economic competition to be 'natural', like the survival of the fittest, and therefore right (such doctrine was called 'social Darwinism'). In our own day several popular books have used the idea that our evolution from ape-like ancestors is the key to our true nature: Robert Ardrey in *The Territorial Imperative* and other books, Desmond Morris in *The Naked Ape*, and Arthur Koestler in *The Ghost in the Machine*. But one of the main sources of their ideas is Lorenz's work. So a critical examination of his ideas should equip the reader to look at these recent popular works with a sympathetic but sceptical eye.

Like Freud, Konrad Lorenz is a product of the scientific and cultural traditions of Vienna who has pioneered a new area of scientific study with deep implications for mankind. In his technical papers on animal behaviour he has interpreted his very extensive and careful observations of many species, and some of the concepts he introduced have passed into the common currency of modern biological science. But he has also written for the general reader, and in *King Solomon's Ring* (1950), *Man Meets Dog* (1954), and *On Aggression* (1963), he displays style, humour, an engaging personality, and an awareness of deep issues of epistemology and society. The first two books introduce ethological themes by a variety of anecdotal descriptions, mostly of the pets Lorenz himself has kept. The latter concentrates on aggressive behaviour and attempts a diagnosis of man's condition, so my page references will be to it (for the American edition see the end of this chapter).

THEORY OF THE UNIVERSE

Lorenz is a biological scientist, so the most important of his background assumptions is the theory of evolution which I have summarized above. To explain the existence of any particular organ or behaviour pattern he looks for its survival value for the species (pp. 8–9). As an ethologist, he denies that all behaviour is conditioned by the environment (p. 41), and devotes himself to studying instinctive behaviour patterns. What is distinctive of these is that they do not always need an external stimulus to set them off, but happen spontaneously, as if driven by causes within the animal itself. Thus a male dove deprived of its mate would begin to perform its courtship dance to a stuffed pigeon, a piece of cloth, or even the empty corner of its cage (p. 42). And a hand-reared starling which had never caught flies or seen any other bird do so would go through fly-catching movements even when no flies were there (p. 43). Lorenz holds that there are many such patterns of animal behaviour which are 'hereditary co-ordinations' or 'instinct movements'; they are innate rather than learned, and for each there is a 'drive' which causes the behaviour to appear spontaneously (p. 74). But he also suggests, somewhat vaguely and tentatively, that such fixed action patterns are often at the disposal of one or more of the four 'big drives'—feeding, reproduction, flight, and aggression (p. 75). He thinks that any one piece of behaviour is usually caused by at least two drives or inner causes (pp. 73, 84), and that conflict between independent impulses can give firmness to the whole organism, like a balance of power within a political system (p. 80).

In *On Aggression* Lorenz devotes most of his attention to the natural history of aggressive behaviour, which he believes to be instinctive, driven by one of the major drives. He is concerned with fighting and threats between members of the *same* species, not with the attack of predator on prey, the mobbing of predators by prey, or the self-defence of any cornered animal (pp. 18–22). Concentrating thus on intra-specific aggression, he asks what its species-preserving function can be, and comes up with several answers. Firstly it can space out the individuals of a species evenly over the available territory, so that there is enough food for each (pp. 24–30). On a coral reef, each kind of fish has its own peculiar source of food, and each individual will defend its 'territory' against others of the same species although it easily tolerates fish of other species. The set-up is like a series of villages, in each of which there is a living for only one butcher, one baker, and one candlestick-maker. Secondly and thirdly, aggression between rival males of a species ensures that the strongest individuals leave offspring, and are available for defence of family and herd (p. 31). Lastly, aggression can serve to establish and maintain a 'pecking order' or hierarchy in an animal community, which can be beneficial in that the oldest and most experienced animals can lead the group and pass on what they have learned (pp. 35–7).

But how can intra-specific aggression have such survival value without leading to injury and death, which obviously contradict survival? The remarkable fact is that despite aggression being so widespread among vertebrate animals, it is rare for an animal to be killed or seriously injured in the wild by members of its own species. Much aggressive behaviour takes the form of threats or pursuits rather than actual physical combat. Lorenz theorizes that evolution has produced a 'ritualization' of fighting, so that it can produce the above advantages without actually causing injury (pp. 93–8). Especially in heavily armoured animals, which must co-operate for breeding and perhaps for hunting, there is a need for a mechanism by which aggression can be inhibited (p. 110). So typically there is some kind of appeasement gesture or ritual submission by which a weaker animal can inhibit the aggression of a stronger. Beaten dogs, for instance, offer their vulnerable neck to the jaws of their opponent, and this seems to activate some specific inhibition mechanism, for it is as if the victor *cannot* then bring himself to administer the fatal bite (pp. 113–14) but just accepts that victory has been conceded.

THEORY OF MAN

Lorenz sees man as an animal who has evolved from other animals. Just as our bodies and their physiology show a recognizable continuity with those of other animals, so Lorenz expects our behaviour patterns to be fundamentally similar to those of animals. To think of ourselves as different in kind, whether in virtue of free will or anything else, is an illusion. Our behaviour is subject to the same causal laws of nature as all animal behaviour (pp. 190–2, 204, 214), and it will be the worse for us unless we come to recognize this. Of course, we are different in *degree* from the rest of the animal world, we are the 'highest' achievement so far reached by evolution (p. 196). To explain our behaviour causally does not necessarily take away from our 'dignity' or 'value', nor does it show us not to be free, for increasing knowledge of ourselves increases our power to control ourselves (pp. 196–202). Though Lorenz does not take discussion of these philosophical questions very far, he shows himself much more sensitive to them than Skinner.

The crucial point of Lorenz's view of human nature is the theory that like many other animals we have an innate drive to aggressive behaviour towards our own species. He thinks that this is the only possible explanation of the conflicts and wars throughout all human history, of the continuing unreasonable behaviour of supposedly reasonable beings (pp. 203–4). He suggests that Freud's theory of the death instinct is an interpretation of the same fundamental fact of human nature (p. 209). Lorenz seeks an evolutionary explanation for our innate aggressiveness, and for its peculiarly *communal* nature (for the most destructive fighting is not between individuals but between groups). He speculates that at a certain stage of the evolution of our ancestors, they had more or less mastered the dangers of their non-human environment, and the main danger came from other human groups. So the competition between neighbouring hostile tribes would be the main factor in natural selection, and accordingly there would be a survival value in the 'warrior virtues' (p. 209). (Natural selection can determine the evolution of cultures as well as of species (p. 224).) At this postulated prehistoric stage, those groups that banded together best to fight other groups would tend to survive longest. Thus Lorenz explains the existence of what he calls 'militant enthusiasm', by which a human crowd can become excitedly aggressive and lose all rationality and moral inhibitions (pp. 231–5): it has evolved from the communal defence response of our pre-human ancestors (p. 232).

DIAGNOSIS

'All the great dangers threatening humanity with extinction are direct consequences of conceptual thought and verbal speech' (pp. 204–5). Thus our greatest gifts are very mixed blessings. Men are omnivorous creatures, physically quite weak with no great claws, beak, or teeth, so it is quite difficult for one man to kill another in unarmed combat. Accordingly there was no evolutionary need for strong inhibition mechanisms to stop fighting between ape-men. The heavily armed carnivores have such mechanisms (p. 207), but other animals do not; this explains why the dove—the very symbol of peace—can uninhibitedly peck to death a second dove which is enclosed in the same cage and cannot escape (see *King Solomon's Ring*, p. 184). But cultural and technological development puts artificial weapons in our hands—from the sticks and stones of pre-human ancestors, through the arrows and swords of history, to the bullets and bombs of today. The equilibrium between killing potential and inhibition is upset (p. 207). Thus Lorenz explains how it is that human beings are the only animals to indulge in mass slaughter of their own species.

Appeals to rationality and moral responsibility have been notoriously ineffective in controlling human conflict. Lorenz explains this by his theory that aggression is innate in us—like the instincts in the Freudian id, it must find an outlet in one way or another. Reason alone is powerless, it can only devise means to ends decided on in other ways, and it can only exert control over our behaviour when it is backed by some instinctual motivation (p. 213). So, like Freud, Lorenz sees a conflict between the instincts implanted in us by evolution, and the moral restraints necessary to civilized society. He speculates that in pre-human groups there must have been a primitive morality which condemned aggression within the tribe (pp. 215–16), for any tribe which fought within itself would soon lose the competition with other tribes. But the pressures of that competition produced an instinct for aggression against other tribes. Thus our technology of weapons has far outstripped the slow development of appropriate instinctive restraints on their use, and we find ourselves in the highly dangerous situation of today, with both the power to destroy the world and the *willingness* to do so in certain situations.

PRESCRIPTION

If aggression really is innate in us, then there might seem to be little hope for the human race. For we have seen the uselessness of mere appeals to reason and morality, and if we try to eliminate all stimuli that provoke aggression, the inner drive will still seek outlets. Theoretically, we could try to breed it out by deliberate eugenic planning of human reproduction. But even if this were morally and politically possible, Lorenz thinks it would be highly inadvisable since we do not know how essential the aggressive drive may be to the make-up of human personality as a whole (p. 239). If we eliminate aggression we might destroy at the same time many of the highest forms of human achievement.

Nevertheless, Lorenz avows optimism in his final chapter, and believes that 'reason can and will exert a selection-pressure in the right direction' (p. 258). For the more we begin to understand the natural causes of our aggression, the more we can take rational steps to redirect it. Self-knowledge is the first step to salvation (another echo of Freud, Sartre, and Socrates!). The next is sublimation, the redirection of aggression to substitute objects in harmless ways (p. 240). We can smash cheap crockery to express rage, and we can channel group-competitiveness into team games. We must break down mistrust between human groups by promoting personal acquaintance between individuals of different nations, classes, cultures, and parties (pp. 243–4). And we must redirect our enthusiasm to causes which can be genuinely universal among all peoples— Art, Science, and Medicine (pp. 244–9). Lastly, Lorenz avows great confidence in the human sense of humour, as something which promotes friendship, attacks fraud, and releases tension without getting out of rational control (pp. 253–7). So humour and knowledge are the two great hopes of civilization. In such means he sees hope that in future centuries our aggressive drive can be reduced to a tolerable level without disturbing its essential function (pp. 257–8).

CRITICAL DISCUSSION

Lorenz's theory is a persuasive one, for he seems to combine the insight of Freud with the scientific rigour of Skinner. Nevertheless there are important doubts to be raised about his theory and diagnosis of man. Unless we are professional researchers into animal behaviour, we can hardly be qualified to discuss the details of Lorenz's theories. Some of his factual claims about certain species—for instance, the alleged 'bloody mass-battles' of the rat (pp. xi, 139)—have been disputed. Here of course we need the facts to be ascertained. What we *can* begin to discuss without leaving our armchairs is the method-

ology of postulating instincts or inner drives to explain behaviour. We found this to be one of the weakest parts of
Freud's theories, yet we could not agree with Skinner's total
rejection of such postulation. Has Lorenz found the right
middle path between these extremes? The crucial question is
whether his application of the concepts of drive and instinct is
falsifiable by observation and experiment. Now when he postulates a drive to explain a specific fixed-action pattern in a
particular species—like the fly-catching routine of the starling
—there do seem to be clear tests of the proposition. We can
establish that a given action pattern is innate by showing that
all normal individuals of the species of the relevant age and
sex will perform the action, without previous learning from
other individuals or from trial and error. If we also find that
the stimulus which usually releases the action does not always
do so with the same effectiveness (mating behaviour varies
with the season) and if we also find that the action can sometimes be produced by less than the usual stimulus (like the
isolated dove which courts the corner of its cage), then it is
reasonable to say that there is some internal driving factor
which varies in its strength.

So the presence of varying drives for specific fixed-action patterns is testable. But what is more dubious about Lorenz's
methodology is his suggestion that such 'little partial drives'
are often at the disposal of one or more of the 'four big drives'
(feeding, reproduction, flight, and aggression) (pp. 74–6). He
holds that a 'self-contained function' is never the result of one
single drive (p. 73), and even suggests that aggression is one of
the driving powers which 'lie behind behaviour patterns that
outwardly have nothing to do with aggression, and even appear to be its very opposite' (p. 35). On the face of it, this
would seem to permit us to attribute any kind of behaviour at
all to aggression, and thus make such attribution untestable
and unscientific. (It is exactly parallel to Freud's theory of
'reaction formation', by which an inner tendency can be
expressed in the opposite behaviour.) There *may* be ways of
testing such talk of basic drives, intermingling of drives, and
diversion of drives to different behaviour, but until the testability is shown, such theorizing is not scientific. And until the
tests give confirmation, there is no reason to suppose it true.

Apart from these methodological questions about the general theory, there must be considerable doubt about the way in which Lorenz argues from animals to men. (This was also a major defect of Skinner.) In *On Aggression* Lorenz takes most of his examples from fish and birds, few from mammals, and hardly any from our closest relatives, the great apes. Yet he is prepared to argue by analogy that if fish and birds are innately aggressive, then human behaviour is subject to the same basic laws (p. 204). The analogy must surely be judged a weak one. It would be stronger if he had made detailed studies of chimpanzees and gorillas, as recent researchers like Jane van Lawick-Goodall have done (see her *In the Shadow of Man*). But even evidence about these nearer relations is very far from showing us the essential nature of man, although popular writers such as Morris would have us believe so. For the *differences* between men and other animals may be as important as the similarities. In general, to show that X has evolved out of Y does not show that X *is* Y, or is nothing but Y, or is essentially Y. Even if it could be shown that sectarian conflict (e.g. in Ulster) is evolved from the territorial defence mechanisms of tribes of ape-men, this still does not show the former to be nothing but the latter. In any case, theories of pre-human behaviour, such as Lorenz's suggestions of what competition between hostile tribes must have been like, are highly speculative, and it is hard to see how we could now find any evidence for or against them.

These doubts must therefore infect the crucial feature of Lorenz's theory of human nature—the idea of innate aggression. For if the analogy from animals does not prove this, we must make direct observation of human behaviour to test it. At this level, Lorenz is as amateur as the rest of us who are not anthropologists or sociologists. We must look not to his speculations but to the facts. Anthropologists have described some societies in which aggression is notably absent (see some of the papers in *Man and Aggression*—described below). This would suggest that it is more socially learned than innate. In modern industrial societies it does seem that overt violence varies somewhat according to social background. No doubt it will be suggested that middle-class economic competition is just as 'aggressive' as working-class gang warfare; but then the term is being extended to cover more than physical violence and the threat of it. Clearer definition of the term is a prerequisite of further inquiry; and that inquiry looks like being at least as much sociological as biological. We must judge Lorenz's theory of man as a speculative generalization from his observation of animals. But it points us to a vitally important area for research into human nature.

FOR FURTHER READING

Basic text: *On Aggression*, translated by Marjorie Latzke (Methuen, London, University Paperback 1966); translated by Marjorie K. Wilson (Bantam Books paperback, New York).

The two volumes of Lorenz's *Studies in Animal and Human Behaviour* (Methuen, London, 1970 and 1971; Harvard University Press, Cambridge, Mass., 1970 and 1971) give more details both of his ethological studies and of the philosophy of science underlying them. Although more technical than the above, these are still intelligible without previous knowledge of science or ethology.

For criticism of Lorenz and other ethological writers, see *Man and Aggression*, edited by M. F. Ashley Montagu (Oxford University Press Galaxy Books paperback, New York, 2nd edn., 1973).

For Darwin's theory of evolution, see his *Origin of Species*, reprinted in Pelican Classics 1968, and in a Mentor paperback (New American Library, New York).

Page references in this chapter are to the Methuen edition of *On Aggression*. Readers of the Bantam Books edition should use the references below.

Stevenson	*Bantam Books paperback*
page 110 refers to pages	9–11; 47–8; 48–9; 49–50; 83–4; 85; 82, 94; 90; 21–6; 28–35
111	35–6; 41–3; 104–10; 123; 127; 214–16, 229, 240; 220–1
112	221–7; 228–9; 235; 235; 251; 259–64; 261; 230
113	233; 233; 240; 241–2
114	268–9; 290; 269–70; 273–4; 274–80; 283–8; 289–90; xi–xii, 157
115	83–6; 82; 40
116	229

PART THREE   Conclusion

CHAPTER 10

Philosophy and
Further Inquiry

IF the reader is expecting this book to conclude with 'the truth' about human nature, then he will be disappointed. I have no eighth, Stevensonian, theory of human nature to offer. I have merely an invitation to further inquiry in a variety of directions. The whole book has been only an introduction to theories, problems, and areas of continuing research.

Although we have treated our seven theories rather as if they were rivals for the prize of truth, they are not necessarily all incompatible with each other. Unless one has an ideological or personal commitment to a particular theory, one will probably see them as emphasizing different aspects of the total truth about man. For despite their individual defects, some of which we have noted in our critical discussions, every one of these seven theories has made a positive contribution to our understanding of ourselves and our place in the universe. Each has permanently changed our view of human nature, and will no doubt continue to influence it. And there are of course many more theories than the seven we have covered here.

So we can see these various theories as adding up, rather than cancelling each other out. But there are of course *some* major disagreements between them. There are five main unsolved problems which I see emerging from our discussion. The first is the general question of how much in human nature is innate, and how much is learned from the social environment. There are many ways of putting this contrast: between the biological and the cultural, between heredity and environment, between nature and nurture, between the individual and society, between the instinctual and the conditioned, between what is universal, inevitable, and unchangeable, and what is culture-relative, subject to change and reform. That some is innate and some learned is agreed by all. The question is which, and how much? Plato, Marx, and Skinner emphasize the extent of social conditioning, and our power to change individuals by changing social structures and practices. Christianity, Freud, and Lorenz emphasize the limits to such change in the innate universal nature of man. The questions to be answered here are mainly empirical, so it is to the sciences of psychology, ethology, and sociology that we must look for the answers.

The other four big questions are primarily philosophical in nature. They are not empirical, for no conceivable observations of facts will settle them, although many facts are highly relevant and should contribute to more adequate understanding. They are questions that demand the logical analysis of concepts; we cannot merely accept the question as clearly understood and set out to find evidence to answer it, we have to examine and perhaps criticize the very terms in which the question is put and the assumptions on which it may rest. Typically the result will be not a yes or no answer, but a re-phrasing of the question, perhaps splitting up into several questions, some of which may be dismissed as misconceived because based on wrong assumptions, some of which may be genuine empirical questions to be handed on to one or other of the sciences for investigation, and some of which may remain as puzzling problems which demand further philosophical treatment. Such is the nature of progress in philosophy. It is thus more a *method* of logical analysis than the study of a particular *subject matter* differentiated from others. But there are certain problems, or problem areas, which are perennial topics of philosophical analysis, and the four following are among the most important.

The question of determinism against free will has recurred at several points in this book. Marx, Freud, and Skinner assert in their different ways that we are not as free as we like to think, but are influenced in ways we do not usually recognize. Marx points to the influence of the economic basis of our society. Freud suggests the influence of factors that are within our own minds, and yet hidden from ourselves. Skinner maintains that we are all conditioned by the influence of our past and present environment. But these theorists can hardly be saying that human choices do not take place, they can at most be suggesting that our choices are determined by factors that are outside our control. Christianity and Sartre agree that our choices are *not* determined for us, and that this is the most important fact about us: the freedom to choose our attitudes, values, and whole way of life is what makes us truly human. Is there or is there not a real contradiction between these views? And if so, how can we decide which is correct? These questions are the beginning of the philosophical problems of free will. The proper treatment of these problems must involve a careful analysis of the concepts of action, choice, freedom, causation, necessity, etc.

Next there are the questions of materialism against dualism. Is man made of matter alone, or is consciousness necessarily non-material in nature? In what way, if any, is it logically possible for a man to survive his own death? Are mental states (sensations, thoughts, desires, drives, etc.) and brain states (the electrical and chemical goings-on investigated by neurophysiology) two different sorts of things, or just two aspects of one set of events? These questions too have arisen but have not been discussed, at various stages of this book. Plato is definitely a dualist, and Skinner a materialist, but some of the other theories are less obviously one or the other. We decided that Christianity, although it asserts survival after death, is not necessarily dualist in its view of man, and that Marx although 'materialist' in general outlook and approach to history and society, was probably not a materialist on the question of the relation of mind to body. Except on the life-after-death issue, the question has perhaps less immediate practical bearing than that of free will. But it is undoubtedly one of the central questions of pure philosophy, and continues to excite discussion.

Another central question of philosophy is that of the nature of moral values. Plato asserted their objectivity, in his theory of Forms. Skinner finds no basis for them at all, except in terms of the survival of the species. Christianity asserts that moral values are ultimately given by God; Marx, Freud, and Lorenz attribute them to the various pressures of society, and Sartre says we choose them for ourselves. These disagreements are fundamental, and the problems they raise are mainly philosophical. They are the special concern of moral philosophy.

Perhaps this is the place to draw attention to the understanding of man offered by the great moral philosophers. In Aristotle's *Nicomachean Ethics*, Hume's *Treatise of Human Nature*, Kant's *Groundwork of the Metaphysic of Morals*, John Stuart Mill's *Utilitarianism*, and in their modern successors, we find ethical views based on a general view of human nature (as the title of Hume's three-volume treatise makes explicit). And although the philosophical bases of these ethical systems differ in many ways, we can perhaps discern some features in common. They can be seen as basing their prescriptions for the good life on certain general and uncontroversial facts about human nature—that men wish to avoid pain, they need food, shelter, and the society of other men, they want to find a purpose in life, and to enjoy exercising their manifold abilities free from interference. The description and analysis of these facts need not involve any transcendent hypotheses about the nature of the universe, whether Platonic Forms or Christian God. So perhaps they can form the basis of a 'humanist' ethic which leaves religious questions open, unlike the aggressively anti-religious stance of Feuerbach, Nietzsche, and Bertrand Russell.

The fourth main area of philosophical questions arising from our discussions is of course that of the existence of God, and the more general problems of the nature of religion and religious beliefs. The evaluation of religious claims is one route which leads us into what are acknowledged as the central and fundamental problems of philosophy—those of meaning, knowledge, and metaphysics.

On all these problems the empirical sciences of human nature have much to contribute. Discussion must be inter-disciplinary to be fertile, for human nature is a topic which not only spreads across the physical and social sciences, but ultimately breaks down the boundary between the sciences and what have traditionally been called 'the humanities'. Our urgent social problems cry out for more understanding of human nature. So, more than ever before, it is true that the proper study of mankind is man.

FOR FURTHER READING

For introductions to psychology and sociology, see:

G. A. Miller, *Psychology: The Science of Mental Life* (Penguin, London, 1966; 2nd edn. by G. A. Miller and R. Buckhout, Harper & Row, New York, 1973).

P. Worsley and others, *Introducing Sociology* (Penguin, London, 1970).

On freedom and determinism, and the mind–body problem, see:

Bernard Berofsky (editor), *Free Will and Determinism* (Harper and Row, New York, 1966).

Antony Flew (editor), *Body, Mind and Death* (Macmillan, New York, 1964).

For a historical introduction to moral philosophy, see:

Alasdair MacIntyre, *A Short History of Ethics* (Routledge & Kegan Paul, London, 1967; Macmillan paperback, New York).

On religion (as well as the reading recommended after Chapter 4) see: I. G. Barbour, *Issues in Science and Religion* (S.C.M. Press, London, 1966; Harper & Row Torchbook paperback, New York, 1971), which is an introductory survey of the relationships of religion to the physical and social sciences, and indeed to philosophy and all questions about the nature of man.

For an introduction to the main problems of philosophy, see: Antony Flew, *An Introduction to Western Philosophy* (Thames & Hudson, London, 1971; Bobbs-Merrill paperback, Indianapolis, Ind., 1971). This combines excerpts from the philosophical classics with critical discussion of the issues.

Index

Watching DALLAS

WATCHING
DALLAS

Soap opera and the
melodramatic imagination

Ien Ang

Translated by
Della Couling

R

ROUTLEDGE · London and New York

First published as *Het Geval
Dallas* by Uitgeverij SUA
Amsterdam
© 1982 Uitgeverij SUA
Amsterdam
English translation (with
revisions) first published in
1985 by Methuen & Co. Ltd

Reprinted 1989 by
Routledge
11 New Fetter Lane,
London EC4P 4EE
29 West 35th Street,
New York NY 10001

© 1985 Methuen & Co. Ltd

Photoset by
Rowland Phototypesetting Ltd,
Bury St Edmunds, Suffolk
Printed in Great Britain by
Richard Clay Ltd,
Bungay, Suffolk

*British Library Cataloguing in
Publication Data*

Ang, Ien.
Watching Dallas: soap opera
and the melodramatic
imagination.
1. Dallas (Television program)
I. Title   II. Het geval Dallas.
English
791.45′72   PN1992.77.D3

ISBN 0 416 41630 6
      0 415 04598 3 Pbk

*Library of Congress Cataloging
in Publication Data*

Ang, Ien.
Watching Dallas.
Translation of: Het geval
Dallas.
Bibliography: p.
Includes index.
1. Dallas (Television program)
I. Title.
PN1992.77.D3A5313   1985
791.45′72   85-15481

ISBN 0 416 41630 6
      0 415 04598 3 (pbk.)

Contents

Preface

When I wrote the original Dutch version of this book in 1982 I had several things in mind. I wanted first of all to intervene in the heated debate on *Dallas* in the Dutch media, which, to my mind, was characterized by a certain measure of ignorance, whether deliberate or not, as to the cultural specificity of this widely popular but highly controversial television serial from the United States. I wanted to encourage serious reflection on the phenomenon itself and, in order to do this, I deemed it useful to introduce the interested Dutch reader to theoretical perspectives on television and television serials, perspectives which stem mainly from Anglo-Saxon media and cultural studies. Dutch intellectual communities were largely unacquainted with these theories. The book, therefore, acquired a somewhat 'pedagogic' character.

Apart from presenting a framework within which *Dallas* could be taken seriously, however, I also wished to contribute to further problematization and understanding of the social, cultural and political role of serials like *Dallas*. Thus, I also deal

with issues which come to the fore as soon as one adopts a position acknowledging that *Dallas* does matter, especially bearing in mind its popularity: issues concerning pleasure and its vicissitudes, its relations with ideology and cultural politics. Parts of the original text were more or less extensively re-written in order to overcome the difficulties arising from its originally being written within a Dutch national context. *Dallas*, however, matters internationally and it is my belief that the Dutch experience is not altogether a unique one.

Of those who have made this translation possible, I should especially like to thank Paul Willemen and Jessica Pickard. There were many others who supported me in one way or another in pursuing the project: Mieke Aerts, Tjitske Akkerman, Jane Armstrong, William Boddy, Christine Gledhill, Dick Hebdige, Johan Meijer, Antoine Verbij and, last but not least, the readers of the women's magazine *Viva*, who so kindly wrote to me about the (dis)pleasure that *Dallas* had afforded them. I am grateful to them all.

I.A.

Amsterdam, May 1985

Introduction

The moment of DALLAS

If we are to believe the plethora of studies, commentaries and warnings from journalists, critics and even politicians, the beginning of the 1980s was marked for the world's television viewing public by a new, spectacular phenomenon: *Dallas*. This unique status is due first and foremost to the extraordinary but undeniable popularity achieved by this American dramatic serial about a rich Texan oil family. That popularity has been wellnigh worldwide: in over ninety countries, ranging from Turkey to Australia, from Hong Kong to Great Britain, *Dallas* has become a national craze, with the proverbial empty streets and a dramatic drop in water consumption when an episode of the serial is going out. In the Netherlands, for example, over half the population watched *Dallas* every week in the spring of 1982, when its popularity reached its peak. No other fictional programme, foreign or domestic, has ever achieved such high viewing figures.

This almost inconceivable popularity has caused *Dallas* to

develop into a modern myth. It became the symbol of a new television age. Euphoric articles were written, especially in the serial's country of origin, on the success of the *Dallas* phenomenon. *Time*, for example, asserted with satisfaction in a cover story that 'the program's high gloss handsomeness brings a touch of class to the ruck of commercial series TV'.[1] But this American pride is countered in the rest of the world by quite different preoccupations. Of course, the Western European popular press was fascinated by the success story of *Dallas* and eagerly contributed to the myth-making. In more serious circles, however, its very success and popularity were fastened on for renewed expressions of concern over the steadily growing influence of American consumer capitalism on popular culture. *Dallas* was regarded as yet more evidence of the threat posed by American-style commercial culture against 'authentic' national cultures and identities. In February 1983, for instance, Jack Lang, the French Minister for Culture, during a conference in Paris to which he had invited a selection of prominent intellectuals and artists ranging from Ettore Scola to Susan Sontag, had even proclaimed *Dallas* as the 'symbol of American cultural imperialism'.

Of course, the problem raised here is real enough. On the eve of a period in which the structure and organization of the world of mass communications are about to undergo drastic changes, through the advance of the so-called 'new technologies' (cable, satellite), national governments and media institutions find themselves compelled to reflect on the social, political and cultural consequences involved and on the policy measures to be taken at this level. If nothing is done, the assumption is, the dominance of the American culture industries will just grow and grow. In this context the *Dallas* phenomenon functions as an alarming bogey. As Michèle Mattelart has put it, 'It is not for nothing that *Dallas* casts its ubiquitous shadow wherever the future of culture is discussed: it has become the perfect hate symbol, the cultural poverty [. . .] against which one struggles.'[2]

But the mere idea of a threatened 'cultural identity' contains elements which do more to conceal than to clarify the nature of the phenomenon and the problems described. Mattelart *et al.* have pointed out how, in the name of its defence, policy measures have been adopted which will not contribute to real alternatives.[3] It can, for example, lead to a misguided form of protectionism, based on a static, exclusively territorial definition of 'cultural identity', such as the setting of a quota system on imported films. For example, British television is allowed to fill a maximum of 14 per cent of its programming time with foreign programmes. But it can also lead to an unoriginal and unimaginative copying of American success formulae, so that viewers are served up a Dutch or French version of *Dallas*, which will inevitably be of poorer quality than the American original, for the very simple reason that the Americans have far greater financial and organizational means of production available. An average episode of *Dallas* costs at least $700,000, which the television industry of a small country like the Netherlands could not possibly afford.

Moreover, a stubborn fixation on the threat of 'American cultural imperialism' can lead one to lose sight of the fact that since the 1950s the mass consumption of American popular culture has been integrated to a greater or lesser degree into the national 'cultural identity' itself, especially in Western Europe. As a result, the popularity of a programme such as *Dallas* becomes a totally incomprehensible and elusive issue, a whim of the 'silent majority'. It becomes hard to understand, in other words, why such a large section of the television audience *en masse* watches *Dallas*. Often this position does not seem to get beyond the somewhat rueful realization that non-American peoples have a 'disturbing susceptibility to American media products'.[4] But this 'disturbance' probably looms only in the ivory towers of the policy-makers and other guardians of the 'national culture'. In the millions of living rooms where the TV set is switched on to *Dallas*, the issue is rather one of pleasure.

For we must accept one thing: *Dallas* is popular because a lot of people somehow *enjoy* watching it.

On the other hand we should not make the opposite mistake and let ourselves be blinded by the fabulous popularity of *Dallas*. The enormous fuss made of it can easily lead to a mystification of the phenomenon, to considering it as something unique. The temptation is great to reach for essentialist explanations, which are both too general and too specific. For example, the exceptional attraction of the villainous J. R. Ewing, one of the main characters in *Dallas*, is often cited as an explanation. Or, as the American television critic Horace Newcomb has done, an essential narrative foundation is sought that is assumed to express the Zeitgeist. According to Newcomb, *Dallas* succeeds in an inspired way in transplanting the old values of the Western into the new world of the American West, the world of express highways and stunning skyscrapers. He asserts: 'Probably without knowing it, the show's creators pump nourishment into the audience's veins. Their timing is perfect. As a nation we are actually growing older and developing the caution that comes with age. It is a time of decline, of recession and restriction, a time of real trouble. The grand old cities of the East and the Midwest are burdened with financial failure and bitter winters. Small wonder that the Sunbelt flourishes and *Dallas* leads the ratings.'[5]

This is all well and good, but the 'Americo-centricity' of such a speculative explanation totally loses its force when the worldwide success of the series is at issue. It is in any case somewhat risky to trace the appeal of *Dallas* to one hidden message or meaning, for it is not plausible that Moroccan, Italian or English viewers are all just as open to such a 'message' as Americans are – if indeed we could even lump all Americans together. The oil industry, for example, does not have everywhere the charged mythical significance that it has in American cultural history. Furthermore, popularity is never the unique accomplishment of one isolated cultural product. It is also dependent on and connects with the context in which it is consumed. In

this connection we must not forget that people have become so used to American television programmes – their production values, their style and pace, their language – that merely the expectations they arouse and their familiarity give any new American product a certain advantage. None the less, this does not get over the fact that *Dallas*, just like Michael Jackson or E.T., has exercised a particular fascination exceeding the cultural significance of the average popular cultural attraction. On the contrary, *Dallas* appears in some way or other to have appealed in an exceptional manner to the popular imagination, although – just like any fashion – this is now on the wane. Stuart Hall has described how the popularity of *Dallas* in Britain peaked and declined: 'At a certain moment the programme achieved a kind of popularity other than merely in terms of numbers of viewers. It had repercussions on the whole culture, the involvement of the viewers became of a different order. At a certain moment you could no longer avoid talking about the popularity of *Dallas* when people started using categories from it to help interpret their experiences. This is a secondary type of popularity which it has now completely lost. The same number of people still watch it, but it is no longer active in the collective cultural consciousness.'[6] *Dallas* is nowadays, then, simply a popular television programme. Where viewing figures are concerned it has even been beaten in several countries by one of its own imitations, *Dynasty*.

In short, popularity is an extremely complex phenomenon. No simple answer is possible on the question of why *Dallas* is (was) so popular, just as it is not possible to explain fully how it is that Michael Jackson or E.T. have exercised such mass attraction. Very divergent factors, including historical ones, contribute to this, and it seems almost pointless to try to examine the success of *Dallas* without taking into account the wider social context of the postmodernist media culture. This book sets itself a more modest role. No attempt will be made to give the definitive answer to the burning question: why is *Dallas* so popular? Instead I want to concentrate my attention

on a phenomenon, one aspect of popularity which is in itself complex enough: pleasure.

However, before turning to this topic, it is necessary to first describe what viewers are offered when they watch *Dallas*. As it is the way in which this programme is received and consumed which will be the focus of this study, I will not go into its production context here. I will confine myself to giving a short and simple summary of the *Dallas* story line; a more structural analysis of the programme will follow in the next chapters.

DALLAS: television fiction without an end

Dallas is a continuous fictional television serial which can, in principle, go on *ad infinitum*. The story centres around the very rich Ewing family who live in the luxurious Southfork Ranch, situated a few miles outside the city of Dallas (Texas).

At the beginning of the story, seven members of the family are living in the ranch: Jock and Ellie Ewing, the parents, their sons John Ross (known as 'J.R.') and Bobby, with their respective wives Sue Ellen and Pamela, and Lucy, daughter of their wayward son Gary.

The dramatic complications always revolve around the weal and woe of this family. J.R. plays a central role in this; he runs the family concern, Ewing Oil, in a villainous manner, treats his wife like dirt and only shows respect for his parents when it suits him. But it cannot be said that J.R. plays the main part: all the other characters in principle are just as important. Jock is the patriarch of the family who, around forty years ago, came to seek his fortune with his friend Digger Barnes in the oilfields of Texas. When success came he dropped Digger and set up Ewing Oil, which has since developed into a powerful concern. Furthermore, he also pinched Digger's girl friend, Ellie Southworth, daughter of the owner of Southfork Ranch. Ellie married Jock but has continued to have a soft spot for Digger. Meanwhile Digger has married another woman, Rebecca, and had a son and a daughter: Cliff and Pamela Barnes. Fate (or the

plot) wills that the beauteous Pamela marries Bobby Ewing, Jock and Ellie's youngest son. Thus Pamela finds herself in a difficult predicament: on the one hand she belongs to the Barnes family and is loyal to her father and brother, on the other hand she is married to a scion of the Ewings, something her brother Cliff in particular cannot stomach because he is firmly resolved to avenge his father and destroy Ewing Oil. Cliff Barnes and J. R. Ewing are arch enemies. Cliff tries to fight J.R. through his work as lawyer and politician (something he hardly ever succeeds in doing because J.R. always manages to outwit him), but also by beginning an affair with J.R.'s wife Sue Ellen. The latter lives on a war footing with J.R. but also quickly gets fed up with Cliff. She is in a constant state of crisis: she goes to a psychiatrist, takes to the bottle from time to time and would like to leave J.R. but does not know how. Pamela has had more luck with Bobby, although the fact that she cannot have children (she has had a few miscarriages) casts a shadow over the happiness of their marriage. Fortunately her work for a fashion shop offers her some diversion. Meanwhile Lucy, who is around twenty years old, lives her own life. Now and then her father Gary comes back to Southfork Ranch with his wife Valene. He had previously left because he wanted to have nothing to do with the oil business of his father and J.R. (Here Bobby occupies a middle position: he likes the cowboy life on the ranch but is also fascinated by the modern business life in the city.) Gary is the favourite son of Miss Ellie, who is also suspicious of the oil business because it lays waste the virgin land around the ranch, and she sees the disintegration of the family with regret. The ranch is run by the cowboy Ray Krebbs who, surprise, surprise, later turns out to be an illegitimate son of Jock's.

As can be seen, mutual relations are extremely complicated. This is made even worse by the fact that from episode to episode secondary figures keep coming and going. For example, there is Kristin, Sue Ellen's sister, who starts an affair with J.R., but tries to shoot him when he deserts her; Alan Beam, a

puppet of J.R., who is given the task of getting rid of Cliff Barnes, makes up to Lucy in the hope of getting rich through an advantageous marriage (which does not come off); Donna Culver, an honest businesswoman and politician who, after a short, unsuccessful affair with Cliff Barnes, marries Ray Krebbs; Dusty Farlow, a rich cowboy who falls in love with Sue Ellen, tries to get her out of J.R.'s grip but at the crucial moment has a flying accident and becomes an invalid; and Mitch Cooper, a poor medical student who gets hooked by Lucy.

This is only a brief summary, jotted down around half-way through the second *Dallas* season (at the time when I began this study). Since then relations and details have kept changing. Jock dies, not long after his former friend Digger. Sue Ellen divorces J.R. but not much later marries him again. Pamela and Bobby's marriage enters a crisis. Pamela finds her mother Rebecca again, who appears to be very well-to-do and is the head of Wentworth Industries, which are brought in by Cliff Barnes as a new weapon against J.R. And so on and so on.

But the basic structure of every *Dallas* episode always remains the same. In twenty to thirty short scenes the complications surrounding each of the characters are set out. In each episode a main story-line can be distinguished from a number of secondary stories. One main story, for example, is that Miss Ellie discovers a tumour in her breast. In various scenes we get her reactions to this: her fears, her visit to the doctor, the wait for the diagnosis, her doubts about how she is to tell Jock about it, and so on. Between these scenes there are others keeping us up with the lives of the other characters – for example, how Dusty and Sue Ellen are getting on, how J.R. pulls off his latest tricks, how Pamela indulges her 'mother instinct' by looking after Sue Ellen's baby, and so on. The number of locations for the action is limited: most scenes take place in recognizable locations such as the various rooms in Southfork Ranch and in the city of Dallas (the Ewing office, Cliff Barnes' flat, various restaurants, etc.). Nearly all the scenes consist of conversation; what we see the characters doing mostly is just talking to one

another. In these discussions problems and mutual conflicts are expressed, generally of a psychological nature. Physical violence, and even milder forms of action, play a marginal part in *Dallas*. And this continues endlessly, in one episode after another. When one problem is still unsolved, another looms on the horizon.

Although this ever continuing story may sound ridiculous and terribly exaggerated to the disengaged reader, it is treated in an entirely serious manner within the programme. All themes and events are dramatized without any humorous distancing devices.

As far as visual style is concerned, *Dallas* offers no surprises: there are hardly any unusual camera movements, no experiments with lighting and so on; there are no diversions from the normal conventions of the production rules of prime time television programmes. In short, *Dallas* is in every respect an expertly made sample of mainstream Hollywood television.

Watching DALLAS: pleasure and ideology

Why do people watch *Dallas*? Clearly because they find it enjoyable. Nobody is forced to watch television; at most, people can be led to it by effective advertising. What then are the determining factors of this enjoyment, this pleasure?

Sociologists often start with the premise that media-use is determined by people's needs and the gratifications they expect. However, the attention given to the socio-psychological constitution of (individual) viewers implies a functionalist conception of pleasure in which its essence is regarded as the experience of satisfaction whenever a certain pre-existent need is fulfilled. What is completely ignored in this conception are the *mechanisms* by which pleasure is aroused. What are the characteristics of *Dallas* that organize the viewer's pleasure? This question indicates that pleasure must be conceived of as not so much the automatic result of some 'satisfaction of needs', but rather as the effect of a certain productivity of a

cultural artefact. Evidently, *Dallas* offers entertainment, but what is it about *Dallas* that makes it a favourite item of entertainment, and what precisely does its entertainment value consist of? How, in short, does *Dallas* present itself as pleasurable?

In order to answer such questions we should not inquire what are the social, economic and psychological characteristics of the public, but should rather ask ourselves what happens in the process of watching *Dallas*. It is in the actual confrontation between viewer and programme that pleasure is primarily generated.

In order to obtain information on the way in which people experience watching *Dallas*, I placed a small advertisement in a Dutch women's magazine called *Viva*, which read as follows:

> I like watching the TV serial *Dallas*, but often get odd reactions to it. Would anyone like to write and tell me why you like watching it too, or dislike it? I should like to assimilate these reactions in my university thesis. Please write to . . .

I had forty-two replies to this advertisement. Letters, all addressed personally to me, varying in length from a few lines to around ten pages. All the letters except three were written by individuals. One letter was written by two boys and two girls, two letters by two girls. Only one letter was anonymous, all the others were provided with the sender's name and in most cases the address too. From these names it emerges that only three letters were from boys or men. The rest were written by girls or women.

These letters form the empirical material on the basis of which I shall be trying in the following chapters to say something about what it can mean to watch *Dallas*. Of course, these letters cannot be regarded as representative of the way in which *Dallas* is received in general. Nor can we assume that they are speaking for the way in which a specific social category (women, for example) handles *Dallas*. Interest in this study, however, is based not so much on the quantitative demo-

graphic distribution of the different ways the programme is received. Rather the central question is *how* these letter-writers experience *Dallas*, what it means when they say they experience pleasure or even displeasure, how they relate to the way in which *Dallas* is presented to the public.

It would, however, be wrong to regard the letters as a direct and unproblematic reflection of the reasons why the writers love or hate *Dallas*. What people say or write about their experiences, preferences, habits, etc., cannot be taken entirely at face value, for in the routine of daily life they do not demand rational consciousness; they go unnoticed, as it were. They are commonsensical, self-evident; they require no further explanations. This means that we cannot let the letters speak for themselves, but that they should be read 'symptomatically': we must search for what is behind the explicitly written, for the presuppositions and accepted attitudes concealed within them. In other words, the letters must be regarded as texts, as discourses people produce when they want to express or have to account for their own preference for, or aversion to, a highly controversial piece of popular culture like *Dallas*. To do this they will have to call on socially available ideologies and images, which channel the way in which such a television serial attains its meanings. It is by tracing these ideologies and images in the letters that we can get to know something about what experiencing pleasure (or otherwise) from *Dallas* implies for these writers – what textual characteristics of *Dallas* organize that experience and in which ideological context it acquires social and cultural meanings. If one general theme is central in this book, then it is the relation between pleasure and ideology.

But it is obvious that this book can never offer an all-embracing unravelling of that relation. There are many ways of enjoying *Dallas*, based on various understandings of what *Dallas* is all about, but only a few ways will be dealt with here – not last because I will be limiting myself to the evidence that can be traced in the relatively small number of letters.

Moreover, any study always bears the traces of the subjec-

tivity of the researcher. Doubtless for that reason my own ambivalent relation to *Dallas* will also have its repercussions. This ambivalence is on the one hand connected with my identity as an intellectual and a feminist, and on the other hand with the fact that I have always particularly liked watching soap operas like *Dallas*. At one time I really belonged to the category of devoted *Dallas* fans. The admission of the reality of this pleasure also formed the starting point for this study – I wanted in the first place to understand this pleasure, without having to pass judgement on whether *Dallas* is good or bad, from a political, social or aesthetic view. Quite the contrary; in my opinion it is important to emphasize how difficult it is to make such judgements – and hence to try to formulate the terms for a progressive cultural politics – when pleasure is at stake. 'Any research is a sort of autobiography', as the anthropologist Georges Dévereux once said. It is for others to judge whether the analyses and arguments presented here are also recognizable and convincing in a more general sense.

1

DALLAS
between reality and fiction

Manipulation or fascination?

Some of the letter-writers dislike *Dallas*, others find it amusing to watch — at least that is what they say. 'Hating *Dallas*' or 'loving *Dallas*' are only labels people stick on the way in which they relate in general to the programme. These are names for the way in which they experience the programme — an experience which can go either in a negative or in a positive direction. But what is hidden behind those apparently unambiguous labels? In fact no single experience, certainly no experience of something as complex as a long-running television serial, is unambiguous: it is always ambivalent and contradictory. The 'totalizing' labels of love and hate conceal this. It is not therefore surprising that in various letters passages can be found in which ambivalences come to the surface — mostly implicit, but sometimes quite explicit, such as in these extracts:

> pleasant or not, you are curious as to what is happening to them. For me it is a cosy and sometimes exciting half hour (or

how long does it last?) though sometimes I get really annoyed. (Letter 11)

When I saw *Dallas* for the first time I found it a very amusing serial and decided to follow it. But after a few months it became so tedious that I didn't find it at all interesting any more. But three weeks ago I just happened to watch it once and now I just have to watch it, however boring I find it. It's strange because I don't like watching TV much and so I find this really ridiculous. (Letter 27)

These ambivalent feelings must make us realize that it is difficult to determine what the letter-writers really think of *Dallas*. Indeed, the search for a total and definitive explanation for the way in which different groups of viewers experience the programme would seem to be particularly frustrating because at a certain moment we have to acknowledge that we are chasing an illusion: such an all-embracing explanation is a rationalistic fiction. We must keep this in mind when interpreting the statements of the letter-writers. What they say about *Dallas* is no more than a snapshot of their reception of the programme, an attempt to put a diffuse viewing experience into words. And when something is put into words there are always things which remain unexpressed and implicit.

Nevertheless, one thing is certain. Not a single letter-writer is indifferent to *Dallas*. And they all watch it. How otherwise could they give such detailed descriptions of it? In particular for those who regard themselves as *Dallas*-haters, this is an awkward absurdity. Letter-writer 31, for example, who describes herself as an ardent opponent of *Dallas*, nevertheless betrays intense involvement in the vicissitudes of the Ewings. In great detail she describes everything which in her opinion is wrong with the *Dallas* characters, but paradoxically she even fantasizes on possibilities for their future life. 'But who knows, perhaps Pamela will start an extramarital affair (I must admit she's really beautiful); that would be something to smack your lips over' (Letter 31).

It is as though the attraction of *Dallas* is running counter to her self-declared hatred. How can we explain this contradiction? Is she perhaps being manipulated by the swanky advertising business surrounding *Dallas*? She herself explicitly refers to this:

In England, where I was in the summer, there was an absolute craze. Besides badges, mugs, spoons, handkerchiefs, teatowels, T-shirts, tablecloths, etc. of Charles and Diana, you could also buy this stuff with J.R.'s head on and 'I love J.R.' or 'I hate J.R.' written on it. I nearly bought a badge with the latter on but I realized that I had nearly got caught in the *Dallas* net. (Letter 31)

It is true: the commercial machinery that has to sell *Dallas* is going full blast. In the Netherlands too, week after week the popular press writes about the ups and downs of the *Dallas* stars. *Dallas* books are on sale everywhere. And there is even a special monthly *Dallas* strip cartoon. But hadn't this letter-writer already been 'caught in the *Dallas* net', even without coming into contact with the J.R. badges? Is it not really the case that watching *Dallas* itself has caught her (in an unpleasant way), in spite of the resistance arising from her commitment to the ideology of mass culture?[1]

It would be naïve to suppose that the marketing practices of the commercial culture industry have no effect whatever on the involvement of the viewers. How great and what that effect is cannot be established here, however. On the other hand it would be far too easy to ascribe the popularity of *Dallas* totally to advertising. We must make a distinction between the programme itself as it can be seen week by week on television, and the advertising practices surrounding it. One letter-writer, who says that she likes *Dallas*, writes the following:

I had read quite a lot about *Dallas* in *Privé*, *Story* and other such magazines.[2] In America millions watch it, and that wasn't expected over here. In short, an awful amount of fuss

was made of it. In America there were 'J.R. hats', stickers, buttons, posters, etc. And that seemed to me terribly over-done. I don't know if you ever read gossip magazines, but if you do you know how it is. If you cut your finger, you put a plaster on it, and that's that. If Larry Hagman or Linda Gray cut a finger, there are great headlines: 'J.R. (or Sue Ellen) temporarily laid up' or something like that.

Altogether *Dallas* didn't interest me much at first, and when the serial began I didn't watch it. From my colleagues and other girl friends I did hear that it was amusing, but people tend to say that easily. So for quite a time I didn't watch it. When it had been going for about half a year, one of my colleagues suddenly said to me (the day after a *Dallas* episode): 'Hey, you really must watch *Dallas*, it's really fantastic.' She is not the type to fall under the influence of a serial either, so when she said that it had to be worth the effort. (Letter 20)

After that, as she recounted, she was done for: after she had seen the programme once, she didn't miss a week. A tall story, perhaps too tall. But in any case it makes us aware that the advertising of one's own social group can be more effective than that of the popular press. The popular press can perhaps fasten the attention of (potential) viewers on the existence of a programme or arouse curiosity for it, but it is improbable that it can have a straightforward and direct influence on the way in which *viewing* a programme is experienced.[3] As one letter-writer says: 'The women are really as beautiful as the gossip magazines say they are and they have one simple recipe for it. But that's not the point here' (Letter 7).

Relatively independent of the competing discourses revolving around *Dallas* – in the popular press, in advertising, but also by television critics, journalists and other intellectuals – the programme has made its way into the experiential worlds of millions of viewers. There's no doubt the programme does exercise a certain fascination. Against the background of prev-

alent notions of 'good television', this fascination is itself an ambivalent experience: 'I find the quality rather bad *but* it does have a certain attraction' (Letter 26, my italics). This attraction appears to elude rational explanation. The pleasure of *Dallas* is presented here as something incomprehensible and against the grain: this is a case of what the German sociologist Dieter Prokop has called 'the *nevertheless* fascinating'.[4] In other words, the pleasure of *Dallas* seems to be an enigma.

In this chapter and the next I want to try to unravel something of this enigma. But I do not claim to solve it fully – that would conflict with my conviction that an all-embracing explanation of the way in which viewers experience *Dallas* is impossible. Instead, I want to use as a starting point the statements the letter-writers who say they like *Dallas* make about their attitude to the programme. For these statements reveal, albeit obliquely, something about the way in which *Dallas* is received by *these* viewers. I shall try to interpret these statements and I shall indicate how they link up with the pleasure these viewers experience from *Dallas*. But first it is necessary to explain the theoretical perspective on the basis of which I shall be tackling the problem of pleasure.

Consumption, use-value and pleasure

Placing emphasis on the *pleasure* that people experience from *Dallas* is not a harmless theoretical (and political) choice. By so doing we are acknowledging that people can have a positive relationship with *Dallas* – a hedonistic attitude which is at odds with the doctrine that mass culture primarily manipulates the masses. According to Adorno and Horkheimer, for example, the experience of pleasure in mass culture is a false kind of pleasure, even part of the trick of manipulating the masses more effectively in order to lock them in the eternal status quo of exploitation and oppression. 'Marxists, in particular, have interpreted the fact that people *enjoy* mass culture as a reason for gloom', Simon Frith[5] asserts in his book on rock

music. Stuart Hall even talks of the stubborn refusal of the left to consider pleasure. 'The project of the left is directed at the future, at the socialism that has still to come, and that is at odds with the direct experience of pleasure here and now. That causes all sorts of mental blocks when theorizing about the problem.'[6]

Put simply, the current Marxist idea is as follows: because the production of culture is subject to the laws of the capitalist economy, cultural products are degraded into commodities to make as much profit as possible on the market. The exchange value of those products is therefore essential for the producers, leading to a neglect of quality. The capitalist market economy is only interested in the production of surplus value and as such is indifferent to the specific characteristics of the goods: caring only that they are sold and consumed. Mass culture is the extreme embodiment of the subjection of culture to the economy; its most important characteristic is that it provides profit for the producers.

But this is a one-sided presentation of the case. Marx himself stated that 'a commodity only has exchange value in so far as it is at the same time a use-value, i.e., as an object of consumption; it ceases to have an exchange value if it ceases to have a use-value.'[7] In other words, one cannot succeed in selling a commodity if it does not have a certain usefulness. And it is here that the contradictory character of the capitalist mode of production lies. From the standpoint of production the product only features as a commodity, but from the standpoint of consumption the same product features as use-value.

The way in which a cultural product is consumed can therefore not be directly deduced from the way in which it is produced; it is also dependent on all sorts of socio-cultural and psychological conditions. Terry Lovell has explained in a simple and clear way how unmanageable the relation between the commercial and the entertainment value of mass culture can be: 'There will be no guarantee that the use-value of the cultural object for its purchaser will even be compatible with its

utility to capitalism as bourgeois ideology [. . .] For example, the utility of a television programme for a producer who buys advertising time is the ability of that programme to enhance the sale of the advertised product, by giving the producer access to the audience which is watching the programme. But the viewer will be watching the programme for its entertainment value and there is some evidence that these two interests may conflict. A programme which is a best seller and which its audience rates very highly on entertainment value may actually be less effective as a vehicle for impressing advertised products and increasing their sales than a less entertaining programme.'[8]

But what is the entertainment value that Lovell is discussing here? Both in common sense and in more theoretical ways of thinking, entertainment is usually associated with simple, un-complicated pleasure — hence the phrase, for example, '*mere* entertainment'. This is to evade the obligation to investigate which mechanisms lie at the basis of that pleasure, how that pleasure is produced and how it works — as though that pleasure were something natural and automatic. Nothing is less true, however. Any form of pleasure is constructed and functions in a specific social and historical context.

How then is the pleasure of *Dallas* constructed? As a product of the commercial culture industry, *Dallas* is explicitly offered to the public as an object for pleasurable consumption. The promise of pleasure is the use-value by which the industry tries to seduce viewers to watch *Dallas* on their television sets. But to achieve this aim the producers have to have a definite idea of what the audience will find pleasurable; they must have a certain self-confidence that their own definition of pleasure will coincide with that of (large sections of) the public. There-fore the strategy of the producers will be directed at the elaboration of what they already know about popular pleasures. Their previous experience in the business will be of assistance to them in this. Hence it is not very likely that the pleasure offered in *Dallas* will be structurally new, ex-perimental or provocative. It will keep within the guidelines of

existing and accepted definitions and routines of popular pleasure. In order to attract a large audience the format of *Dallas* will therefore tend to accord with easily accessible and current patterns of what is pleasurable and entertaining. This does not, however, mean that the producers will be fully aware of the effectiveness of their product. As a matter of fact, it is only necessary for them to know that the mechanisms *work* – something they try to discover, for example, by audience ratings and programme testing – not *how* and *why* they work. From their pragmatic viewpoint they are not interested in cultural theory.

We, however, do wish to know how and why the mechanisms of pleasure function – we have indeed set ourselves the task, if not to solve the riddle of the pleasure of *Dallas*, then at least to unravel it to some degree. In 'The aristocracy of culture',[9] Pierre Bourdieu has explained that popular pleasure is characterized by an immediate emotional or sensual involvement in the object of pleasure. What matters is the possibility of identifying oneself with it in some way or other, to integrate it into everyday life. In other words, popular pleasure is first and foremost a pleasure of recognition. But what do *Dallas*-lovers recognize in *Dallas*? This is now the main question confronting us.

DALLAS as television entertainment

But is it really possible to isolate pleasure in *Dallas* from pleasure in television in general? Could it not be said that pleasure in *Dallas* is connected not so much with the specific characteristics of the programme itself, as with the pleasure of watching television as such? And would it not be nearer the truth to say that the audience watches *Dallas* because it has little choice, because television just is not offering anything better?

The consumption of *Dallas* is not an isolated phenomenon, but is embedded in a network of other activities and associ-

ations which are connected with those activities. We should not inflate the pleasure in *Dallas* into something unique and therefore elusive. We have to take into account the socio-cultural context in which *Dallas* is consumed. These conditions of consumption are of course not the same for all social categories and groups. Quite the contrary – an enquiry into the *different* ways in which the television serial is received by various population groups and subcultures could in fact yield particularly useful insights and apply a corrective to the prevalent image of 'passive consumption'.[10] But this would demand a wide-scale sociological examination and that is not my intention. Instead I will confine myself here to describing some general socio-cultural and ideological conditions of television viewing.

For the great majority of the population, television viewing is associated with entertainment: it means relaxation, resting after the day's work. Entertainment belongs to the domain of leisure, and leisure is regarded in the everyday experiential world as 'time for yourself', as liberation from the chafing bonds of the official world of factory, school or office, or from the worries of running the home.[11] Entertainment has for most people expressly positive associations; it is seen as a right, as something earned. And if one thing is associated with watching television as a cultural practice, then it is the right to be entertained in one's own living room. The fact then that *Dallas* is presented as an entertainment programme already offers the promise of pleasure. No one will regard watching *Dallas* as an irksome duty.[12] One letter-writer described it like this: 'a programme it's nice to sit/lie watching, intellect set at nil, the rare luxury of doing sweet nothing' (Letter 19). And another letter-writer gives the following reason why she watches it: 'It's a "penny dreadful" but relaxing. You don't have to strain yourself to understand the story. Just the thing after a hard day's work' (Letter 42).

Pleasure in *Dallas* is therefore associated with the pleasure of the freedoms of entertainment, in which people feel released

from the prohibitions and demands of society. Although many leisure practices are organized socially, in the day-to-day reality leisure time is experienced as an enclave to which one can retreat, 'be oneself'. And in this the weekend occupies a special place; it has the most pleasant associations. 'I just find it a pity that it isn't on Friday any more, because I found that a really good evening for it. But never mind, I'll still watch it on Tuesdays. This evening I'll be sitting there ready and waiting at half past nine' (Letter 2).

But why does it have to be *Dallas*? Isn't this programme just one of many entertainment programmes and is not its pleasure merely something fortuitous? There are three lines of argument which seem to suggest that the popularity of *Dallas* derives not so much from its own qualities as from the fact that it is a *television* programme.

In the first place, *Dallas* is usually televised at prime time. If in addition the other television channels are broadcasting few attractive popular programmes (which has certainly been the case in the Netherlands for a season)[13] it is not surprising that large groups of viewers set to watching *Dallas* – apparently just because they want to watch television, not because they are particularly interested in it. Of course this situation will have a positive influence on the *size* of the audience. But in spite of that it cannot explain the extremely high viewing figures attained by *Dallas* (which are only a quantitative indication of the popularity of the programme anyway).

The second argument points to the nature of television viewing as such. According to Raymond Williams watching television is strongly influenced by the 'flow' character of programming: a coming and going of programmes without their individuality leaving any especially deep impression, because there is no time. Before one programme has finished, another has begun. '[M]ost of us say, in describing the experience, that we have been "watching television", rather than that we have watched "the news" or "a play" or "the football on television". Certainly we sometimes say both, but the fact that

we say the former at all is already significant', Williams states.[14] Formally speaking, then, our contact with particular programmes is shortlived, casual and superficial. Furthermore, television viewing is one of the most obvious and easy-to-realize forms of leisure activity: because the television set is permanently available – it nearly always occupies a central place in the living room – television viewing has almost become an extension of daily life and routine activity. All these socio-cultural characteristics of television viewing as such do indeed set limits on the unique nature of watching *Dallas*. But that does not mean that the programme does not occupy a special place within those limits: the very fact that so much has been said and written about it proves that *Dallas* plays a prominent role in the cultural consciousness of society (at least for the time being: even popular pleasures are subject to fashion to a large degree).

Finally, there is yet a third argument about why we cannot just take the pleasure of *Dallas* on its own terms. This has to do with the authoritarian character of television programming: it is the television networks which decide which programmes are to be broadcast and which not. The audience can only wait and see what menu it will be served. In this sense the television audience is 'passive'. It could then be reasoned that people watch *Dallas* for lack of anything better. But the remarkable thing about television programming, certainly that of commercially run networks, is that it is dominated by the idea of 'giving the public what it wants'.[15] This self-image of the television network is of great influence in the selection of programmes to be broadcast. Certainly where entertainment programmes are concerned there is no doubt that those programmes are selected which are *thought* likely to take the fancy of the public at large. Of course such a programming policy does run the risk that the law of the 'greatest common denominator' will come to prevail. On the other hand, however, ironically enough, this strategy also has the advantage that it does have to take account of the general wishes and preferences of the public. A

commercial television network, from the point of view of its own economic logic, cannot allow itself to become paternalistic; quite the contrary, a populist attitude belongs as it were 'spontaneously' to the professional ideology of the commercial culture industry. It is therefore undeniable that the principles of commercialism do tend to lead to serious considerations of (some of) the wishes of the audience. The fact that the preferences and feelings of the audience are capricious and unpredictable explains why the culture industry feels the need to put so much money and energy into market research – although the motives for this are dubious, being purely pragmatic and egoistic. In short, to use Frith's words, ' "giving the public what it wants", the classic huckster's phrase, describes in fact a complicated relationship between "supply" and "demand" '.[16]

The audience itself didn't ask for *Dallas*: it got it 'thrown into its lap', as it were, as a present from a distant uncle in America. But once it had got it, it then started 'playing' with that present – it was clearly happy with it, happier than with most other 'presents' offered by television. This manifest preference of the audience is certainly limited by the range of what is on offer, but this does not necessarily mean that *Dallas* is consumed in a passive and resigned way. In fact, viewers put a lot of emotional energy into it and experience pleasure from it. Once again, then, the question of pleasure confronts us.

DALLAS as text

In reading the letters we encounter an avalanche of self-given 'reasons' why lovers of *Dallas* like watching the programme. The letter-writers extensively describe their viewing experiences and state what does and does not appeal to them.

> I find *Dallas* a super TV programme. For me it means relaxation twice a week, out of the daily rut. You may wonder why twice a week – well, that's because I watch it on

Belgian TV too. You have to switch over, but you quickly pick it up again. I'm interested in the clothes, make-up and hair-dos too. Sometimes it's quite gripping too, for example in Miss Ellie's case. [. . .] And I think Ray Krebbs is wonderful. But I think J.R. is a monster, a hypocrite, etc. (Letter 1)

The reason I like watching it is that you can easily get really involved in their problems. Yet all the time you know it will all turn out all right again. In fact it's a flight from reality. (Letter 5)

Why do I watch *Dallas* every Tuesday? Mainly because of Pamela and that wonderful love between her and Bobby. When I see those two I feel warmth radiating from them. I am happily married myself too and perhaps I see myself in Pamela. I find her very beautiful too (which I myself am not). (Letter 8)

First of all it's entertainment for me, part show, expensive clothes, beautiful horses, something I can just do with by the evening. (Letter 11)

I think it's marvellous to project myself into *Dallas* and in my mind to give J.R. a good hiding when he's just pulled off yet another dirty trick, or admire Miss Ellie because she always tries to see the best in everyone or to bring it out in them. (Letter 13)

I find *Dallas* marvellous, though it isn't an absolute 'must' for me. Reasons:
Everyone is so kind to one another (leaving aside J.R.) and they form a real family, being sociable, having their meals together, for example.
Witty dialogue.
Fast, characteristic of an American product. (Letter 17)

My absorption in *Dallas* has to do with the fact that I follow everything coming from America. I have been there once – last year – and I started watching *Dallas* just to see the American city scene: those beautiful apartment blocks (espe-

cially the really beautiful one you see during the titles) and
the cars. (Letter 21)

I don't find everything entertaining. The farm doesn't interest me much. Now and then you get a whole episode with
nothing but cowboys and cattle. I find that boring, I'm not
keen on Westerns. Too macho. Like the episode when the
Ewing men went hunting and were chased. Boring. After
that it got better again, fortunately. [. . .] I like the pictures of
the city too a lot. The office buildings in Dallas. The talks
about oil. I really enjoy that. (Letter 23; this letter is from a
man)

I find the situations always so well chosen and excellently
fitting together and everything runs so well from one thing
into another. Then I find the milieu (a rich oil family, etc.)
very well chosen. (Letter 40, also from a man)

It is clear that there is not just one 'reason' for the pleasure of
Dallas, which applies for everyone; each has his or her own
more or less unique relationship to the programme. What
appeals to us in such a television serial is connected with our
individual life histories, with the social situation we are in, with
the aesthetic and cultural preferences we have developed, and
so on.

But though the ideas of each of the letter-writers are of
course personal, they cannot be regarded as a direct expression
of their 'motives' or 'reasons' for watching *Dallas*. They can at
most be regarded as indications or symptoms of deeper psychological incentives and orientations. Furthermore, although
these ideas can *appear* to be strictly personal for the letter-
writers themselves, ultimately all these ideas are structured in a
specific socio-cultural manner. And so we must take a look
behind these ideas; we must subject them to a 'symptomatic
reading' to be able to say something about the pleasure of
Dallas that rises above the merely individual level.

It would be going too far to say that viewers are completely
free to handle *Dallas* as they want, as the possibilities of

experiencing pleasure in it are not infinite. *Dallas* itself, as an object of pleasure, sets its own limits on those possibilities. From the letter excerpts I have just quoted it emerges that the ideas expressed by these viewers contain many elements referring to what is to be seen in the programme – to its textual characteristics. This fact makes it necessary to go into the specific way in which *Dallas*, as a cultural object, is structured.

Dallas is a weekly television programme. A television programme consists of a series of electronic images and sounds which emerge from a television set. These images and sounds represent something: people talking, walking, drinking, high-rise apartment blocks, moving cars, and so on. From this standpoint a television programme can be looked on as a *text*: as a system of representation consisting of a specific combination of (visual and audible) signs.[17] The problem here, however, is that *Dallas* is a discontinuous text: it is a television serial consisting of a large number of episodes, each more or less forming a separate whole. Each episode can then in its turn be called a textual unit. For the sake of clarity I shall view the television serial *Dallas* as a whole as an incomplete, 'infinite' text.[18]

A text functions only if it is 'read'. Only in and through the practice of reading does the text have meaning (or several meanings) for the reader. In the confrontation between *Dallas* and its viewers the reading activity of the latter is therefore the connecting principle. And this reading does not occur just anyhow. As David Morley says: 'The activity of "getting meaning" from [a] message is . . . a problematic practice, however transparent and "natural" it may seem.'[19] A reader has to know specific codes and conventions in order to be able to have any grasp of what a text is about. So it is not by any means a matter of course for viewers to know directly that in *Dallas* they are dealing with a fictional text and not, for example, with a documentary. A great deal of cultural knowledge is necessary to be able to recognize a text as fiction. In *Dallas* – as is the custom in all television serials – certain hints

ven for this, such as the titles, presenting the actors one ..... another, the music, etc.

Any text employs certain rhetorical strategies to arouse the interest of the viewers, and obviously *Dallas* succeeds in attracting the attention of millions of people with very varied social, cultural and psychological backgrounds, and maintaining their involvement in the programme. Very general and widespread structural characteristics of television programmes such as *Dallas* contribute to this.

The function of characters

How do viewers get involved in a television serial like *Dallas*, and what does this involvement consist of? The Belgian media theoretician Jean-Marie Piemme, in his book on the television serial genre,[20] asserts that this involvement occurs because viewers are enabled to participate in the 'world' of the serial. This participation does not come of its own accord, but must be *produced*:

> If, in the serial [. . .] participation can be brought about, this is certainly because this activity has psychological foundations, but it is also because these psychological foundations are confronted by a type of discourse allowing them to be activated. In other words, the structure of the discourse which sustains the serial produces the participation as well as the psychological attitude.[21]

The structure of the text itself therefore plays an essential role in stimulating the involvement of viewers. More importantly still, according to Piemme, it is impossible to watch a television serial without some degree of personal involvement. 'To watch a serial', he states, 'is much more than seeing it: it is also involving oneself in it, letting oneself be held in suspense, sharing the feelings of the characters, discussing their psychological motivations and their conduct, deciding whether they are right or wrong, in other words living "their world".'[22] But

what is there so particular about the textual structure of television serials thát makes them able to effect such profound involvement?

In commonsense explanations of the attraction of television serials, textual structure and its effects are generally ignored. Often single elements of the story are held responsible for the popularity of a serial. Commentary in the press about *Dallas*, for example, shows a special preference for the striking role of the 'baddie' J.R. One of the letter-writers, however, mentions her preference for another *Dallas* character: 'Sue Ellen is definitely my favourite. She has a psychologically believable character. As she is, I am too to a lesser degree ("knocking one's head against a wall once too often") and I want to be (attractive). Identification, then' (Letter 17). But such identification with one character does not take place in a vacuum. One does not just recognize oneself in the ascribed characteristics of an isolated fictional character. That character occupies a specific position within the context of the narrative as a whole: only in relation to other characters in the narrative is her or his 'personality' brought out. In other words, identification with a character only becomes possible within the framework of the whole structure of the narrative.

Moreover, the involvement of viewers cannot be described exclusively in terms of an imaginary identification with one or more characters. Several other aspects of the text contribute to this, such as the way in which the story is told, or the staging. This does not mean, however, that the characters play a subordinate role in the realization of participation. According to Piemme, in a television serial the characters even function as the pre-eminent narrative element which provides the point of impact for the involvement of viewers. But it is not so much the personalities ascribed to the characters in the story, as their formal narrative status that matters. In a fictional text like the television serial the characters are central. Through the characters the various elements of the text (situations, actions, locations, indications of time and so on) obtain a place and function

in the plot. Because the viewer imagines the characters as active subjects, those elements are stripped of their arbitrariness and obtain meaning in the narrative. Furthermore, the 'lifelike' acting style ensures that the distance between actor and character is minimalized, so that the illusion is created that we are dealing with a 'real person'. The character therefore appears for the viewer as a person existing independently of the narrative situations shown in the serial. The character becomes a person appearing to lead an autonomous life outside the fiction of the serial; she or he becomes a person of flesh and blood, one of us. The popular press regularly plays on this illusion: the names of actors and actresses and those of the characters are often used interchangeably or merged – Larry 'J.R.' Hagman.

Being able to imagine the characters as 'real people' thus forms a necessary precondition for the involvement of viewers and is an anchor for the pleasure of *Dallas*. This theoretical assertion is reflected in the letters. When the letter-writers comment on the characters, it is almost always in the same way as we talk about people in daily life: in terms of character traits. The characters are not so much judged for their position in the *Dallas* narrative, as for *how they are*.

That at least is the case for the letter-writers who like *Dallas*. Those who dislike *Dallas* appear to keep a little more distant from the characters. Some of them even criticize their 'unreal' nature.

> One of them (his name escapes me) is always the bastard with his sneaky ideas and tricks, the other son is the goody together with his wife, J.R.'s wife (found the name now) is always 'sloshed' and going off alone to her room. (Letter 32)
>
> When they can't think up any more problems they send Digger after Miss Ellie and change Sue Ellen around a bit again, while J.R. (over the top) is well away with Sue Ellen's sister. (Letter 36)
>
> I find the characters appearing in the serial very caricatured [. . .] J.R. with his crazy ideas: always the same teeth-

gritting. He is also a very caricatured figure, that is obvious. Oh, how bad he is. It's really laid on thick. I find his wife the most lifelike figure in the serial. I think because she was in such a difficult position the writers had most chances with her. What I really can't stand though is the facial expression she has on. Has on, I can't call it anything else. It looks as though her head is cast in plastic. (Letter 41)

What is striking in these reactions is not only a rejection of the 'personalities' of the *Dallas* people, but also an indignation over their constructedness. Those who like *Dallas*, on the other hand, write much more sympathetically about them. In their descriptions a much greater emotional involvement emerges in the characters as people, even when they find them unsympathetic. As one fan of *Dallas* writes:

Actually they are all a bit stupid. And oversensational. Affected and genuinely American. [. . .] And yet [. . .] the Ewings go through a lot more than I do. They seem to have a richer emotional life. Everyone knows them in Dallas. Sometimes they run into trouble, but they have a beautiful house and anything else they might want. (Letter 21)

The personalities of the characters are for some fans apparently so important that they have spontaneously included a whole list of characterizations and criticisms in their letters. They make clear to us how central the characters are in their viewing experience.

I don't know whether it's what you want but I'll write what I myself think of the characters too.
Miss Ellie: a nice woman.
Jock: mean, doesn't know himself exactly what he wants, I think.
Bobby: someone who has respect everywhere and for everyone (except for J.R. but that's understandable).
J.R.: Just a bastard. I personally can't stand him but I must say he plays his role well.

Pamela: a nice girl (I find her a woman of character; she can be nice, but nasty too).

Sue Ellen: has had bad luck with J.R., but she makes up for it by being a flirt. I don't like her much. And she's too sharp-tongued.

Lucy: she has rather too high an opinion of herself, otherwise she's quite nice (she's made up too old).

I don't know so much about the rest who take part in *Dallas* so I won't write about them. If you need what I've said here about these characters then I hope you can use it. If not tear it up. (Letter 3)

Now I'll describe the main characters a little, perhaps that might be useful for you too. Here we go then.

Jock: a well-meaning duffer, rather surly and hard-headed, a very haughty man.

Miss Ellie: very nice, sensitive, understanding, courageous, in other words a real mother.

J.R.: very egoistic, hard as nails, keen on power, but a man with very little heart.

Sue Ellen: just *fantastic*, tremendous how that woman acts, the movements of her mouth, hands, etc. That woman really enters into her role, looking for love, snobbish, in short a real woman.

Pamela: a Barbie doll with no feelings, comes over as false and unsympathetic (a waxen robot).

Bobby: ditto.

Lucy: likeable, naïve, a real adolescent. (Letter 12)

On the characters: Sue Ellen is definitely my favourite. She has a psychologically believable character. [. . .] (Her friend, Dusty, really loves her and for that reason, although the cowboy business in the serial irritates me and so he does too a bit, I do like him as far as I can judge.)

Miss Ellie is all right too. She looks good, always knows the

right thing to do (conciliatory and firm) within the family and her breast cancer gave her some depth.
Lucy has guts, but is a wicked little sod too.
The others don't offer much as characters, I believe. Pamela pouts, and is too sweet. I have absolutely nothing to say about Jock and Bobby; J.R. is really incredible, so mean. (Letter 17)

What is interesting in these extracts is not so much the content of the character descriptions (although the difference in sympathies in itself is worth some attention), but the fact that 'genuineness' forms the basis for evaluation. The more 'genuine' a character appears to be, the more he or she is valued. But what is even more remarkable is that even for the severe critics 'genuineness' is the criterion by which they judge the characters. The only difference is that the severe critics tend to see them as 'unreal', whereas among the fans the opposite is the case. Characters who are 'caricatures' or 'improbable' are not esteemed, characters who are 'lifelike' or 'psychologically believable' are. Also, casually dropped remarks from fans quoted above ('I must say he plays his role well', 'she's made up too old' and 'tremendous how that woman acts, the move-ments of her mouth, hands, etc.') make clear that these letter-writers are very well aware that they are only dealing with fictional 'real people'. Such remarks indicate that these viewers would like that fictional element eliminated as far as possible. In their eyes actor and character should merge:

. . . then I find that all the actors and actresses act very well. So well even that, for example, I really find J.R. a bastard, or Sue Ellen a frustrated lady. (Letter 18)

. . . Because in my opinion they have chosen awfully good actors. I mean suitable for the role they are playing. The whole Ewing family is played so well that they are really human. Sometimes you get a film or a play and you think: God, if I really had to do that, I'd react quite differently. Then it seems so unreal. But usually *Dallas* could really

happen, and the actors and actresses make it credible. (Letter 20)

The people taking part in it act terribly well. (Letter 4)

The effect of 'genuineness' is then the most important thing these viewers expect. Only when they experience the fiction of the serial as 'genuine' can they feel involved in it. They have to be able to believe that the characters constructed in the text are 'real people' whom they can find pleasant or unpleasant, with whom they can feel affinity or otherwise, and so on. It could be said that such involvement is a necessary condition for the pleasure of *Dallas*.

The (un)realistic quality of DALLAS

But genuine-seeming *people* alone are not enough. According to Piemme, the fictional *world* in which the characters live must seem equally real. But how 'real' or 'realistic' is this world? This rather vague concept of 'realism' also seems to play an important part in the letters. 'Realism' seems to be a favourite criterion among viewers for passing judgement on *Dallas*. And here 'realistic' is always associated with 'good' and 'unrealistic' with 'bad'. So it is not surprising that many haters of *Dallas* express their dislike by referring to its – in their opinion – 'unrealistic' content. Here are some letter extracts:

In *Dallas* no attention at all is paid to any realistic problems in this world. The problems of ordinary people. (Letter 31)

... in my eyes the characters appearing in it are totally unreal. (Letter 38)

It is a programme situated pretty far outside reality. The mere fact that a whole family is living in one house comes over as rather unreal. What happens in this serial you would never run into in the street or in your circle of acquaintance: very unreal events. The family relations that are so weirdly

involved: this one's married to the sister of the enemy of his brother, etc., etc. (Letter 41)

1. It is an improbable story because:
    1.1 Such a rich family would scarcely live as three families in one house (at least in a Western society), so that privacy for each family is minimal:
        1.1.1 They breakfast together, etc.
        1.1.2 Other than the common rooms each family only has one bedroom (no separate sitting room or study, etc.).
        1.1.3 The whole family concerns itself with everything.
    1.2 Too much happens in the short time and then it's all dramatic situations, not only for the main characters, but for the minor characters as well. This latter makes things confusing.
    1.3 The actors are rather clichéd types, i.e. they keep up a certain role or attitude. Normal people are more complex.
2. Thanks to the constant drama there is a certain tension in the story, but this is exaggerated. Even in a more realistic story there can be tension and I actually find that nicer. (Letter 42)

In these extracts a number of things are striking. In the first place these letter-writers find *Dallas* 'unrealistic' because in their opinion the world and the events in the story do not coincide with the world and events outside *Dallas*: reality 'as it is'. A text is called 'realistic' here if the 'reality' standing outside and independent of the text is reflected in an 'adequate' way. But – and this is the second striking point – the letter-writers each invest the notion of 'reality' with a different content. For some the represented reality must coincide with the social reality of 'ordinary people' (i.e. 'real' problems such as unemployment and housing shortages and not the 'mock problems' of the rich); for others that reality must be 'recognizable',

i.e. comparable to one's own environment; and for others again the world presented must be 'probable', i.e. cohere, be 'normal'. Finally, a text is also occasionally called 'unrealistic' if people find that it simplifies the 'real' reality (whatever that may be), exaggerates it or reflects it in clichés.

As we can see, the significance of the notion '(un)realistic' can assume different forms. Clearly there is no unambiguous definition of what 'realism' contains. But in the way in which the term is used by the letter-writers quoted, at least an essential community of ideas can be discerned: they all call *Dallas* 'unrealistic' because in their opinion it gives a 'distorted image of reality'. This definition of realism, in which a comparison of the realities 'in' and 'outside' a text is central, we can call 'empiricist realism'.[23] This empiricist concept of realism often fulfils an ideological function in television criticism in so far as its standards are used to furnish arguments for criticizing programmes and to strengthen the concept itself. From this point of view, a text which can be seen as an 'unrealistic' rendering of social reality (however that is defined) is 'bad'. And as we have seen, *Dallas* is often subjected to this judgement.

But having said this, we are immediately confronted by an apparently baffling contradiction. Contrary to the critics and those who dislike *Dallas*, who regard it as particularly 'unrealistic', many fans do find it 'realistic'. Some letter-writers even see the – in their eyes – realistic content of *Dallas* as a reason for the pleasure they experience.

> I find *Dallas* super and for this reason: they reflect the daily life of a family (I find). (Letter 3)

> It is realistic (for me anyway), other people think I'm mad, things happen in it we might well find happening to us later (or have had). (Letter 12)

How should we interpret this contradiction? Should we ascribe to these letter-writers a 'false consciousness' because their judgement on the 'realistic' content of *Dallas* is totally wrong?

Or is there more to it? Reasoning from an empiricist-realistic standpoint, we can simply say these letter-writers are misled. In *Dallas*, according to this reasoning, the 'daily life of a family' is certainly not being reflected – for, as one letter-writer suggests: 'I wonder why these people in Heaven's name carry on living in the same house!' (Letter 36). Furthermore, it could be said that the things that happen in it are certainly not things 'we might well find happening to us', for it is clear that in *Dallas* there is an improbable accumulation of sensational events, such as airplane accidents, weird diseases, kidnappings, etc. In short, if *Dallas* is regarded as a mirror of 'the' reality, then we should recognize that it is a big distorting mirror, or more seriously, 'a twisted image of reality'.

But this empiricist conception of realism presents problems for a number of reasons. I shall cite two difficulties here. First, it is wrongly based on the assumption – and this is inherent in empiricism – that a text *can* be a direct, immediate reproduction or reflection of an 'outside world'. This is to ignore the fact that everything that is processed in a text is the result of selection and adaptation: elements of the 'real world' function only as raw material for the production process of texts. The empiricist conception denies the fact that each text is a cultural product realized under specific ideological and social conditions of production. And so there can never be any question of an unproblematic mirror relation between text and social reality: at most it can be said that a text constructs its own version of 'the real'. As Raymond Williams says: 'The most damaging consequence of any theory of art as reflection is that [. . .] it succeeds in suppressing the actual work on material [. . .] which is the making of any art work.'[24]

The second difficulty is connected with this. The empiricist conception of realism cannot do justice to the fact that a large number of *Dallas* fans do seem to *experience* it as 'realistic'. Must we regard this experience merely as the result of incorrect reading and must we, consequently, accuse the letter-writers who read 'wrongly' of a lack of knowledge of reality? It is, to

say the least, unsatisfactory just to dismiss this very prevalent way of responding to the programme. A more structural explanation must be possible.

DALLAS and the realistic illusion

In the empiricist conception of realism the thematic content of the narrative becomes the guideline for the assessment of the 'realistic' nature of the text. Some literary and film theoreticians on the other hand make the way in which the story is told responsible for what is called the 'realistic illusion': the illusion that a text is a faithful reflection of an actually existing world emerges as a result of the fact that the constructedness of the text is suppressed. Piemme states that it is this suppression which fosters the involvement of viewers in the serial: 'Participation can only function by denying itself as product of discourse. What produces it must suppress the marks of its production in order that the illusion of the natural, the spontaneous, the inevitable, may function.'[25] In other words, the realistic illusion is not something to be blamed on the ignorance or lack of knowledge of the viewers, but is generated by the formal structure of the text itself; the thematic content plays only a subordinate role here.

The film theoretician Colin MacCabe calls a (literary or film) text which arouses such a realistic illusion a 'classic realistic text'.[26] Characteristic of such a text, for which the nineteenth-century realistic novel is the model, is the dominant role which the story in itself plays.[27] It is told in such a way that the viewer or reader is unaware that the narrative has a narrator. In a classic realistic text 'narrative must deny the time of its own telling – it must refuse its status as discourse [. . .] in favour of its self-presentation as simple identity, complete knowledge'.[28] In short, the classic realistic text conceals its own status as narrative and acts as though the story 'speaks for itself'.

With regard to film, in this connection the term 'transparent

narrative cinema' is used: 'transparent' because the screen appears to be a transparent window on the events taking place in the film story. The classic-realistic method of narration is the most common in the history of the cinema, but it is mainly in classical Hollywood that the conventions of transparent narrativity have been perfected to the utmost. What then are these conventions?[29]

A Hollywood-story is always about individual characters who want or desire something. The characters perform actions to achieve their goals, but can encounter opposition to this from other characters who have other wishes or desires. From this schema flows a chain of events which are in a cause/effect relationship with one another. This chain forms the framework of the story.

This story must be told filmically, i.e. translated into a concrete sequence of images and sounds. Countless technical and aesthetic means are necessary to translate an abstract narrative into a concrete film story: the narrative must be divided into scenes, the sequence of the scenes and shots determined, locations must be sought, actors selected and their acting style defined, the camera must focus the *mise-en-scène* in a specific way and the individual shots must finally be assembled together. It is characteristic of a transparent narrative film that all these filmic operations are made subordinate to the demands of the story. Everything we see or hear in the film has a narrative function: 'meaningless' images and sounds are deemed redundant and tend to be excluded. Through this the illusion arises that the story is unrolling before our eyes without any mediation: the narrating instance has been effectively eliminated.

In Hollywood since the beginning of this century certain iron rules of cinematography have been developed (such as continuity editing, classic montage, etc.) to create this suggestion of narrative spontaneity. But we no longer experience these rules as rules, because we have become so used to this dominant American film language that we no longer even recognize it as a

language. This is the socio-cultural background of the realistic illusion.

The television serial *Dallas* also uses the classical Hollywood rules to a great degree. The story concerns the members of the Ewing family: it is their desires and wishes that propel the narrative, their actions (and the mutual conflicts they have as a result of these) fill the narrative. The whole construction of the serial is also directed at showing those actions and their consequences. All the elements in the film are at the service of the narrative. Because the narrative wants the characters to be rich a beautiful ranch is chosen as their house, they drive luxury cars and the women wear expensive clothes. And the camera only portrays what is necessary for understanding the story: where something is happening, there stands the camera. A scene is broken off the moment the dramatic action in it has come to an end: there is no point in remaining at that place any longer. Moreover, the successive scenes run smoothly into one another: jumps in time and space must take place in such a way that the viewer does not find them disturbing, for this can lead to a loss of illusion of narrative continuity and coherence. This illusion is strengthened even more by the strictly chronological sequence in which the course of the narrative is set forth; what first happens in the story we get to see before later events. (The only exception to this is the 'flashback', which is, however, announced so explicitly as a retrospection of one of the characters that no misunderstandings can arise over it.)

According to MacCabe and others[30] it is precisely this constructed illusion of reality which is the basis for pleasure. It is pleasurable to be able to deny the textuality and the fictional nature of the film and forget it: it gives the viewers a comfortable and cosy feeling because they can 'let the narrative flow over them' without any effort. The apparent 'transparency' of the narrative produces a feeling of direct involvement, because it ensures that the viewer can act exactly *as though* the story really happened. In other words, according to this theory pleasure in *Dallas* could be regarded as a pleasure in the

obvious, apparently natural meaningfulness of the ups and downs of the Ewing family and the people around them. It is the *form* of the narrative which produces pleasure, not its content.

Yet this explanation of pleasure is not totally satisfactory, precisely because it abstracts from the concrete narrative-content.[31] Transparent narrativity alone is not enough to get pleasure out of a text; not all transparent narrative texts are experienced as equally pleasurable. On the contrary, the thematic differences between such texts are of interest, as one of the letter-writers states: 'For me *Dallas* is comparable to *Dynasty*. Other American series (*Magnum, Hulk, Charlie's Angels, Starsky and Hutch*, in short, violence) I can appreciate less' (Letter 17). Thus the pleasure of *Dallas* is not only to do with the illusion of reality which is produced by its transparent narrativity – although it might be said that this illusion is a general condition of pleasure as it is experienced by a lot of viewers. *What* is told in the narrative must also play a part in the production of pleasure.

DALLAS and 'emotional realism'

Why then do so many fans call *Dallas* 'realistic'? What do they recognize as 'real' in its fictional world?

A text can be read at various levels. The first level is the literal, denotative level. This concerns the literal, manifest content of the *Dallas* narrative: the discussions between the characters, their actions, their reactions to one another, and so on. Is this literal content of the *Dallas* story experienced as realistic by viewers? It does not look like it. Indeed, we can say that the above-quoted letter-writers who dislike *Dallas* are talking on this literal narrative-level when they dismiss the programme as *un*realistic. Let us repeat a letter extract:

It is a programme situated pretty far outside reality. The mere fact that a whole family is living in one house comes

er as rather unreal. What happens in this serial you would
ver run into in the street or in your circle of acquaintance:
very unreal events. The family relationships that are so
weirdly involved: this one's married to the sister of the
enemy of his brother, etc., etc. (Letter 41)

This indicates that the *Dallas* narrative at the level of denotation is not exactly regarded as realistic; literal resemblances
are scarcely seen between the fictional world as it is constructed
in *Dallas* and the 'real' world. Again the inadequacy of the
empiricist-realistic approach becomes clear here. It is only
sensitive to the denotative level of the narrative. Therefore it
can only see the fact that so many *Dallas* fans obviously do
experience the programme as realistic as a paradox.

A text can, however, also be read at another level, namely at
the connotative level.[32] This level relates to the associative
meanings which can be attributed to elements of the text. The
same letter-writer we have just quoted also wrote the following: 'The nice thing about the serial is that it has a semblance of
humanity, it is not so unreal that you can't relate to it any more.
There are recognizable things, recognizable people, recognizable relations and situations in it' (Letter 41).

It is striking; the same things, people, relations and situations which are regarded at the denotative level as unrealistic,
and unreal, are at connotative level apparently not seen at all as
unreal, but in fact as 'recognizable'. Clearly, in the connotative
reading process the denotative level of the text is put in
brackets.

But what does make *Dallas* so 'recognizable' at that connotative level? What does that 'semblance of humanity' consist
of that this letter-writer is talking about?

In the letters we come across all kinds of descriptions which
can give us some indication of the associative meanings these
viewers ascribe to *Dallas*. From the heterogeneous stream of
signs with which viewers are confronted when they watch the
television serial, they pick up only certain things; they find only

certain elements of the whole text relevant, striking – pleasurable. In other words, a text is never read in its totality; during reading a selection process is always taking place. As Roland Barthes has noted in *The Pleasure of the Text*, 'it is the very rhythm of what is read and what is not read that creates the pleasure of the great narratives. [. . .] Thus, what I enjoy in a narrative is not directly its content or even its structure, but rather the abrasions I impose upon the fine surface: I read on, I skip, I look up, I dip again.'[33] In a similar way, we could say that the letter-writers only name those elements from *Dallas* which are important for them in some way or other, which for them make up the special and pleasurable quality of *Dallas*.[34]

Many lovers of *Dallas* say that they find it pleasurable because it is 'realistic'. From their letters we can now get an impression of how they reach that judgement, or more precisely, which elements of the text they select which lead to its 'realism' at a connotative level. Note the similarity between the meanings which emerge in the following letter extracts.

I find *Dallas* super and for this reason: [the characters] reflect the daily life of a family (I find). You sometimes see serials where everything runs smoothly. Never any rows or anything. Not a damn thing wrong. Every family has rows sometimes. It's not always smooth sailing. In *Dallas* there are rows, desperate situations. (Letter 3)

Do you know why I like watching it? I think it's because those problems and intrigues, the big and little pleasures and troubles occur in our own lives too. You just don't recognize it and we are not so wealthy as they are. In real life too I know a horror like J.R., but he's just an ordinary builder. That's why I see so many aspects and phases of life, of your own life, in it. Yes, it's really ordinary daily problems more than anything that occur in it and that you recognize. And then it's so marvellous the way they solve them better than you've solved your own problems. (Letter 4)

You have to see the reality of life, and reality occurs there the

way it is in real life too, the intrigues, especially with people living together in the same house. The wealth is the only difference, I'm not rich (financially, materially speaking). (Letter 6)

I'll tell you why I like watching *Dallas* and what I find so disgusting about it. The good thing about it is that so many different things in it are taken from life, so to speak. Such as Miss Ellie's illness, and Sue Ellen with her marital problems. . . . The disgusting thing I find is the exaggeratedly difficult life these people (in the serial) have, this one's having a great row with that one, and they keep climbing in and out of one another's beds. I get really fed up with that. But that's life, just look around you. There are so few people left living happily and harmoniously with one another. (Letter 10)

I also find some elements true to life. Take the story of Sue Ellen. (Letter 11)

But *Dallas* could really happen. . . . For example, I can sit very happy and fascinated watching someone like Sue Ellen. That woman can really get round us, with her problems and troubles. She is really human. I could be someone like that too. In a manner of speaking. (Letter 2)

Two things stand out in these extracts. The first is that the writers find *Dallas* 'taken from life'; what happens to the Ewing family is in their own eyes not essentially different from what they themselves (can) experience in life. The second point is more important for us, for it reveals the mechanism used for realizing this at first sight puzzling 'experience of reality': in order to be able to experience *Dallas* as 'taken from life' these letter-writers seem to abstract from the denotative level of the text. In naming the 'true to life' elements of *Dallas* the concrete living circumstances in which the characters are depicted (and their wealth in particular springs to mind here) are, it is true, striking but not of significance as regards content; the concrete situations and complications are rather regarded as symbolic representations of more general living experiences: rows, in-

trigues, problems, happiness and misery. And it is precisely in this sense that these letter-writers find *Dallas* 'realistic'. In other words, at a connotative level they ascribe mainly emotional meanings to *Dallas*. In this sense the realism of *Dallas* can be called an 'emotional realism'.

And now it begins to become clear why the two previous conceptions of realism discussed above, empiricist realism and classical realism, are so unsatisfactory when we want to understand the experience of realism of *Dallas* fans. For however much the two approaches are opposed to one another – for the former realism is a token for a 'good' text, and for the latter for a 'bad' text – in both a cognitive-rationalistic idea dominates: both are based on the assumption that a realistic text offers *knowledge* of the 'objective' social reality. According to the empiricist-realists a text is realistic (and therefore good) if it supplies 'adequate knowledge' of reality, while in the second conception a classic-realistic text is bad because it only creates an illusion of knowledge. But the realism experience of the *Dallas* fans quoted bears no relation to this cognitive level – it is situated at the emotional level: what is recognized as real is not knowledge of the world, but a subjective experience of the world: a 'structure of feeling'.[35]

It is emotions which count in a structure of feeling. Hence emotions form the point of impact for a recognition of a certain type of structure of feeling in *Dallas*; the emotions called up are apparently what remain with the letter-writers most. Thus the following letter-writer describes *Dallas* as a sequence of ever-changing emotions:

> Now I'll tell you why I like watching *Dallas*. Here goes!
> 1. There is suspense in it.
> 2. It can also be romantic.
> 3. There is sadness in it.
> 4. And fear.
> 5. And happiness.
> In short, there is simply everything in that film. (Letter 16)

What we can deduce from this is the notion that in life emotions are always being stirred up, i.e. that life is characterized by an endless fluctuation between happiness and unhappiness, that life is a question of falling down and getting up again. This structure of feeling can be called the *tragic* structure of feeling; tragic because of the idea that happiness can never last for ever but, quite the contrary, is precarious. In the tragic structure of feeling emotional ups and downs occupy a central place: 'All that rowing and lovemaking I find marvellous to watch' (Letter 9). Isn't it precisely the radical contrast between the emotional associations of quarrelling and lovemaking that is so fascinating for her?

Life presents a problem according to the tragic structure of feeling, but that does not mean that life consists solely of problems. On the contrary, problems are only regarded as problems if there is a prospect of their solution, if, in other words, there is hope for better times. Here too we are dealing with a contrast between misery and happiness. So it is not so odd that some letter-writers want to place emphasis on 'happiness':

> Why do I watch *Dallas* every Tuesday? Mainly because of Pamela and that wonderful love between her and Bobby. When I see those two I feel warmth radiating from them. . . . I also find the relationship between Jock and Miss Ellie nice, but I'm scarcely interested at all in J.R. and Sue Ellen and certainly not in the Ewing empire. (Letter 8)

It seems as though the 'wonderful love' of Pamela and Bobby takes on greater glory against the background of the loveless relationship between J.R. and Sue Ellen. According to another letter-writer, lovelessness is even the normal condition: 'Mutual relationships and communications are often so cool that it seems as though they are just wrapped up in themselves' (Letter 7). Or, as expressed briefly but succinctly by one letter-writer: 'a bed of roses it is not' (Letter 6).

Between reality and fiction

Let us summarize what has been said above. Many letter-writers contend that the pleasure of *Dallas* comes from the 'lifelike' character of the serial. If we subject their statements to closer analysis, then it appears that what is experienced as 'real' indicates above all a certain structure of feeling which is aroused by the programme: the tragic structure of feeling. In this many letter-writers who like *Dallas* seem to recognize themselves, and therefore experience it as 'real'. And precisely this recognition arouses pleasure: 'I myself enjoy *Dallas* and the tears start to flow when anything tragic happens (in nearly every episode then)' (Letter 14).

The realism of *Dallas* is therefore produced by the construction of a *psychological* reality, and is not related to its (illusory) fit to an externally perceptible (social) reality. It could even be said that in *Dallas* an 'inner realism' is combined with an 'external unrealism'. The external manifestation of the fictional world of *Dallas* does also contribute to pleasure, not because of its reality value though, but because of its stylization:

a bit of a show, expensive clothes, beautiful horses. (Letter 11)

the serial is very relaxing to watch: beautiful people, a carefree life, restful surroundings. (Letter 19)

I also pay attention to the clothes, make-up and hair-dos. (Letter 1)

Then it's nice to see the clothes of the *Dallas* women. (Letter 9)

There are a few minor details(!) which make the serial attractive, such as the splendid house and the beautiful landscape. (Letter 2)

I started watching *Dallas* just to see the American city scene: the beautiful apartment blocks (especially the really beautiful ones you see during the titles) and the cars. (Letter 21)

It is probably the glamorous *mise-en-scène* of *Dallas* referred to in these letter extracts that is responsible for the fact that viewers are well aware they are watching a fictional world. The illusion of reality is therefore not total. Moreover, the fictional world is not uncritically accepted either. Various letter-writers show quite explicitly that they are aware that *Dallas* is a textual construction.

> You have to keep in mind the reality of life, and there's reality in it too the way it is in real life . . . Although now and then I do find things a bit over the top. (Letter 6)

> The good thing about it, I think, is that lots of things happen in it taken from life, so to speak. Such as . . . Sue Ellen with her marital problems, though I do find that in the longer run that is a bit overdone, she makes a game out of it. I think the serial writers do that deliberately, because lots of men find it terrific to watch her. And would even like to help her. Oh well. Those gallant Don Juans. (Letter 10)

> If they (the writers) write Pamela (or Bobby) out of the serial it will be over for me. The good relationship between those two is my reason for watching. But then, I still believe in 'true love'. (Letter 8)

All these remarks suggest a distance between the 'real' and the fictional world. And precisely because the letter-writers are aware of this, it appears, they can indulge in the excessive emotions aroused in *Dallas*.

> After a serial like that of poverty and misery, where spiritual character is concerned, because financially nothing is lacking, I often think with relief, now I can come back to my own world and I'm very happy in it. To have seen all those worries gives me a nice feeling – you're looking for it, you're bringing it on yourself. (Letter 10)

> Yes, it's actually ordinary daily problems that occur in it mainly and that you recognize. And then it's so marvellous that they solve them better than you've solved your own

problems. Perhaps for me it's relativizing my own problems and troubles or just escaping them. (Letter 4)

'Escape.' This word definitely sounds familiar. It is a term with a negative charge: it is generally not viewed as a sign of strength or courage if people seek refuge in a non-existent fantasy world. It is regarded as a lack of 'sense of reality'. Furthermore, the term often comes up in public discourses over mass entertainment: it is their supposed 'escapist' character that so often leads to a negative judgement of popular entertainment forms.[36] But precisely the fact that this view is so current should warn us to be cautious when we encounter it in the letters. What is the term 'escape' actually referring to, what does it mean for the letter-writers themselves? The term is misleading, because it presupposes a strict division between reality and fantasy, between 'sense of reality' and 'flight from reality'. But is it not rather the case that there is interaction between the two? One of the letter-writers formulates it as follows:

> The reason I like watching it is that it's nice to get dizzy on their problems. And you know all along that everything will turn out all right. In fact it's a flight from reality. I myself am a realistic person and I know that reality is different. Sometimes too I really enjoy having a good old cry with them. And why not? In this way my other bottled-up emotions find an outlet. (Letter 5)

'And you know all along that everything will turn out all right.' This is a key sentence, clearly defining the nature of the 'flight'. The 'flight' into a fictional fantasy world is not so much a denial of reality as playing with it. A game that enables one to place the limits of the fictional and the real under discussion, to make them fluid. And in that game an imaginary participation in the fictional world is experienced as pleasurable:

> I really like watching it, and especially Pamela and Bobby

because it comes over (in the film) as real affection, although it's only a film. (Letter 6)

I try to find more and more in the various characters. After each shocking event I try to imagine what they'll do. . . . In future there will be more sex in the serial. That is one aspect of a further illustration of the characters. But there are many more. It would be good too if the actors' thoughts were put in. (Letter 7)

I find it's marvellous to project myself into *Dallas* and in my mind to give J.R. a good hiding when he's just pulled off yet another dirty trick, or admire Miss Ellie because she always tries to see the best in everyone or to bring it out in them. Also, I find it awfully nice to imagine myself in that world, such as: 'What would I do if Sue Ellen said that to me?' Or to see myself running round in a big city like Dallas. (Letter 13)

Thus, whatever there is to be said about the pleasure of *Dallas*, the field of tension between the fictional and the real seems to play an important part in it. Or, as a more theoretically minded letter-writer put it: 'It is easier and loads more pleasurable to dash away a tear because Ma Dallas has cancer – because she's only acting – than because of whatever annoying things are in your own life, and at least you have got rid of that tear' (Letter 22). A constant to and fro movement between identification with and distancing from the fictional world as constructed in the text therefore characterizes the involvement of the letter-writers who like *Dallas*. But one question still remains unanswered. How does Dallas succeed in producing those tears, that 'dizziness'? In other words, how does *Dallas* construct the tragic structure of feeling which is recognized by these viewers? This is the subject of the next chapter.

2

DALLAS
and the melodramatic imagination

DALLAS and genre

A television serial like *Dallas* is made according to certain rules and conventions which belong to a specific genre. A genre is, one might say, a complex of themes, narrative structures and styles that groups of individual films or television programmes have in common with one another.[1] Because we know these rules and conventions, and have become familiar with them, we often know quite quickly whether a film is a Western or a thriller and we entertain certain expectations of the course of the film, although each Western or thriller has its own idiosyncrasies. But the general characteristics of the genre set limits on the individual genre film, which renders it simpler for the audience to follow. A genre is in other words a formula and each individual genre film is a specific 'application' of the rules and conventions of the genre. This application can succeed to greater or lesser degree, be more or less inventive, opening new ground for the genre to a greater or lesser degree. In analysing a genre film, then, one must constantly move between the general

and the particular, between the established structures and the specific application. In this chapter we shall be trying to do that with *Dallas*.

In order to discover which television genre *Dallas* should be classified under, we must take a look at the structural characteristics of this serial. The first structural characteristic that deserves our attention is its episodic character. For as we shall see later on, this genre-characteristic plays an essential role in the construction of the emotional realism stemming from the tragic structure of feeling.

The episodic character of television fiction can assume two forms: that of the *series*, in which the individual episodes are completely separate from one another from a narrative viewpoint (only the hero(ine) of the series and the basic situation are the connecting elements between the individual episodes), and the *serial*, i.e. the continuous narrative. Programmes like *Magnum* and *Charlie's Angels* are examples of series, while *Dallas*, but also *Hill Street Blues*, are examples of the serial. The separate episodes of a serial cannot in principle be watched in any order, because the precise sequence of the episodes creates a notion of the continuance of time, a continuance which is linear and irreversible. Of course each episode is more or less a separate whole: not only is there in each episode of *Dallas* one more or less central narrative line, but each episode also gets its own title and is divided off by recognizable beginning and end credits.

But in contrast to a series, in which the time between two episodes is of no narrative importance whatever, the time between two episodes in a serial does play a role – though merely an imaginary one – in the way in which viewers experience the narrative. 'The characters in a serial, when abandoned at the end of an episode, pursue an "unrecorded existence" until the next one begins', states Christine Geraghty, in a summary of the formal characteristics of the television serial.[2] The television serial thus appeals to a historical sense of time: it constructs the feeling that the lives of the

characters go on during our absence – i.e. between two episodes. Thus the idea of 'unchronicled growth' is aroused in viewers.

This feeling can, however, only arise if the end of an episode offers the possibility for it. The end of an episode of a serial is mostly in the shape of a so-called 'cliffhanger': the narrative is broken off at a moment of very great suspense, so that the viewers are encouraged to see the following episode if they want to know how the story goes on. In earlier film serials the cliffhanger consisted mainly in an abruptly broken off action: or at the very moment the hero threatens to be pushed over the cliff by his enemy, the words 'to be continued' appear – as if to tease the audience – on the screen. The following episode then takes up the thread at the same action, at the same moment in the story. In such cases there is no question of an imaginary passage of time between two episodes.

This type of 'cliffhanger' is, however, seldom used in television serials,[3] although they do occur in fact, by way of exception, in *Dallas*. Just think of the episodes that ended with an attempt on J.R.'s life or with the moment when Southfork is going up in flames. But in by far the majority of cases in *Dallas* a psychological cliffhanger is used: an episode ends most often at the moment when one of the characters lands in a new, psychologically conflictual situation. The last shot of an episode is then nearly always a close-up of the face of the character concerned, which emphasizes the psychological conflict she or he is in. In one of the following episodes – it does not necessarily need to be the very next one – we are then shown how she or he handles the conflict, but meanwhile time proceeds and life goes on as normal. The very next episode usually begins with a new day. Such a construction offers viewers the possibility of having the feeling that time in *Dallas* more or less keeps pace with the time in which the viewers themselves are living. This fact in itself takes care of a specific dimension of 'everyday realism' – the life of the Ewings in Dallas flows on just like our own life.

But an even more important characteristic of *Dallas* that helps to arouse this idea is the fact that there is no narrative ending in sight. The structure of the *Dallas* narrative is radically different from that of a feature film or an episode of a series such as *Kojak* or *Lou Grant*. In classic narrative theory narrative is defined in terms of the schema: order/disturbance of order/restoration of order. A narrative consists of 'a movement between equilibriums which are similar but not identical':[4] at the end all the problems which have disturbed the equilibrium of the opening situation have been resolved. This narrative scheme, however, will not work for an endlessly running television serial like *Dallas*. Although in each episode problems are solved, at the same time new ones are created, which form the point of departure for the following episodes, and so on and so on.

The 'endless' character of a serial is typical for a special genre of television fiction: the soap opera. Soap opera is a long-standing radio genre which was 'invented' and developed at the end of the 1920s by American, mainly female, radio programme makers. The soap opera, which rapidly developed into one of the most popular entertainment forms on radio, was characterized by an accent on human relations, domesticity and daily life; it is home, garden and kitchen problems which are discussed and solved by the characters.[5] The 'soaps', so called because it was mainly soap manufacturers who sponsored the programmes, shot up like mushrooms and built up a faithful following, especially among housewives – not least because they were broadcast almost every day. The soap opera was alleged to be able to provide some (surrogate) company for housewives living in isolation; they listened to their favourite soaps while doing the ironing, cooking or other domestic work.[6]

With the coming of television the soap opera finally disappeared from the American radio stations, but the genre took on a new and flourishing existence in the new medium. Although soap opera is not an exclusively American phen-

omenon – British, Australian and Brazilian television, for example, are richly provided with home-grown soap operas – the genre is almost totally unknown on Dutch television. *Peyton Place* and *Coronation Street* could be seen at the beginning of the 1970s on Dutch television, and they were quite popular, but the American 'daytime serials', as they are officially called, have never been screened in the Netherlands – in contrast to the parodies of them: *Mary Hartman! Mary Hartman!* and *Soap!* which are esteemed mainly by an intellectual audience! Only with the arrival of *Dallas* on the screen did the Dutch television audience get handed another American soap opera.

But *Dallas* is not a daytime soap opera. Just like *Peyton Place*, *Dallas* is made to be shown at prime time. Of course this has its consequences. An important formal difference between *Dallas* and the daytime soap opera is the much greater attention to visualization in *Dallas*. In contrast to daytime soaps, which have always kept a radio-like character and in which the visual element is kept to a minimum (very sparse locations, very simple camera work, etc.), *Dallas* looks chic – because of the high production values which generally apply for prime time programmes – and it is made with filmic expertise. A lot of attention is paid to the visual attractiveness of the locations, the stars' costumes, and so on. This is doubtless a background which should not be neglected when accounting for its worldwide popularity. The hegemony of American television (and film) has habituated the world public to American production values and American *mises-en-scène*, such as the vast prairie or the big cities, the huge houses with expensive interiors, luxurious and fast cars and, last but not least, the healthy- and good-looking men and women, white, not too young, not too old. Such images have become signs which no longer merely indicate something like 'Americanness', but visual pleasure as such. The television audience has, over the years, become familiar with all this and tends to recognize it as pleasurable; it is as though for large groups of people these American images

fulfil a signal function, they imply the promise that the story will be suspenseful and exciting. As Simon Frith states: 'America, as experienced in films and music, has itself become the object of consumption, a symbol of pleasure.'[7]

The fact that *Dallas* is a prime time programme also has consequences for the structure of the narrative content. Prime time is the time in which the whole family usually watches television, in contrast to the morning or afternoon hours (during which housewives, pensioners and the unemployed form the largest group of viewers). A popular programme must therefore, at least according to the commercial logic of the American television industry, appeal to the whole family. In a certain sense this could explain why in *Dallas* themes from other genres such as the Western are worked in, to attract the interest of a broad mass audience. Similarly the fact that men and masculine themes such as business life play a much more central part in *Dallas* than in the average daytime soap could be connected to this.[8] Therefore *Dallas* is not a soap opera in the traditional sense.

DALLAS as prime time soap opera

But in spite of the differences we have cited between *Dallas* and the daytime soaps, there are sufficient structural similarities between them to justify calling *Dallas*, as an American television encyclopedia[9] has done, a 'prime time soap opera'. The similarities lie in the first place in the narrative structure dictated by the endless character of the serial. Each episode of a soap opera always consists of various narratives running parallel. In every episode one of these narratives gets the greatest emphasis, but the other narratives keep 'simmering' as it were in the background, to reach a climax in some subsequent episode. As one letter-writer puts it:

> I watch *Dallas* pretty regularly because I find it a free serial. By that I mean that the writer can go in any direction in every

episode. One time Bobby is the central figure, then it can be J.R. or Sue Ellen or another member of that 'immense' family. (Letter 5)

In this sense a soap opera is therefore a continuous coming and going of mini-narratives, in an uneven rhythm. This characteristic of the soap opera can explain why many letter-writers who dislike *Dallas* find it longwinded: 'Every time I watch it again I'm curious as to what has happened. But then *Dallas* ends and even more questions have arisen. I find that really stupid' (Letter 37). But this 'longwindedness', this steady continuance of the story, this 'indefinitely expandable middle',[10] is essential for the soap opera as genre. Those who like *Dallas* will therefore tacitly agree to this convention. They are not expecting the definitive dénouement; quite the contrary, the (promise of) endlessness itself is a source of pleasure. 'I can't get enough of it' (Letter 9), says one letter-writer. According to Sheila Johnston, the primary source of involvement in a soap opera is not situated in the *suspense* of the narrative, as in many other popular television genres, but in 'the creation and slow consolidation of a complex fictional world'.[11] The repetitive character of *Dallas* can therefore be very important for *Dallas* fans:

> It's reassuring to see the same characters again and again. Then you are far more involved in it. At least, I feel that. When I sit down to watch, I always get the idea that I belong to the family in a way too, because I have seen so much of them. I can enter into all the characters, because they are so familiar. I know them through and through. (Letter 20)

But there are other characteristics which are typical for the structure of the soap opera and which also apply for *Dallas*. Not only do different narratives exist side by side, sometimes to touch and intersect one another, and sometimes to run completely parallel. The fact that not just one (or a few) but many main characters are involved is also an important aspect of soap operas. Of none of the main characters in *Dallas* can it be

said that he or she occupies the most important position from a narrative viewpoint. (In the press, it is often assumed that J.R. is the main character in *Dallas*. Although his actions do in fact often play a central part in the propulsion of the narrative, to reduce all the other characters to secondary roles shows a misjudgement of the multi-dimensionality of the *Dallas* narrative. Furthermore, considering J.R. as the main character only results from a very specific reading, which may be characterized by a masculine bias. For many letter-writers the role of J.R. is not that important at all; they are not that interested in him.)

In fact the unity of the soap opera is not created by all the individual characters together, but by the community in which they live. In that community (Dallas) they each occupy an established position. This community also appears to determine which possibilities of action are open to the various characters. Not a single one of the characters escapes the 'rules' of that community; in this sense the soap-community is an enclosed community, like a village, a street, a hospital. Although new characters can enter the community – and that happens regularly: the soap opera steadily encroaches as it were on its surroundings in the course of years – as soon as they have made their entrance they are subjected to the laws and the logic of the community.

In *Dallas* the Ewing family forms the centre of the community. At the beginning of the serial Jock, Miss Ellie, J.R., Sue Ellen, Bobby, Pamela and Lucy have an established structural position within the family, positions ('father', 'mother', 'son', 'daughter-in-law', 'husband', 'wife', 'granddaughter') which are pretty unalterable. Of course later on alterations do occur in the status of the characters within the family: for example, Sue Ellen first divorces J.R. and later marries him again; and Ray Krebbs was initially not a member of the family then later turns out to be an (illegitimate) son of Jock's, so that suddenly he does belong to the family. But the fact remains that within the family itself the positions are established. The family is the

central point of reference. Gillian Swanson, who has analysed the narrative structure of *Dallas*, has shown that 'it is their identity as a family which is the central standard around which relations are made and according to which characters are defined and events are constructed'.[12]

The Ewing family is a community within the wider community of *Dallas*, for other characters who do not belong to the family belong to that larger community. Of these characters Cliff Barnes is certainly the most important: he is the personification of the counter-forces within the larger community which try to disrupt the Ewing family. The community as a whole is therefore by no means a harmonious one – on the contrary, conflict and strife are the order of the day.

This brings us to a third important characteristic of the soap opera. This concerns the themes of the story. A soap opera follows the individual lives of the characters of a community, but it is not interested in their whole lives. In other words, it does not reveal all their doings, all their experiences. The soap opera is selective; it tells us a lot about the different characters, but it also leaves large parts of their life histories untold. A familiar complaint levelled at soap operas is, for example, that they lack social relevance: social problems and conflicts get short shrift or are not dealt with in an adequate, that is, structural way. But anyone expressing such a criticism overlooks the fact that leaving out or cutting out questions which are seen as important in the social reality is functional for the soap opera as genre. In other words, the soap opera generally ignores too concrete social or cultural references because it concerns itself with a completely different aspect of life.

According to Charlotte Brunsdon the ideological problematic of soap opera, that is, the perspective from which events in the narrative take on meaning, is that of 'personal life'. 'More particularly, personal life in its everyday realization through personal relationships. This can be understood to be constituted primarily through the representation of romances, families, and the attendant rituals – births, engagements, marriages,

divorces and deaths.'[13] However, this does not imply that only the so-called private sphere of life is dealt with. Questions from the public sphere have a place too. The way in which they are handled and take on meaning is, however, always from the standpoint of the private sphere: 'the action of soap opera is not restricted to the familial, or quasi-familial institutions, but as it were *colonizes* the public masculine sphere, representing it from the point of view of the personal', writes Brunsdon.[14] Thus in *Dallas* the business imbroglios to do with Ewing Oil are always shown with an eye to their consequences for the mutual relations of the family members. And the motives of Cliff Barnes in his work – first as politician and lawyer, later as owner and manager of a rival concern – are as it were shrivelled down to that one, all-prevailing motive: revenge on the Ewings. In short, in the world of the soap opera all sorts of events and situations from the public sphere occur only in so far as they lead to problems and complications in the private sphere.

The striking thing is, however, that these problems and complications assume such grotesque shapes. Personal life in soap operas is dominated by conflicts and catastrophes, which are blown up to improbable proportions. None of the following sensational problems has not yet occurred in *Dallas*: murder, suspicion of murder, marital crisis, adultery, alcoholism, rare disease, miscarriage, rape, airplane accident, car accident, kidnapping, corruption, psychiatric treatment, and so on. It is precisely this characteristic of the soap opera, this endless piling up of appalling crises, which often gives rise to incomprehension and ridicule from critics. For example, one well-known Dutch doctor and writer has lamented of *Dallas*: 'I find it admirable the things these people can put up with, for . . . after a tenth of that stress I would be lying in the psychiatric hospital.'[15]

As a prime time soap, then, *Dallas* combines the ideological problematic and the narrative structure of the daytime soaps with the visual style and glamour which are more usual for prime time programmes.

DALLAS as melodrama

Until now we have been describing the most important formal characteristics of *Dallas* as soap opera. Now I want to illustrate how important this formal structure is for the construction of the tragic structure of feeling – the complex of meanings which, as indicated in the last chapter, viewers can read from *Dallas*. Note: *can* read. The tragic structure of feeling as an umbrella meaning of *Dallas* emerges from the level of connotation, and not all viewers will ascribe the same connotative meanings to the programme. In other words, an arousal of the tragic structure of feeling is certainly made possible by the way in which the soap opera text itself is formally and ideologically structured, but whether this meaning is also actually ascribed depends on the cultural orientations of the viewers concerned: the expectations they have of the serial, their attitude towards the genre and television in general, the place television viewing occupies in their life, and so on. In the following chapter we shall see that *Dallas* can also give rise to quite different reactions; that the tragic structure of feeling suggested in it can also provoke ridicule and irony. Moreover, the individual viewer will probably not always make the same emotional associations when watching the programme; it is more plausible to assume that he or she can be gripped at one moment by the tragic structure of feeling, and at another moment can assume a more ironic attitude towards the text – identification and distancing constantly alternate with one another. The tragic structure of feeling is not therefore contained as it were in the nature of *Dallas*. It is a complex of meanings which is central for certain groups of *Dallas* fans, for whom a tragic look into daily life is in principle logical and meaningful.

There is a name for cultural genres whose main effect is the stirring up of the emotions: melodrama. Melodrama is a drama form which is not highly regarded in our culture and is mostly dismissed as 'a sentimental, artificially plotted drama that sacrifices characterization to extravagant incident, makes sen-

sational appeals to the emotions of its audience, and ends on a happy or at least a morally assuring note.'[16] Not all soap operas or aspects of a soap opera can be regarded as melodramatic. The English soap opera *Coronation Street*, for example, has a more socio-realistic nature.[17] Most American soap operas, however, certainly are very melodramatic in character. So is *Dallas*, as I shall illustrate below.

It is difficult to persuade people to take melodrama seriously as a cultural form which is a significant expression of a lived reality, because, according to current notions, it plays on the emotions of the public in a false way: emotional straining after effect is seen as its sole aim. It is also sometimes said that melodrama is failed tragedy: the plot is so exaggerated and overdone that the story becomes ridiculous and bereft of any credibility and sensibility. The characters in a melodrama seem to be so taken up with their own violent emotions that there is no scope for reflection, intellectual distancing and relativizing.

What is unsatisfactory with these attitudes is not so much their descriptive value as the fusion of description and judgement. Melodrama is a cultural form that has been popular since the beginning of the nineteenth century, especially among the 'popular' classes, and as such has also always had the status of inferior culture. And indeed, in the eyes of the literary and literate European culture of the established bourgeoisie, capitalizing on plot at the expense of giving greater depth to the characters is a reason for rejecting melodrama as 'cliché-ridden' and 'banal'. But such a judgement is one-sided, not only because it makes absolute the norms of the European literary tradition, but also because it looks only at the surface, the outward form of melodrama. For us this last point is of particular interest. The application of literary norms to melodrama disregards the *function* of the heightened plot and the exaggerated emotions, while it is this very function that can reveal something of the attraction of melodrama. For what comes over from outside as a simplistic and easy-going pen-

chant for the sensational, can in its structure constitute the strength of the genre.

In *Dallas* too we can perceive this penchant for the sensational: the crises in the Ewings' family life succeed one another at an incredibly rapid speed, at least compared with 'real' life. But although such a plot structure will be viewed by outsiders as pure sensationalism, within the fictional world of *Dallas* it is not sensational at all. On the contrary, such a plot structure is quite normal for the soap opera. To put it more strongly, soap opera would not be able to exist without murders, legal battles, extramarital affairs or serious illness. So it seems that the genre acquires its very strength from such exaggerated occurrences. This at least is the view advanced by the American television critic Horace Newcomb. 'The fact that this story, in the technical reality of soap opera, is so unsensational gives us the clue to its real importance', he states.[18] In the world of soap opera the characters go through all kinds of calamities as though it were the most normal thing in life. The significance of such a plot structure is that through it 'human misery' is exposed in a very emphatic manner. 'Most of the problems forming the centre of soap opera plots can be defined best as being in the areas of psychical or emotional pain', says Newcomb,[19] and it seems as though it is not possible to express that pain other than by means of an overdramatizing of the narrative.

Is this the result of a lack of creativity and subtlety? I do not believe that such a personal reproach levelled at the writers of melodramatic soap operas gives us any insight into the cultural specificity of the genre, as it ignores the structural function of exaggerated plots in soap opera. Exaggerated plots can be regarded as the symbolic lumping together of the diffuse and hard-to-describe notion of 'life's torments' which occur at times in every individual life. They function as metaphors for these 'life's torments'. And the fact that in soap operas the same types of plots are reverted to, the same sorts of narrative situations occur, should not be blamed on a lack of originality, for

at this level a soap opera certainly does not try to be original. (Originality on the basis of individual creativity is a bourgeois literary value which cannot be applied to a popular genre such as soap opera.) Rather I would suggest that such plots and situations are dominant and generally current as metaphors for 'life's torments' in our culture, speaking directly to the imagination of the public.

Within the framework of a popular fiction form like soap opera, exaggerated events such as kidnappings, marital dramas and chance meetings with great consequences should not be regarded and assessed for their referential value, but as bearers of the melodramatic effect. Melodrama does not seek to dramatize the unique experience of a single human character (as is mostly the case in 'serious' drama). In a fascinating article on American film melodrama of the 1950s Thomas Elsaesser points out that melodrama operates on a 'non-psychological conception of the *dramatis personae*, who figure less as autonomous individuals than to transmit the action and link the various locales within a total constellation. In this respect, melodramas have a myth-making function, in so far as their significance lies in the structure and articulation of the action, not in any psychologically motivated correspondence with individualized experience.'[20] In other words, the 'psychological credibility' of the characters in melodrama is subordinated to the functioning of those characters in melodramatic situations, so that the emotional effect is pushed to extremes. That effect can be achieved because these imagined situations are socially and culturally surrounded by myths and fantasies which endow them with a strongly emotional appeal. That appeal draws less on the bare facts of those situations than on the metaphorical role they play in the popular imagination.

Alcoholism is one such metaphor which is often used in melodrama to represent the impotence of a character. As Elsaesser remarks:

Although alcoholism is too common an emblem in films [. . .] to deserve a close thematic analysis, drink does become interesting in movies where its dynamic significance is developed and its qualities as a visual metaphor recognized: wherever characters are seen swallowing and gulping their drinks as if they were swallowing their humiliations along with their pride, vitality and the life-force have become palpably destructive and a phoney libido has turned into real anxiety.[21]

The symbolic effectiveness of drunkenness is employed not only in films like John Huston's *Under the Volcano*. Anyone who has followed *Dallas* faithfully will know how Sue Ellen took to drink and regularly appeared drunk on the screen. Her alcoholic inclination was used as a visual externalizing of her feelings of impotence in a life-situation in which she felt fettered: to be married to a man whom she loathed and who was unfaithful to her, but who at the same time had her completely in his power. Sue Ellen's alcoholism therefore has a metaphorical function here: the intention is not so much that viewers start worrying about the concrete drinking problem (from a financial point of view, for example, it will never be any problem for Sue Ellen to get a drink: pots of money), much rather, the depiction of alcoholism should enable viewers to have some idea of Sue Ellen's psychological state, of her suffering, of the emotional conflicts she is battling with.

Such a metaphor derives its strength from a *lack* of originality and uniqueness: precisely because it constantly recurs in all sorts of popular narratives, it takes on for viewers a direct comprehensibility and recognizability. We could even say that viewers must be ready to read all sorts of events and situations in the narrative in a metaphorical way, in order to be able to understand and evaluate their full implications. Insight into the metaphorical value of the plot is the basis for the pleasure of many faithful viewers of soap operas – an insight missed by the

intellectual who only watches a soap opera now and then with a mistrustful attitude and seeks to evaluate the narrative only on the basis of its literary value.

I cannot go into the question here of why exactly these events and situations fulfil a metaphorical function and precisely which common-sense meanings they contain. That would require a separate cultural-historical essay. Why, for example, in addition to murders, misfortunes or diseases are there so many illegitimate children, unknown fathers or mothers (for whom the adult children passionately and restlessly search), or secret pasts (with fatal results for the present)? All these plot elements are incorporated in *Dallas* too! In *Dallas*, however, not only are existing metaphors adapted in the narrative in an ingenious way, but these metaphors are sometimes modernized as well, adapted to the sensibilities of the present.

An example is the metaphor of illness. It is not surprising that characters in melodramas and soap operas are so often ill, as this can propel the narrative forward in a marvellously melo-dramatic way. As Susan Sontag has illustrated, the phenom-enon of illness is liberally surrounded by all sorts of emotional-ly loaded associations and images. Being ill means not only physically being out of order but also being excluded from the world of the healthy, being overcome by an unknown and uncontrollable force, etc. And some illnesses, such as tubercu-losis and cancer, have a uniquely terrifying aura. Being ill therefore has far-reaching cultural consequences extending far beyond the biological fact of illness itself.[22]

In soap operas there are often cases of illness for which the diagnosis remains unknown or the physical results of which remain invisible. For example, in *Dallas* Cliff Barnes and Pamela Ewing at a certain moment are told the unpleasant news by their doctor that they are suffering from an incurable illness inherited from their father Digger, called 'neurofibro-matosis' – a mysterious illness which does exist according to the medical encyclopedia, but the symptoms of which in fact are not such as they are shown in *Dallas*! But only a killjoy

would point that out. It is not the illness itself that is relevant for the narrative, but the dramatic consequences of it for the sick person. In the case of Pamela the illness functions as a metaphor for the drama that a powerful desire can never be fulfilled: beyond her own control, she can never achieve what she wants (to have children), for the illness prevents her. (Later the plot becomes even more involved when it emerges that Pamela is not Digger's daughter at all. . . .)

In stark contrast to the vagueness of Pamela's illness, how-ever, is the hard realism of the illness that strikes Miss Ellie: breast cancer. From a content-analysis it has emerged that the diagnosis of cancer hardly ever occurs in soap operas:[23] the illness is apparently so terrifyingly real that it cannot be fitted into the mythical world of soap opera. The fact that it does occur in *Dallas* and in such an emphatic way (two episodes were totally taken up by Miss Ellie's illness), can be regarded as 'modern' or in any case as daring, the more so as Miss Ellie's breast cancer is dramatically mobilized as a metaphor for a form of 'life's torment' which certainly does not enjoy any general social recognition: the sexual objectifying of the female body by men. Miss Ellie realizes that a mastectomy has far-reaching results for her attractiveness to men. She does not believe what her husband Jock says: that it makes no difference to him (for, she muses, 'he has an eye for a pretty girl') and she tells him that men cannot understand what she is feeling. From other scenes it emerges how Miss Ellie's mastectomy releases a feeling of menace among the other female family members (Sue Ellen, Pamela and Lucy) which has to do with their sexual identity. In particular for Lucy the thought of such a mutilation of the body is so unbearable that at first she refuses to see the sick Miss Ellie and has to be persuaded by Pamela to visit her grandmother in the hospital. For Miss Ellie herself too, the illness leaves deep traces for years. Although initially she seems to recover well from the illness and has been able apparently to forget the torment, years later her mutilated body causes her to shrink from entering a new marriage – with Clayton Farlow – a

fear which she has to be argued out of by Donna Krebbs ('He loves you!'). In this way a theme which has been brought into the open by feminists is recycled in *Dallas*!

As melodramatic soap opera therefore, *Dallas*, by means of 'a sentimental, artificially plotted drama that sacrifices characterization to extravagant incident' makes visible areas of internal psychological disturbance. It is now time to go into the nature of these disturbances in a little more detail.

DALLAS and family tragedy

'What is implausible in [television melodramas] is the continual necessity for emotional display by the characters. In real life we are rarely called upon to feel so intensely, and never in such neatly escalating sequences. But the emotions dramatized by these improbable plots are not in themselves unreal, or at least they need not be', states David Thornburn in an article on television melodrama.[24] It is just as though, under the guise of the sensational, something is brought to the surface which otherwise would remain hidden. The sensational improbability of the narrative must magnify the probability of the conflicts expressed by it.

In most soap operas the conflicts forming the foundation of the dramatic development of the narrative always have to do with difficult family situations: it is the conflictual relations between family members – husband/wife, parents/children, brothers/sisters – which again and again give rise to tensions, crises and emotional outbursts. We have indicated earlier that the ideological problematic of the soap opera is personal life; we can now add that, certainly in *Dallas*, the development of personal life *within the family* is set up as the ideological norm. The family is regarded as the ideal cradle for human happiness. At least, it should be.

This focusing on the area of the personal and on the problem of psychological well-being distinguishes the soap opera in a crucial way from other genres of popular television fiction,

such as the police or adventure series. These genres are pre-occupied with overcoming a danger or an enemy, and there is usually little room there for emotional uncertainties or psycho-logical conflicts relating to individual, personal existence. The (almost always male) hero is in this regard completely sure of himself. Even more, precisely this certainty forms an important ingredient of his invincibility: he never doubts, knows precisely what he has to do and never dwells on his own insignificance. He is invulnerable.

This type of popular fiction appeals to the public in a radically different way from soap opera. Just as in film melo-drama, 'its excitement comes from conflict not between enem-ies but between people tied by blood or love'.[25] That is why there is no invincibility in soap operas: as a value, invincibility does not count in family relationships. Even J.R., who shrinks from nothing and no one to get his way, from time to time has to face the fact that he can lose. And that applies even more for all the other characters. No one is invulnerable, however heroic, powerful or strong he or she might be. Which is tragic.

Family life is not actually romanticized in soap operas; on the contrary, the imaginary ideal of the family as safe haven in a heartless world is constantly shattered. In *Dallas* this is done in an extremely sophisticated way. In contrast to most traditional soap operas *Dallas* concentrates totally on the ups and downs of one family: the Ewings. All the actions in the narrative are ultimately directed at the position of this family within the *Dallas* community. And for the characters it is of particularly great significance whether they are inside or outside the family. Any new marriage, such as that between Miss Ellie and Clayton Farlow, any divorce, such as between Pamela and Bobby, or the birth of a child also inevitably causes some disturbance, because here the profile of the family is at stake. The continuance of and harmony within the Ewing family is paramount in *Dallas*. Whereas the characters of other soap operas can still find inner peace and happiness outside their family life (such as in the intimacy and camaraderie between

two women friends), the belief that one can feel at home in a community not based on family relationships is doomed to failure. Sue Ellen's greatest defeat is that, after she has finally divorced J.R. and tried to build up an independent existence, she nevertheless remarries J.R. and thus – against her better judgement – projects her personal happiness again within the Ewing family. Pamela's happiness too after her divorce from Bobby is only temporary and therefore illusory: Mark, the new man in her life (who is by the way merely a compensation for Bobby, whom she still loves), turns out to be incurably ill and soon dies.

The outside world, i.e. the world outside the family, is presented in *Dallas* as a hotbed of activity threatening to the family. The relationships the Ewing women enter into with people (men) outside the family are, from the standpoint of the family, a danger to the unity of the family. The business contacts of the Ewing men in the Dallas community lead only too often to instability in the family harmony, especially through the continuing discord between J.R. and Bobby. Because the idea of personal happiness can only exist against the background of the unity of the family, this unity must always be safeguarded against attacks from outside and from inside. In short, the conflict between family-strengthening and family-undermining forces is, as Swanson's structural analysis of the *Dallas* narrative shows, the most important motor that propels this soap opera forward.[26]

Family harmony is also offered to the viewers as the norm for the assessment of the situation of the Ewings. The way in which the narrative is told scarcely allows for another point of view. The central role that Southfork plays in each episode, as the place – the haven – where family members sooner or later always return, ensures that the ranch functions as a permanent identification point. The scenes in which the whole family is at home together, at breakfast or in the living room before going to dinner, often form temporary respites in the endless series of complications. One or two of such scenes are included

in each episode.[27] This was particularly true of the earlier episodes. The slow disintegration of the original family makes these family gatherings less and less frequent. In one episode there is even a dramatic scene in which Miss Ellie, the *mater familias*, is sitting quite alone at the head of a luxuriously laid dinner table – her children have not turned up, and her husband Jock is dead. . . . The viewers are thus invited to identify with the idea that the unity of the family is a living condition of prime importance. (Such an identification, however, by no means need coincide with a real attachment of the viewer to the ideology of the family: it is a component of the fantasmatic game the viewer begins when he or she enters into the narrative.)

But this norm of family harmony takes its toll. The individual family members are subjected to its demands. It is the family structure which determines which rules each of the family members must conform to; it is from the standpoint of the family that each family member is, as it were, set in a stereotyped role, such as the loving mother or the worthy son. According to Swanson this subjection of the Ewing characters to a stereotyped role forms a second important structural source of conflict.[28] They do not seem capable of becoming reconciled to the shackles of the family ideal, or they actively try to escape from them, and this leads to new, manifest problems. For example, Sue Ellen's attempts to get away from J.R. cannot be reconciled with holding the family intact: she has to leave the family in order to fulfil her own desires (and staying in the family or returning to it means giving up her desires!). Also, her initial refusal to look after her own newborn child – a refusal of the traditional mother role – does not exactly have a favourable effect on the family peace: it leads to worry for Miss Ellie, to reproach from J.R. and to the (brief) illusion for Pamela that she can take over motherhood from Sue Ellen with baby John Ross. Peace only returns when Sue Ellen accepts her duty as a mother. And above all the poisonous activities of J.R., his countless extramarital relations and his

business intrigues with Ewing Oil, can certainly not be reconciled with the safeguarding of family harmony. But J.R. is pre-eminently someone who is always consciously abandoning his role of son, brother and husband whenever it suits him, and so puts the unity of the family chronically at risk.

Thus the most important characters move constantly between the two poles of a dilemma: either to go their own way in search of personal happiness, or to submit to the social fetters of the family structure. The moments when these two options are in harmony with one another are few. Just as in any soap opera, no marriage in *Dallas* is proof against the ravages of time, not even the almost idyllic marriage of Pamela and Bobby.

What is conveyed in this representation then is the eternal contradiction, the insolubility of inner conflicts, the unbridgeability as it were of the antithesis between pleasure principle and reality principle. As Laura Mulvey puts it, 'beyond or beneath the dramatic mainspring of ideological contradiction that melodrama plays on, lies another contradiction: the impossibility of reconciling desire with reality. The melodrama recognizes this gap by raising problems, known and recognizable, and offering a personal escape similar to that of a daydream: a chance to work through inescapable frustrations by positing an alternative ideal never seen as more than a momentary illusion.'[29] It is this disturbing 'truth' over personal life that viewers are confronted with. What could provide better soil for the tragic structure of feeling?

Soap opera, melodrama and the tragic structure of feeling

But this tragic structure of feeling within *Dallas* would impose itself in a less forceful way on devoted viewers if the conflicts the characters have to go through were not presented in a specifically melodramatic way. 'Characters caught in the world of melodrama are not allowed transcendent awareness or

knowledge', says Mulvey.[30] In other words, although the problems of characters develop from a conflict set structurally in the narrative, the characters themselves are not aware of that structure. They fight for a happier life in the direct immediacy of existence and are not capable of sizing up their objective position. 'The melodramatic characters act out contradiction, achieving actual confrontation to varying degrees and gradually facing impossible resolutions and probable defeats', according to Mulvey.[31] And precisely this *gradual* facing of one's own impotence makes it the more tragic: illusions and ideals are steadily undermined.

The dialogues in *Dallas* – dialogue is *the* narrative instrument of soap opera – never contain any critical and conscious (self) reflection. The characters never ponder on their position in the world, they never philosophize from a detached point of view on themselves and their relations to others. The conversations the characters have with one another, on the other hand, always express the living through or digesting of a conflict, in the here and now. There is never question of an intellectual exposition and exchange of ideas; each spoken word reflects the subjective inner world of a character – his or her desires, fears, moral preferences, etc. But at the same time the dialogues between the characters are not often examples of frank and honest communication. Often they don't say everything, or don't say what they mean, or mean more than they say. In this sense the dialogues in *Dallas* are often elliptical. The status of the spoken word is therefore relativized, as though there are always things which cannot or may not be said. The essence of a situation is not expressed, but lies as it were concealed behind the facial expression of the character who at the end of a scene – as so often in *Dallas* – is shown in close-up and held for a few seconds, before the first shot of the following scene.[32] This melodramatic method produces an enlargement of the tragic structure of feeling: the close-ups emphasize the fact that the character ultimately does not have control of her or his own life, not so much because of the machinations of some super-

human divinity, but because of contradictions inherent in human society itself.

The end of the narrative is always a problem for melodrama. It is often pointed out that a melodrama is only effective when it has an 'open' end: at first sight there may be the possibility of a happy ending, but so many future conflicts are already brewing that the happy end itself is not credible. In fact the end of a melodrama is not actually so important; the main thing is what happens before. As Mulvey notes, 'the strength of the melodramatic form lies in the amount of dust the story raises along the road, a cloud of over-determined irreconcilables which put up a resistance to being neatly settled in the last five minutes.'[33]

However, for the soap opera this problem of the last five minutes is much less acute. It is inherent in the form of soap opera that in principle it goes on endlessly.[34] The soap opera can, therefore, because it is always going along the road, raise an infinite amount of dust without worrying about clearing it up. This lack of an end, this constant deferment of the ultimate 'solution', adds a new dimension to the tragic structure of feeling. The endless repetition of the slogan at the end of each episode of *Soap!*, that tragicomic parody of soap opera, is a striking illustration of this: 'Confused? You won't be after the next episode of . . . *Soap!*' But one is nevertheless confused yet again.

Tania Modleski has pointed out in this connection that in soap opera the so-called 'hermeneutic code' prevails.[35] This code consists of all those elements in a narrative which pose a problem or effect a delay in the solution of a problem: obstacles, errors, devious behaviour, deceptions, half-truths, and so on. In a classic, linear narrative the hermeneutic code is ultimately conquered by the final solution, the moment of complete truth. But in a soap opera delay is the rule, the normal course of affairs. And so the viewer is manoeuvred into a position of permanent expectation which, in the words of Roland Barthes, refers to 'disorder: disorder is [. . .] what is forever added on without solving anything, without

finishing anything'.[36] This position of eternal expectation strengthens a feeling of aimlessness and directionlessness; it 'creates a feeling that things are constantly happening (becoming more complicated) in the narrative, but that, at the same time, nothing ever really happens'.[37] The idea of progress, which is connected with the idea of a fundamental difference between past and present, is absent. The characters in *Dallas* live in the prison of an eternally conflictual present. This places the viewer in a curious position. She knows that the soap opera will never end and that the agony will never let up. Whereas in other narratives the assurance and confirmation of a happy end is a source of pleasure, in soap opera it is precisely the tragic knowledge of the *holding off* of an end satisfactory to all the characters which is the basis for narrative pleasure.

Furthermore, the viewer's position towards the individual characters is also ambiguous. As we have said, in a soap opera various narratives always intersect one another. Whereas at one moment we can sympathize with Sue Ellen's marital woes and get a glimpse of her having a good cry at her psychiatrist's, the next moment we are witness to Pamela's dilemma about whether to tell Bobby of her illness. All the characters live their own lives without necessarily having anything to do with or being in touch with the problems, actions and plans of the others. They are wrapped up in their own preoccupations and view any situation purely and simply from their own subjective standpoint. Viewers, however, know 'everything' about each of them and thus find themselves in a powerful, omniscient position. But strangely enough this power is based on a realization of powerlessness, because they know that the relational structure in which the life of all the characters is embedded is immovable and leads to all kinds of tensions, without the characters themselves being aware of them.

An example: Miss Ellie hesitates to tell Jock that she has breast cancer, because she is afraid that then he will turn away from her. (She experiences exactly the same fear, as we have

noted, much later when Clayton has asked her to marry him.)
At the same time Jock does not know how he can tell Miss Ellie
that he was married before, because he is frightened of her
reaction. In both there is doubt and uncertainty, and therefore
mistrust, without their knowing it of one another, which leads
repeatedly to all kinds of irritations and misunderstandings.
Viewers, however, are informed of both secrets and must, in
order to be able to continue to follow the narrative, put
themselves in the position of both. This appeal to 'multiple
identification'[38] means that viewers cannot simply identify
with one character in order to understand and judge all the
developments from that character's point of view, as is mostly
the case in an adventure story.

This floating viewer-position is strengthened even more by
the fact that the characters are sometimes particularly incon-
sistent in their behaviour and within a short period can completely change their attitude. An American television critic has
noted that a total instability of behavioural codes prevails in
Dallas,[39] so that neither the characters themselves nor the
viewers know where they stand. For example, instead of
handing her over to the police, J.R. puts Sue Ellen's sister
Kristin on the plane out of Dallas with a thick wad of bank-
notes, after he has learned that she was the one who had tried to
shoot him. And so Sue Ellen's feelings for J.R. after the attempt
on his life veer right round: although she hated him before, she
suddenly realizes that she does in fact love him . . . only to find
out some weeks later that J.R. does not deserve her love. There
is a lack of 'any secure sense of what constitutes the status quo',
says Sheila Johnston.[40] And Modleski comes to the conclusion
that soap operas implicitly announce a frightful truth about
life: 'soaps continually insist on the insignificance of the individual life'.[41] The world of the soap opera is therefore totally
ambiguous. It is a world in which the area of the personal is
all-prevailing, but in which at the same time all personal lives
are perverted. For not a single individual in a soap opera is free
to construct his or her own life history. On the contrary, it is the

structures and contradictions in which they are caught that determine developments.

In *Dallas*, however, one figure escapes these shackles: J.R. This villain constantly ignores the laws and rules of society and bends developments to his own will. Through his dishonest dealings and intrigues he is the most important cause of misery in *Dallas*. Modleski points out that the villain has an essential function in the soap opera narrative: he or she is the one who does not submit but resists. But paradoxically enough, J.R.'s actions tend to strengthen the tragic structure of feeling. He demonstrates that power can only be coupled with badness and immorality, while those who want to live a 'good' life are constantly bereft of power and doomed to suffer. But that does not mean that the villain always wins. On the contrary, because in the soap opera ambivalence and temporality are the rule, J.R. has to keep on trying to get his way. According to some it is precisely this unremitting and indefatigable attempt to break out which explains the attraction of the villain. As Horace Newcomb says, 'what we see in J.R. is a refusal to give up. He persists.'[42]

But the villain fulfils a second function in the world of soap opera. Not only is he not an outsider, set apart from an otherwise harmonious community, but he also belongs to the community. Moreover, he is the one who brings the community to life and sees to it that things happen. The evil is therefore woven into the order of the community itself, so that the community by definition is conflictual because it bears the core of the conflict within itself: harmony only exists as unattainable Utopia. Thus, the Ewing family and *Dallas* would certainly cease to exist if J.R. were put out of action: family life, in the logic of *Dallas*, can only exist by the grace of the one who regularly jeopardizes the very survival of the family!

Finally, let us return to the meaning of the glamorous *mise-en-scène* which characterizes *Dallas*. The Ewings are very rich people and can afford everything material: luxury homes, splendid clothes, exclusive dinners, expensive presents, etc.

This wealth does not, however, seem to have many fundamental consequences for the general plot structure of *Dallas* as soap opera: here money has more of an *instrumental* function for the composition of conflict and agony. Money as such is never the source of agony in *Dallas*: rather the ease with which millions of dollars are thrown about gives an extra sensational and bombastic dimension to the interpersonal conflicts with which *Dallas* is preoccupied. It is therefore questionable whether the glamorous *mise-en-scène* does primarily fulfil a *narrative* function, as expressed in the phrase 'money can't buy happiness', which according to some critics is the ideological message of programmes like *Dallas*. Such an explanation ignores the fact that the visual excess of *Dallas* can also produce meanings which are relatively independent of the narrative. The sun-drenched prairie around Southfork, the luxurious swimming pool, the tall, spacious office buildings, the chic restaurants and the elegant women and handsome men – they seem rather to belong to the optimistic image world of advertising, an optimism that does not fit in with the pessimistic world of soap opera, so that the *mise-en-scène* in itself produces a chronic contradiction. It intensifies in this way the claustrophobic sphere of the closed community in which the characters live, in which hysteria can break out any moment, but is also curbed time and again. For in *Dallas* life always goes on normally, whatever happens.

The melodramatic imagination

It is thus the combination of melodramatic elements and the narrative structure of soap opera that evokes a tragic structure of feeling. This tragic structure of feeling does not, however, consist of being bowed down by the Great Tragedy of Man, as is expressed, for example, in classical Greek tragedy, but of a half-conscious realization of the tragic side of ordinary everyday life. Not high-flown *Weltschmerz*, but a completely pedestrian form of suffering. In Newcomb's words, it is a matter here

of the simple idea that survival is 'complicated by ambiguity and blurred with pain even in its most sought-after accomplishments'.[43]

But I have said earlier that the tragic structure of feeling, which is inscribed in the meaning-structure of *Dallas*, will not automatically and obviously agree with the meanings viewers will apply to *Dallas*. That will only happen if they are sensitive to it. In other words, the tragic structure of feeling suggested by *Dallas* will only make sense if one can and will project oneself into, i.e. recognize, a *melodramatic imagination*. Viewers must therefore have a certain cultural competence or orientation to understand and evaluate *Dallas* in a melodramatic way. As Charlotte Brunsdon has so aptly put it: 'Just as a Godard film requires the possession of certain forms of cultural capital on the part of the audience to "make sense" [. . .] so too does [. . .] soap opera.'[44] In the case of *Dallas*, the melodramatic imagination seems central to that cultural orientation.

The melodramatic imagination is characterized by Peter Brooks as a type of imagination in which a (semi-desperate) attempt is made 'to bring into the drama of man's quotidian existence the higher drama of moral forces'.[45] The melodramatic imagination should be regarded as a psychological strategy to overcome the material meaninglessness of everyday existence, in which routine and habit prevail in human relationships as much as elsewhere. In other words it is a matter of making 'the world we inhabit one charged with meaning, one in which interpersonal relations are not merely contacts of the flesh, but encounters that must be carefully nurtured, judged, handled as if they mattered'.[46] The melodramatic imagination is therefore the expression of a refusal, or inability, to accept insignificant everyday life as banal and meaningless, and is born of a vague, inarticulate dissatisfaction with existence here and now. This then is the tragic structure of feeling: it is not about the great suffering which plays such a prominent role in the history of humankind and which is generally known as human tragedy – the sufferings of war, concentration camps, famine, etc. – but is

rather about what is usually not acknowledged as tragic at all and for that very reason is so difficult to communicate. There are no words for the ordinary pain of living of ordinary people in the modern welfare state, for the vague sense of loss, except in half-ironic, half-resigned phrases such as: 'You win some, you lose some.' By making that ordinariness something special and meaningful in the imagination, that sense of loss can – at least for a time – be removed. It is in this world of the imagination that watching melodramatic soap operas like *Dallas* can be pleasurable: *Dallas* offers a starting point for the melodramatic imagination, nourishes it, makes it concrete.

We may wonder about the social and historical roots of the melodramatic imagination. No single form of imagination, as a way in which the everyday, practical consciousness makes sense of and accounts for the living experiences it is confronted with, just appears out of the blue. To which cultural-historical circumstances does the melodramatic imagination form a fantasmatic answer? Here we can only go into this question briefly.

Peter Brooks connects the melodramatic imagination to the fragmented character of modern society, in which no single system of values is capable any longer of functioning as the binding element for the great variety of events and impressions. The melodramatic is, he says, 'a form of the tragic [. . .] for a world in which there is no longer a tenable idea of the sacred'.[47] In a life in which every immanent meaning is constantly questioned and in which traditions no longer have a firm hold, a need exists for reassurance that life can in fact have meaning and therefore life is worth the trouble, in spite of all appearances to the contrary. According to Brooks the explanation can also be found here for the tendency to sentimental exaggeration which is so characteristic of melodrama. It is as though the melodramatic imagination must impress itself so emphatically because what it wants to express is so uncertain, so difficult to grasp, and therefore too so difficult to justify. When the meaning of life threatens to elude us, the 'larger than life'

emotions of the melodramatic imagination offer an anchor.

Other authors have ascribed a specific function to the serial as fiction form on the basis of such considerations. The French semiologist Violette Morin points out, for example, that the popularity of the television serial could derive from the fact that the life depicted in it seems to proceed *more slowly* than real life. According to her this effect is achieved by cramming each scene with meaning, even when it is not directly of interest for the continuance of the narrative: 'People eat, talk, walk about in a TV serial in tune with the rhythm of a constant semantic "braking"; as if they were afraid to be happy at living, as if they were more slow, more cautious than in real life and at all events more healthy in their attitude to the pace of life than everyday existence.'[48] According to Morin, this slow-motion idea of life responds to a desire to slow down, to put the brakes on the hasty nature of modern life. We could conclude from this that the serial form is an extremely suitable vehicle for the melodramatic imagination, because in itself it ascribes more meaning to everyday things than is usual in real life.

But such explanations, in which the melodramatic imagination is linked to the characteristics of modern society, are not specific enough. They take into consideration solely some general, formal characteristics of modern daily life, such as the fragmenting of experience, the transitory nature of time and the break with tradition, and therefore abstract from the socio-cultural differences between the living conditions of different groups of people. It is, however, precisely the concrete, practical living situations of people which demand psychological assimilation and which form the raw material for imagination and fantasy. Not everyone living in an urban, industrialized society will be equally sensitive to the melodramatic imagination. The routes followed by people's imaginative strategies are formed during the course of their personal and subcultural histories and slowly rub through, as it were, into their practical consciousness.

If, as is said of soap opera, it is a 'woman's genre' because it is

mainly women who like watching it, then that would suggest that it is mainly women who are susceptible to the melodramatic imagination, a type of imagination which appears to express mainly a rather passive, fatalistic and individualistic reaction to a vague feeling of powerlessness and unease. This 'susceptibility', however, has not so much to do with the material social situation of women (housewives) – this would imply a sociological reductionism – as with the way they have become accustomed to facing situations psychologically and emotionally. The ideologically dominant association of the 'women's area' with a concern for the private sphere and with the caring function is an important determining factor in this, for example.[49]

Moreover, we must not overrate the role of the melodramatic imagination in everyday consciousness. Commonsense thinking is not one-dimensional. On the contrary, it is of a very heterogeneous nature.[50] And there are many other ways in which experiences can be lived and assimilated: a melodramatic manner of perceiving the world can alternate with a humorous, romantic, rebellious or other imaginative strategy. The sense of the melodramatic, the tragic structure of feeling, surfaces only occasionally, often cutting in on a sober acceptance of daily existence. Mostly, too, people only experience melodramatic *moments*. Such a moment can, for example, occur when someone is watching *Dallas*. Then *Dallas* is pleasurable because it makes the melodramatic imagination present and palpable.

Of course this does not mean that there are no other ways of experiencing pleasure from *Dallas*. Viewers can also read it in a completely different way; they can attend to other aspects of the text and respond to them: the ingenious way in which the plots are intertwined, the mythical Western-elements, the technical discussions on oil, J.R.'s venomous humour, and so on. *Dallas* offers points of contact for many types of imagination.

In conclusion, then, we can say that the pleasure of *Dallas* consists in the recognition of ideas that fit in with the viewers'

imaginative world. They can 'lose' themselves in *Dallas* because the programme symbolizes a structure of feeling which
connects up with one of the ways in which they encounter life.
And in so far as the imagination is an essential component of
our psychological world, the pleasure of *Dallas* – as a histori-
cally specific symbolizing of that imagination – is not a *compensation* for the presumed drabness of daily life, nor a *flight*
from it, but a *dimension* of it. For only through the imagination, which is always subjective, is the 'objective reality' assimilated: a life without imagination does not exist.

Pleasure and theory

But the above is a theoretical construction. And theoretical
constructions by definition never coincide with immediate
experience: they can only shed light on that experience in a
onesided way. The capricious and contradictory nature of
experience is nullified by this.

As immediate experience, pleasure in *Dallas* is a more or less
'spontaneous' phenomenon: a person enjoys watching it, or
otherwise, in some way or other. Experiencing pleasure is not a
conscious, directed activity (although one can strive for it), but
something that 'happens', something which comes over the
viewer according to his or her feelings. The experience is
diffuse, bound to time and context, heterogeneous: so much is
going on in the viewer's head.

In analysing the pleasure of *Dallas* we have started with the
premise that the programme is a text with a specific structure.
Pleasure is then connected with the way in which viewers read
the text from a specific subject-position. But generally viewers
do not approach *Dallas* as text. For them watching it is first and
foremost a *practice*. Certainly, in this practice the *Dallas* text
occupies a central place, but the practice itself comprises more
than that. Therefore it is somewhat misleading – or at any rate
inadequate – to deduce the pleasure of *Dallas* totally from its
characteristics as text. Watching *Dallas*, just like watching

television in general, is a cultural practice which has much of the nature of a habit: it is directly available, casual and free. And a habit is always difficult to explain in intellectual terms, because it feels so natural and self-evident.

A theoretical construction has the character and the effect here, then, of a rationalization. And is it not a fact that we can talk of the experience of pleasure only by means of rationalizations? Pleasure eludes our rational consciousness. This applies not only for theoreticians who want to explain this pleasure, but also for the 'witnesses' or 'reporters' of pleasure, on which the theoreticians base their explanations. It seems as though the letter-writers – my 'reporters' – realize that. Some of them do their very best to express in words why they like watching *Dallas*; they recite reason after reason, in order ultimately, quite unexpectedly, to end their account with expressions of uncertainty such as:

> I don't know, but I like watching it. (Letter 4)

> I don't know exactly what it is but *Dallas* really draws me, there is, I find, a sort of charm radiating from the actors and from the thing itself. I just really love watching it. (Letter 13)

> In a word, there's a bit of everything in that film. Perhaps it's crazy to think so but that's what I see in it. (Letter 16)

> Finally I must just say that, funnily enough, last year I just couldn't stand *Dallas*. Unfortunately I can't say why. (Letter 17)

> I think *Dallas* is a serial for sensitive people, but of course I could be completely wrong. (Letter 18)

> I hope my story has been of some use to you, but I find it really difficult to state exactly why I like *Dallas*. (Letter 20)

> Looking into it more closely, I can imagine you haven't got much from my reaction because it's a bit shallow as an analysis, but I'll send it anyway. (Letter 22)

> Here are some opinions from my brother and from a girl living in our house. They like watching it, amusing and

good-looking people are in it and it is well produced. According to them. My father just says it's shit. I hope this has been some use to you. Unfortunately there's not much you can say about it. (Letter 37)

It is as though the pleasure of *Dallas* eludes the rational consciousness of these letter-writers. They do their utmost to give explanations for that pleasure, but somehow they know that the explanations they can put into words are not the whole story, or even perhaps the 'right' story.

Pleasure is therefore obviously something uncertain and precarious. 'Everyone can testify that the pleasure of the text is not certain: nothing says that this same text will please us a second time; it is a friable pleasure, split by mood, habit, circumstance, a precarious pleasure', writes Roland Barthes.[51] A theoretical (re)construction can therefore never fully comprehend pleasure, because theory makes it something substantial and presumes it to be permanent and static. Nor do we have to agree with Barthes when he asserts that 'we are scientific because we lack subtlety'[52] (scientific subtlety may in fact exist, but this is of a different order from the subtlety of pleasure) to be able to conclude that any theoretical look at pleasure by definition falls short. A conclusion which, however paradoxical it might sound, gives rise to optimism.

3

DALLAS
and the ideology of mass culture

DALLAS and boredom

In the preceding chapters we have seen that the letter-writers who like *Dallas* have difficulty in stating why they do. Many of them finally have to admit that they don't know. This uncertainty is not surprising, as the experience of pleasure is not rationally motivated. On the contrary, pleasure always arises as a spontaneous feeling of well-being. You feel good when you are watching *Dallas* and that makes it enjoyable: no explanation appears to be necessary. People rarely wonder why something is pleasurable to them. Pleasure is one of the things in life regarded as self-evident and which as a rule people don't think about.

Hence, in order to say something about the determinants and structurings of pleasure in *Dallas* one needs to make a theoretical diversion. The letters do not, it is true, contain any straightforward explanations, but they do describe how the letter-writers watch the programme, what aspects of *Dallas*

they find most important and most valuable, and what meanings they ascribe to them. I have read the letters 'symptomatically', as it were, to try to find out what it means when the letter-writers say they like *Dallas* and I have reached the conclusion that, at least for *these* fans, it is a sense of emotional realism that appeals to them. More specifically, this realism has to do with the recognition of a tragic structure of feeling, which is felt as 'real' and which makes sense for these viewers. Then by means of an analysis of *Dallas* as a melodramatic soap opera I have set out how this tragic structure of feeling is organized (concretized, made material) in the narrative structure of the serial: the ideological problematic of personal life; the emphasis on the unavoidably contradictory and conflictual character of interpersonal relations, etc., which is reinforced by the fact that the narrative goes on indefinitely.

But what about the letter-writers who don't like *Dallas*? What is their attitude towards this construction of the tragic structure of feeling? The following letter extracts illustrate that the lack of narrative progress, which for *Dallas* fans contributes so much to their pleasure, is for these letter-writers a source of annoyance:

> The stupid thing about the serial, I find, is that in every episode it comes down to the same thing. . . . This serial never changes, every episode is the same. (Letter 32)

> There is absolutely no variation in it. (Letter 33)

> It always revolves around the same thing. One of them has been up to dirty tricks again and someone else is waiting for something and then at the last moment something else happens. Really funny. (Letter 34)

> For *Dallas* you only have to read that little bit in the programme guide and then you can dream up the rest. Quarrels – tears – and it all turns out all right in the end, and on to the next episode. (Letter 36)

Every time I watch it again I'm curious to know what's happening. But then *Dallas* is over and even more questions have arisen. I find that so stupid. . . . And it's much too longwinded. (Letter 37)

The imagination of the tragic structure of feeling as presented in *Dallas* would appear to be completely meaningless for these particular letter-writers. Probably they expect something quite different from a good television serial: their definition of what is enjoyable does not seem to coincide with what *Dallas* has to offer them. One letter-writer states this quite explicitly: 'Well, personally I'd rather watch Roald Dahl, because when you think "now such and such is going to happen" you know that you're going to be wrong because you can never predict it' (Letter 36). The 'longwinded' narrative structure of *Dallas*, its 'indefinitely expandable middle' and the consequent lack of progress, is therefore not a source of enjoyment for these letter-writers, but of boredom.

So even among the letter-writers who don't like the programme we encounter references to aspects of its textual structure. But for them these references are markers to an experience of irritation, not of pleasure. They *don't* feel good when they are watching *Dallas*. Boredom and irritation are also feelings which arise quite spontaneously; for these experiences too we don't generally look for causal explanations. Only if asked will one wonder what the reasons might be for these negative feelings. Just as with the letter-writers who like *Dallas*, then, it would not be surprising if its critics find it difficult to give a consistent and rational explanation for their feelings of irritation.

But, and this is striking, those who hate *Dallas* betray no trace of the uncertainty we encounter among lovers of the programme. Quite the contrary, they seem to take their dislike so much as a matter of course that they confidently believe in the rationality of their dislike. This confidence can be very clearly read from the tone of the following letter extracts:

I find very little style in it and the story very bad, it is *simply* a commercial success. (Letter 34, my italics)

It really makes me more and more angry. The aim is *simply* to rake in money, loads of money. (Letter 35, idem)

There's *just* nothing in this serial, it has *just* no content and always turns out well. (Letter 33, idem)

And those women always look good and that is disgusting *of course*. (Letter 38, idem)

Words like 'simply', 'just' and 'of course' in these statements indicate that these letter-writers not only have no difficulty in giving their opinion, but also that they are convinced that they are right. They feel they are on firm ground. Why then do these particular letter-writers appear so self-confident in their opinions?

Hating DALLAS

The letters of those who dislike *Dallas* are characterized not only by a positive and self-assured tone, but also by a large measure of fury, annoyance and indignation. These people seem not just to dislike *Dallas*: they get terribly worked up by it. Many of them also make considerable use of strong language in judging the programme, as though to emphasize yet again the logic of their hatred: 'worthless rubbish', 'a stupid serial', 'the biggest nonsense', 'eyewash', 'dreadful', 'annoying', 'ghastly', 'daft', 'ridiculous', 'disgusting', etc.

But these letter-writers don't just resort to emotional expressions of anger and frustration. They often go to some length to supply a rational explanation for their dislike. For example, some justify their aversion by denouncing the *Dallas* story as 'stereotypical', especially where the representation of women is concerned.

The ideal life – big house, swimming pool, big cars, lots of money, etc., etc., occupy the centre of interest. (Letter 35)

I also find it so disgusting that there are those perfect, beautiful women in it who are really servile too. Take Sue Ellen. She acts as though she's very brave and can put up a fight, but she daren't take the step of 'divorce'. What I mean is that in spite of her good intentions she lets people walk over her, because (as J.R. wants) for the outside world they have to form a perfect family.

Then that wife of Bobby's. Recently I saw an episode in which Bobby was busy in some (self-glorifying) political campaign or other. A group of men (omniscient of course) were on a visit to the Ewing office: Bobby asked whether Pamela wouldn't like to put some coffee on. It almost looked as though she was going to refuse, but like a good little girl she did as she was told. Of course the fact that she hesitated was meant to make you think about it too, but just imagine the shocked faces of the men if she had refused. Yuk, yuk. But who knows? This Pamela may start an extramarital affair (I must admit she's very beautiful). That will be something else to smack your lips over.

These are just two examples of the inferior role of the women in *Dallas*. Then I still haven't said anything about that tubby little blonde and that mother who condemns lots of things in her heart but never does anything about it. Love is blind? Or aren't you allowed to criticize your husband? (Letter 31)

Now about *Dallas*. When the serial began I really disliked it because in my eyes the characters in it are totally unreal, certainly the women – in the whole of *Dallas* there's not one ugly woman, and these women always look good and that is disgusting, of course. Then the men. They are one and all successful businessmen and stinking rich. Women crawl to them and act like that the whole time. (Letter 38)

My personal opinion of *Dallas* is that I find it a horribly cheap serial. I do admire it, the way they can work it all out every time, how they can set up the most crazy dramas in a

series like that. Every instalment the family members all go bawling on non-stop (only the women, of course, men aren't allowed to cry, apparently). (Letter 36)

Such condemnations levelled at the content of *Dallas* can also be combined with disapproval of the presumed insincere intentions of the producers. *Dallas* is a kind of fraud, these letter-writers find, because it is a commercial product:

You wrote [. . .] whether we wanted to write to you what we thought of *Dallas*. Well, I want to write to you that I find *Dallas* absolute nonsense. The whole serial is only concerned with money. It's just like *Peyton Place*. That was another load of old rubbish. (Letter 33)

I find very little style in it and the story very bad, it is simply a commercial success, like lots of serials, not just *Dallas*. (Letter 34)

It really makes me more and more angry. The aim is simply to rake in money, loads of money. And people try to do that by means of all these things – sex, beautiful people, wealth. And you always have people who fall for it. To get high viewing figures. (Letter 35)

But the most comprehensive and total condemnation of *Dallas* is expressed in this letter extract:

My opinion of *Dallas*? Well, I'd be glad to give it to you: WORTHLESS RUBBISH. I find it a typical American programme, simple and commercial, role-affirming, deceitful. The thing so many American programmes revolve around is money and sensation. Money never seems to be a problem. Everyone is living in luxury, has fantastic cars and loads of drink. The stories themselves are mostly not very important. You never have to think for a moment: they think for you. (Letter 31)

All these condemnations have the same function. Categories like 'stereotypical' and 'commercial' are not only used in the

descriptive sense, but invested with a moral status and emotional charge: they serve as explanations for the writers' dislike of *Dallas*. These explanations sound extremely convincing. But, we might ask, are they really as adequate and balanced as they appear at first sight?

It is not my aim here to cast doubt on the sincerity of the feminist and anticapitalist concerns of these letter-writers. But what can be questioned is whether it is really so logical to connect the experience of displeasure, which must in the first instance be an emotional reaction to watching *Dallas*, so directly with a rationalistic evaluation of it as a cultural product. Even if someone does like watching it, he or she can be aware of the 'commercial' or 'stereotypical' character of the programme. Thus, enjoying *Dallas* does not preclude a political or moral condemnation of its production context or its ideological content. The fact that those who hate the serial do make such a connection indicates that categories like 'commercial' and 'stereotypical' exercise a certain attraction, because using them gives the letter-writers a feeling of security. These categories enable them to legitimize their dislike, make it credible and totally comprehensible. They seem to give these letter-writers the conviction that they are right and allow them an uninhibited display of anger.

And so these categories form a central component of an ideological discourse in which the social significance of forms of popular culture is determined in a particular way. This is the ideology of mass culture. In order to understand the self-confidence of those who hate *Dallas* we need now to investigate this ideology more closely.

The ideology of mass culture

Dallas is not only widely watched, but also widely discussed: a lot is said and written about the programme. These public discourses about *Dallas* provide a framework within which answers can be given to questions such as: what must I think

about such a television serial? What arguments can I use to make my opinion plausible? How must I react to people who hold a different opinion? Not all existing discourses, however, are equally capable of formulating satisfactory answers to such questions. Some discourses are more prestigious than others, they sound more logical or convincing, and are more successful in determining the social image of TV programmes like *Dallas*.

In many European countries nowadays there is an official aversion to American television series: they are regarded as a threat to one's own, national culture and as an undermining of high-principled cultural values in general.[1] Against this ideological background, professional intellectuals (television critics, social scientists, politicians) put a lot of energy into creating a consistent and elaborated 'theory' on American television series – a theory which provides a 'scientific' cloak for the aversion. A representative and revealing formulation of this theory comes from the sociology of mass communications:

The most important characteristic of a TV series is that the film content is dependent on its economic marketability. Aiming at a very broad market means that the content must be reduced to universally consumable motifs. This applies in particular to American series which in the United States serve as 'commercial' packaging. [. . .] The commercial character of the TV series hinders the introduction of concrete social and political attitudes, because they might provoke controversies in various groups. [. . .] The film is given a 'universal appeal' character; it deals with familiar, broadly institutionalized ingredients. The necessary ingredients of a successful series include romantic love [. . .] simple patterns of good and evil and the building-up of suspense, climax and relief. [. . .] This reduction to the normal human aspects of existence means that the content is recognizable for a wider audience, but it offers a stereotypical and schematized image of reality. [. . .] In this regard TV series succeed in fulfilling primarily economic functions, and thus in reproducing a

bourgeois ideology, without losing their attraction for different sectors of the audience.[2]

As a description of the working method of the commercial, American television industry this account certainly offers some adequate insights, although one might wonder whether such a direct connection exists between the economic conditions under which TV series are produced and their aesthetic and narrative structures. Such crude economic determinism is often criticized in media studies circles. Nevertheless, the core of this theory tends to be accepted as correct. What interests us here, however, is not the correctness or adequacy of the theory itself, but the way in which some of its elements carry over into the way in which American TV series are evaluated. A theory fulfils an ideological function if it fulfils an *emotional* function in people's heads, to which the assertions contained in the theory are subordinated. As Terry Eagleton puts it, 'what *is* important to recognize is that the cognitive structure of an ideological discourse is subordinated to its emotive structure – that such cognitions or miscognitions as it contains are on the whole articulated according to the demands [. . .] of the emotive "intentionality" it embodies.'[3]

Emotionally, then, the above-described theory on American TV series leads to their total rejection and condemnation. They become 'bad objects'. These then are the contours of what I would like to call the 'ideology of mass culture'. In this ideology some cultural forms – mostly very popular cultural products and practices cast in an American mould – are *tout court* labelled 'bad mass culture'. 'Mass culture' is a denigrating term, which arouses definitely negative associations.[4] In opposition to 'bad mass culture' implicitly or explicitly something like 'good culture' is set up. One letter-writer expresses this dichotomization of 'bad' and 'good' culture very clearly:

> In *Dallas* no attention at all is paid to any realistic problems in this world, the problems of ordinary people, whereas even in America social equality is a long way off. [. . .] I mean, I'd

rather read a good book or watch a programme like *Koot en Bie* [a high-brow Dutch satirical programme]. (Letter 31)

So dominant is this ideology of mass culture where the judging of American TV series is concerned that the chairman of the Dutch Broadcasting Foundation, Eric Jurgens, can say without any hesitation: 'The Dutch broadcasting organizations *of course* don't exist primarily to broadcast *Dallas*. [. . .] *No one* can maintain that these American series are of a high standard as regards content. They are at most cleverly made.'[5] The ideology of mass culture takes on here the status of Absolute Truth. Judgement is passed, no doubts allowed.

The emotional attraction of the ideology of mass culture, however, is not confined to the select circle of professional intellectuals. As we have seen, the letter-writers who dislike *Dallas* also all too easily reach for its categories. Apparently the ideology of mass culture has such a monopoly on the judging of a phenomenon like *Dallas* that it supplies ready-made conceptions, as it were, which sound self-evident and can be used without any strain or hesitation. The dominance of the ideology of mass culture apparently even extends to the commonsense of everyday thinking: for ordinary people too it appears to offer a credible framework of interpretation for judging cultural forms like *Dallas*.

It therefore looks as though the letter-writers who hate *Dallas* have adopted the ideology of mass culture as a guideline for its rejection. Because of this the border between individual experience and social ideology tends to become blurred: the way in which these letter-writers watch *Dallas* is described in terms of the ideologically dominant status of *Dallas* as 'mass culture'. The ideology of mass culture therefore not only offers a (negative) label for the programme itself, but also serves as a mould for the way in which a large number of haters of *Dallas* account for their displeasure. To put it briefly, their reasoning boils down to this: '*Dallas* is obviously bad because it's mass

culture, and that's why I dislike it.' And so the ideology of mass culture fulfils a comforting and reassuring role: it makes a search for more detailed and personal explanations superfluous, because it provides a finished explanatory model that convinces, sounds logical and radiates legitimacy.

Hating *Dallas* need not, however, necessarily coincide with subscribing to the ideology of mass culture. Other factors may be responsible for the fact that one is not attracted to the television serial itself. The letters from those who dislike it, however, are so structured by the schemas of this ideology that they offer us little insight into the way in which they watch the programme, which meanings they attach to it, etc. Hence, despite the confidence of their expressed opinions, it remains even more puzzling why some letter-writers don't like *Dallas* than why its fans do.

The ironical viewing attitude

But not all letter-writers who have adopted the ideology of mass culture seem to dislike *Dallas*. On the contrary, some of them state explicitly that they are fond of it, while at the same time employing the norms and judgements the ideology prescribes. How is this possible? It seems somewhat contradictory to regard *Dallas* as a 'bad object' on the one hand, but on the other to experience pleasure in watching it. But if we read the relevant letters carefully, it emerges that this apparent contradiction is resolved in an ingenious manner. How? Let me give an example.

> *Dallas*. . . . God, don't talk to me about it. I'm just hooked on it! But you wouldn't believe the number of people who say to me, 'Oh, I thought you were against capitalism?' I am, but *Dallas* is just so tremendously exaggerated, it has nothing to do with capitalists any more, it's just sheer artistry to make up such nonsense. (Letter 25)

It is clear how this letter-writer 'solves' the contradiction between the moral of the ideology of mass culture and ex-

periencing pleasure in *Dallas*: with mockery and irony. One group of letter-writers seems to make *Dallas* the object of derision. They assume an ironic stance when watching it, an attitude they refer to in their letters at length and with obvious pleasure. An important element of this ironical viewing attitude is the supplying of commentary. According to Michel Foucault commentary is a type of discourse that has the aim of dominating the object:[6] by supplying commentary to something one affirms a superior relation to that object. Thus *Dallas* too is 'dominated' by the mocking commentary of these viewers, 'put in the corner'. Two 'ardent *Dallas* watchers', as they call themselves, tell us how this can be done:

> We never miss this programme for a single week and sit glued to the box, like two flies to a treacle-pot. At first we watched out of pure curiosity, now because we're hooked on it. Mostly we watch with a group of people and we laugh, scream and roar. . . . We ourselves have given a bit of our own flavour (to this programme) such as changing the names. For example Pamela = Memmela. Miss Ellie = Miss Lellie. Sue Ellen = Sod Ellen, etc. We even have a notice-board in the house devoted to the *Dallas* characters. And if one of us can't watch, then a written report of it is drawn up. This board is also richly illustrated. (Letter 28)

Commenting on *Dallas* has here become a ritual. Apparently these letter-writers don't enjoy *Dallas* itself at all, what they seem to enjoy is the irony they bring to bear on it. According to Freud, irony is based on the mechanism of inversion:

> Its essence lies in saying the opposite of what one intends to convey to the other person, but in sparing him contradiction by making him understand – by one's tone of voice, by some accompanying gesture, or (where writing is concerned) by small stylistic indications – that one means the opposite of what one says.[7]

We could add to this that the effect of irony need not necessarily arise through an inversion of the meaning of words, but can also be realized through an inversion of the meaning of an object. Thus, through a mocking commentary *Dallas* is transformed from a seriously intended melodrama to the reverse: a comedy to be laughed at. Ironizing viewers therefore do not take the text as it presents itself, but invert its preferred meaning through their ironic commentary. This can provide brilliant constructions:

> In some sense this serial is a lot like *Soap!* but less satirical. (Letter 29)

> *Dallas* is sensitive and ludicrous. Another of our favourite programmes is *Soap!* (Letter 30)

It is marvellous that these letter-writers connect up *Dallas* with *Soap!* of all things. *Soap!* is a comedy serial which is an explicit parody of soap operas, exaggerating the melodramatic appeal to emotionality and sentimentality to the point of ridicule. Putting *Dallas* and *Soap!* in the same category, as these letter-writers do, is certainly no accident; such a comparison reveals the functioning of and only makes sense from a certain ideological position. The ideology of mass culture is extremely suitable as a foundation for such a position, because the ideology of mass culture regards *Dallas* by definition as a 'bad object' and therefore turns it into an easy subject for mockery and parody.

But it would be too simple to make that ideology the only responsible determinant of an ironic stance towards *Dallas*. Some forms of mass culture are more easily available to an ironic attitude than others. Melodramatic soap operas are an extremely vulnerable genre here: melodrama stands or falls by the degree to which it can whip up passion, sentiment, despair and drama and still carry the viewers along. In other words, the melodramatic effect only works if the viewer identifies with the excessive world of the soap opera. If that is not the case and the

viewer feels an outsider to this world, then the melodramatic enlargement of emotions becomes completely senseless and laughable. Melodramatic soap operas are therefore an easy prey for irony: any relativizing is disastrous for melodrama.

However, the ironic viewing attitude makes a reconciliation possible between the rules of the ideology of mass culture ('I must find *Dallas* bad') and the experiencing of pleasure ('I find *Dallas* amusing *because* it's so bad'). As these letter-writers put it:

> My feelings are mostly very superior, such as: what a lot of idiots. And I can laugh at it. Often too I find it over-sentimental. One thing in its favour: It's never dull. (Letter 29)

> As you may notice I watch it a lot, and (you may find this sounds a bit big-headed) I find it amusing precisely because it's so ghastly (if you know what I mean). If, for example, I had had to play Miss Ellie's role, when her breast is amputated, I would really kill myself laughing, with that slobbering Jock hanging over me full of good intentions. (Letter 36)

By ironizing commentary a distance is created from the reality represented in *Dallas*. In this way those who subscribe to the norms of the ideology of mass culture can like *Dallas*. Irony then comes to lead its own life and this viewing attitude becomes a necessary condition for experiencing pleasure in the first place. Thus the conflict disappears between the norms of the ideology of mass culture and liking *Dallas*: ironizing, i.e. creating a distance between oneself and *Dallas* as 'bad object', *is* the way in which one likes *Dallas*. This is, for example, the case for the 'ardent *Dallas* watchers' I quoted above. But the viewing attitude of the following letter-writer is also determined to a large degree by the exorcizing power of the ironic commentary:

> Why does a person watch *Dallas* and in my case, why does a serious, intelligent feminist like watching *Dallas*? It releases

primitive feelings in me. I go dizzy, hate, love, loathe, feel disgusted, condemn and often dash away a tear. Personally I keep aloof from Mills and Boon, but I'm ready to play truant from evening school for *Dallas*. . . . My leisure reading consists 90 per cent of feminist books, but when I'm watching *Dallas* with my girl friend and Pamela comes down the stairs wearing a low-necked dress, then we shout wildly: just look at that slut, the way she prances around, she ought to be called Prancela. Bobby is a decent chap, like my eldest brother, and Jock is like my father, so I can hate them intensely too. I can stand Sue Ellen, neurotic as she is, and J.R. laughs just like Wiegel [Dutch right-wing politician] and that has me jumping with rage. Lucy is too beautiful to be true and I don't find Miss Ellie all that marvellous since her breast operation. [. . .] I like to let it all hang out, a sort of group therapy, mostly together with friends. (Letter 24)

The ironic viewing attitude places this viewer in a position to get the better, in a sense, of *Dallas*, to be above it. And in this way, as a 'serious, intelligent feminist', she can allow herself to experience pleasure in *Dallas*. She says in fact: 'Of course *Dallas* is mass culture and therefore bad, but precisely because I am so well aware of that I can really enjoy watching it and poke fun at it.'

The following letter-writer presents her own viewing attitude in the same sort of way:

I watch *Dallas* regularly and I lap it up. All my girl friends watch it, and it's great fun to slate the whole thing. I find the quality rather bad, but it does have a certain attraction. Lots of money, and beautiful people, good and bad clearly distinguished. It's just as much fun to read a gossip magazine. Nothing sticks. You don't think any more about it, but it's fun. [. . .] The same improbable things happen as in romantic fiction. Insidious illnesses, true love, etc. (Letter 26)

And she ends her letter as follows: 'It's wonderful to watch it but sometimes I do need a realistic book or a good film, not to fall into sentimental despair.'

Here again we have the well-known opposition between 'good culture' and 'bad culture': although this letter-writer does not find 'mass culture' 'bad' in the sense that she dislikes it, indeed she can enjoy it, that enjoyment is in her view a completely different, less high-principled sort of enjoyment than that of 'good culture'.

Just as for the letter-writers who dislike *Dallas*, for these ironizing fans the ideology of mass culture has become common sense: for them too it is self-evident that *Dallas* is 'bad mass culture'. But the very weapon of irony makes it unnecessary for them to suppress the pleasure that watching *Dallas* can nevertheless arouse; irony enables them to enjoy it without suffering pangs of conscience. The dismissive norms of the ideology of mass culture are smoothly integrated in the ironic viewing attitude.

We have seen earlier that those who hate *Dallas* have little difficulty in giving reasons for their dislike: they can always draw on the instant judgements of the ideology of mass culture. However, the ironic fans are in a certain sense on even stronger ground. While liking *Dallas* ironically leads to euphoria and merriment, as we have seen, disliking *Dallas* is accompanied by anger and annoyance. And these are not nice feelings. Hence those who dislike *Dallas* run the risk of a conflict of feelings if, *in spite of this*, they cannot escape its seduction, i.e. if they continue to watch. This can lead to almost tragi-comic ups and downs, as this letter-writer relates:

When the serial started I disliked it intensely. [. . .] I myself started watching the serial because I spent a lot of time in the home of people, the husband of whom was from America and the serial made him think a lot about home. So I watched a few episodes because I was forced to in a way and that's now for me the only reason I watch it. I just want to see how

it turns out. The fact is that every time the disasters overlap, so I'm sitting in front of the box and now I never miss a single episode. Fortunately it's on late in the evening so before that I can do some sport or something. I must also add that in every episode there are some things that really annoy me. (Letter 38)

So disliking *Dallas* is certainly not an experience without its ambivalences!

Loving DALLAS

But what about those who 'really' like *Dallas*? How do they relate to the ideology of mass culture?

Ideologies organize not only the ideas and images people make of reality, they also enable people to form an image of themselves and thus to occupy a position in the world. Through ideologies people acquire an identity, they become subjects with their own convictions, their own will, their own preferences. So, an individual living in the ideology of mass culture may qualify him or herself as, for example, 'a person of taste', 'a cultural expert' or 'someone who is not seduced by the cheap tricks of the commercial culture industry'. In addition to an image of oneself, however, an ideology also offers an image of others. Not only does one's own identity take on form in this way, but the ideology serves also to outline the identity of other people. As Göran Therborn puts it, 'in one's subjection to and qualification for a particular position, one becomes aware of the difference between oneself and others'.[8] Thus a dividing line is drawn by the ideology of mass culture between the 'person of taste', the 'cultural expert', etc. and those who, according to this ideology, are not such. Or to be more specific, between those who do recognize *Dallas* as 'bad mass culture' and those who do not.

One *Dallas*-hater thus tries to distance herself from those who like *Dallas*:

I don't understand either why so many people watch it, as there are lots of people who find it a serious matter if they have to miss a week. At school you really notice it when you turn up on Wednesday morning then it's, 'Did you see *Dallas*, wasn't it fabulous?' Now and then I get really annoyed, because I find it just a waste of time watching it. [. . .] Then you hear them saying that they had tears in their eyes when something happened to someone in the film, and I just can't understand it. At home they usually turn it on too, but then I always go off to bed. (Letter 33)

She outlines the identity of the others, those who like *Dallas*, in a negative way, and with a particular degree of confidence: lovers of *Dallas* are almost declared idiots by this letter-writer! Roughly the same pattern, but in somewhat milder terms, emerges in the following extract: 'Reading through it [her own letter], it's a serial a normal person shouldn't watch, because you feel someone else's sorrow and difficulties. For me that's also the reason why so many people find the serial good' (Letter 38). The image of the others, of those who do not recognize *Dallas* as 'bad mass culture', can be summed up shortly but forcefully from the viewpoint of the ideology of mass culture: 'The aim is simply to rake in money, lots of money. And people try to do that by means of all these things – sex, beautiful people, wealth. *And you always have people who fall for it*' (Letter 35, my italics). The ideology of mass culture therefore definitely does not offer a flattering picture of those who like *Dallas*. They are presented as the opposite of 'persons of taste', 'cultural experts' or 'people who are not seduced by the cheap tricks of the commercial culture industry'. How do lovers of *Dallas* react to this? Do they know that this negative image of them exists and does it worry them at all?

In the small advertisement which the letter-writers replied to, I included the following clause: 'I like watching the TV serial *Dallas* but often get odd reactions to it.' It seems to me that the phrase 'odd reactions' is vague at the very least: from

the context of the advertisement there is no way of knowing what I meant. Yet various lovers of *Dallas* go explicitly into this clause in their letters: the words 'odd reactions' seem sufficient to effect an 'Aha!' experience in some fans.

> I have the same 'problem' as you! When I let drop in front of my fellow students (political science) that I do my utmost to be able to watch *Dallas* on Tuesday evenings, they look incredulous. (Letter 19)

> It always hits me too that people react 'oddly' when you say you like watching *Dallas*. I think everyone I know watches it but some of my friends get very worked up over this serial and even go on about the dangerous effects on the average TV viewer. I really don't know what I should think of this. (Letter 22)

These extracts lead one to suspect that the rules and judgements of the ideology of mass culture are not unknown to *Dallas* fans. What is more, they too seem to respond to this ideology. But they tend to do so in a completely different way from those who hate *Dallas* or who love it ironically. 'Really' loving *Dallas* (without irony) would seem to involve a strained attitude toward the norms of the ideology of mass culture. And it is this strained relationship which the fans have to try to resolve.

In contrast to the haters and ironic lovers, who, as we have seen, express their attitude to the ideology of mass culture in a rather uniform and unconflicting way, the 'real' fans use very divergent strategies to come to terms with its norms. One strategy is to take over and internalize the judgements of the ideology of mass culture itself:

> I just wanted to react to your advertisement concerning *Dallas*. I myself enjoy *Dallas* and the tears roll down when something tragic happens in it (in nearly every episode, that is). In my circle too people react dismissively to it, they find it a typical commercial programme far beneath their

standards. I find you can relax best with a programme like this, although you just have to keep your eye on the kind of influence such a programme can have, it is role-confirming, 'class-confirming', etc., etc. And it's useful too if you think what kind of cheap sentiment really does get to you. (Letter 14)

There is a remarkable about-face in this letter. Instead of stating why she likes *Dallas* so much (which was the question I had put in my advertisement), the letter-writer confines herself to reiterating a reasoning which derives from the ideology of mass culture in answer to the 'dismissive reactions' of her milieu. She doesn't adopt an independent attitude towards this ideology but merely takes over its morals. But whom is she addressing with these morals? Herself? Me (she knows from my advertisement that I like watching *Dallas*)? All *Dallas* fans? It is as though she wants to defend the fact that she enjoys *Dallas* by showing that she is in fact aware of its 'dangers' and 'tricks'; aware, in other words, that *Dallas* is 'bad mass culture'. A similar reasoning can be read in the following letter extract:

In fact it's a flight from reality. I myself am a realistic person and I know that reality is different. Sometimes too I really enjoy having a good old cry with them. And why not? In this way my other bottled-up emotions find an outlet. (Letter 5)

In other words: watching *Dallas* is all right if you know that it is not realistic and therefore 'bad'.

But a protective strategy can also be employed by actually challenging the ideology of mass culture.

I am replying to your advertisement as I would like to speak my mind about *Dallas*. I've noticed too that you get funny reactions when you like watching *Dallas* (and I like watching it). Many people find it worthless or without substance. But I think it does have substance. Just think of the saying:

> 'Money can't buy happiness', you can certainly trace that in
> *Dallas*. (Letter 13)

But what has been said here against the ideology of mass
culture remains caught within the categories of that ideology.
Against the opinion 'no substance' (= 'bad') is placed the
alternative opinion 'does have substance' (= 'good'); the
category 'substance' (and thus the difference 'good/bad') is
therefore upheld. This letter-writer 'negotiates' as it were
within the discursive space created by the ideology of mass
culture, she does not situate herself outside it and does not
speak from an opposing ideological position.

But why do these *Dallas* lovers feel the need to defend
themselves against the ideology of mass culture? They obviously
feel under attack. Obviously they can't get round its norms
and judgements, but must stand out against them in order to be
able to like *Dallas* and not to have to disavow that pleasure. But
it is never pleasant to be manoeuvred into a defensive position:
it shows weakness. To have to defend oneself is nearly always
coupled with a feeling of unease.

> You are right in saying that you often get these strange
> reactions. Such as 'So you like watching cheap mass enter-
> tainment, eh?' Yes, I watch it and I'm not ashamed of it. But I
> do try to defend my motivation tooth and nail. (Letter 7)

'Tooth and nail'; the pent-up intensity of this expression
reveals the strong desire of this letter-writer to defend herself
and to justify herself, in spite of her contention that she 'is not
ashamed of it'.

And another letter-writer says:

> Oh well, I'm one of those people who sit in front of the box
> every Tuesday for the *Dallas* programme, actually to my
> own amazement. . . . I must honestly confess that I do like
> watching the serial now. By 'confess' I mean this: at first I felt
> a bit guilty about the fact that I had gone mad on such a

cheap serial without any morals. Now I look at it rather differently. (Letter 11)

'To my own amazement', she writes, in other words 'I hadn't thought it possible'. Her feeling of guilt arises precisely because she has not escaped the power of conviction of the ideology of mass culture, from the branding of *Dallas* as a 'cheap serial without any morals'.

Finally, yet another defence mechanism against the ideology of mass culture is possible. That is, strangely enough, irony again. But in this case irony is not integrated so unproblematically in the experience of watching *Dallas* as in the case of the ironic fans we encountered earlier. On the contrary, here irony is an expression of a conflicting viewing experience. One letter-writer has put this psychological conflict clearly into words. In her account there is an uncomfortable mixture of 'really' liking *Dallas* and an ironic viewing attitude:

Just like you I often get odd reactions when I say that at the moment *Dallas* is my favourite TV programme. [. . .] I get carried along intensely with what is happening on TV. I find most figures in the serial horrible, except Miss Ellie. The worst thing I find is how they treat one another. I also find them particularly ugly. Jock because he doesn't have an aesthetically justifiable head, Pamela because she has to seem so smart, I find that 'common'. I can't stand it that everyone (in the serial) finds her sexy when she looks like Dolly Parton with those breasts. Sue Ellen is really pathetic, she looks marvellously ravaged by all that drink. J.R. needs no explanation. He keeps my interest because I always have the feeling that one day that wooden mask is going to drop. Bobby I find just a stupid drip, I always call him 'Aqualung' (his former role in a series). They are a sad lot, so honest, stinking rich, they want to seem perfect but (fortunately for us!) none of them is perfect (even Miss Ellie has breast cancer, and that cowboy Ray, whom I've really fallen for, is always running into trouble). (Letter 23)

The distance from the *Dallas* characters is great for this letter-writer – witness the annihilating judgement that she passes so ironically on them. Nevertheless her account is imbued with a kind of intimacy which betrays a great involvement in the serial ('I get carried along intensely' . . ., 'I can't stand it' . . ., 'I am interested in him' . . ., 'whom I've really fallen for'). The detached irony on the one hand and the intimate involvement on the other appear difficult to reconcile. So it emerges from further on in her letter that irony gains the upper hand when watching *Dallas* is a social occasion:

> I notice that I use *Dallas* as a peg for thinking about what I find good and bad in my relations with others. I notice this in particular *when I'm watching with a group of people* because then we usually can't keep our mouths shut; we shout disgraceful! and bastard! and bitch! (sorry, but emotions really run high!). We also sometimes try to get an idea of how the Ewings are all doing. Sue Ellen has postnatal depression and that's why she is so against her baby. Pamela is actually very nice and suffers because of Sue Ellen's jealousy. J.R. is just a big scaredy-cat, you can see that from that uncertain little laugh of his. (Letter 23, my italics)

The ironic commentaries are presented here as a *social* practice. This is confirmed by the sudden transition from the use of 'I' to 'we' in this extract. Is it perhaps true to say that the need to emphasize an ironic attitude to viewing, thereby creating a distance from *Dallas*, is aroused in this letter-writer by the social control emanating from an ideological climate in which 'really' liking the programme is almost taboo? In any case intimacy returns further on in the letter as soon as she is talking again in terms of 'I'. And the irony then disappears into the background.

> Actually they are all a bit stupid. And oversensational. Affected and genuinely American (money-appearance-relationship-maniacs – family and nation! etc.). I know all

this very well. And yet. . . . The Ewings go through a lot more than I do. They seem to have a richer emotional life. Everyone knows them in Dallas. Sometimes they run into trouble, but they have a beautiful house and anything else they might want. I find it pleasant to watch. I do realize their ideals of beauty. I look at how their hair is done. I'm very impressed by their brilliant dialogues. Why can't I ever think what to say in a crisis? (Letter 23)

Real love and irony – both determine the way in which this letter-writer relates to *Dallas*. It is clear that they are difficult to reconcile: real love involves identification, whereas irony creates distance. This ambivalent attitude to *Dallas* seems to stem from the fact that on the one hand she accepts the correctness of the ideology of mass culture (at least in a social context), but on the other hand 'really' likes *Dallas* – which is against the rules of this ideology. The irony lies here then in the 'social surface'; it functions, in contrast to the ironizing lovers, for whom irony is interwoven with the way in which they experience pleasure in *Dallas*, as a sort of screen for 'real' love. In other words, irony is here a defence mechanism with which this letter-writer tries to fulfil the social norms set by the ideology of mass culture, while secretly she 'really' likes *Dallas*.

We can draw two conclusions from these examples. First, the fans quoted seem spontaneously, of their own free will, to take the ideology of mass culture into account: they come into contact with it and cannot apparently avoid it. Its norms and prescriptions exert pressure on them, so that they feel the necessity to defend themselves against it. Second, it emerges from their letters that they use a very wide variety of defence strategies: one tries simply to internalize the ideology of mass culture, another tries to negotiate within its discursive framework, and yet another uses surface irony. And so it would appear that there is not one obvious defence strategy *Dallas* fans can use, that there is no clear-cut ideological alternative which can be employed against the ideology of mass

culture – at least no alternative that offsets the latter in power of conviction and coherence. And so the letter-writers take refuge in various discursive strategies, none of which, however, is as well worked out and systematic as the discourses of the ideology of mass culture. Fragmentary as they are, these strategies are therefore much more liable to contradictions. In short, these fans do not seem to be able to take up an effective ideological position – an identity – from which they can say in a positive way and independently of the ideology of mass culture: 'I like *Dallas* because . . .'.

But this weak position the fans are in, this lack of a positive ideological basis for legitimizing their love of *Dallas*, has tiresome consequences. Whereas those who hate the programme can present their 'opponents' as, for example, 'cultural barbarians', 'people with no taste' or 'people who let themselves be led astray by the tricks of the commercial culture industry' (thus implying that they themselves are *not*), the fans do not have such a favourable representation to hand. They are not in a position to hit back by forming in their turn an equally negative image of those who dislike *Dallas*; they can only offer resistance to the negative identities that *others* ascribe to them.

According to Therborn, such a psychologically problematic situation is characteristic for subject positions which get the worst of it ideologically. From an ideologically dominant subject position it is possible to stigmatize 'the others' as it were. For the victims of this dominant ideology, however, no such reassuring position is available: they find themselves in a position which, 'while also involving a perception and evaluation of the differences between ego and alter, tends towards resistance to the Other rather than towards forming him or her. This difference is inscribed in the asymmetry of domination.'[9] This situation can have disastrous consequences for *Dallas* fans who feel pushed into a corner by the ideology of mass culture. They can easily be reduced to silence because they can literally find no words to defend themselves. The ground is cut

from under them. As one of the letter-writers says: 'I personally find it terrible when I hear people saying they don't like *Dallas*' (Letter 2). As finding it 'terrible' is her only word of defence – apparently nothing else occurred to her – isn't that a form of capitulation?

The ideology of populism

It is wrong, however, to pretend that the ideology of mass culture exercises dictatorial powers. The discourses of this ideology are very important, culturally legitimized organizers of the way in which the social meaning of *Dallas* is constructed, but alternative discourses do exist which offer alternative points of identification for lovers of *Dallas*.

Not all letter-writers who like *Dallas* seem to be troubled by the compelling judgements produced by the ideology of mass culture. Some of them just seem to ignore the 'odd reactions' mentioned in the advertisement text, probably because they do not even know what is meant by it, as this letter-writer indicates: 'I have never yet heard odd reactions – as you wrote in *Viva*. People who didn't watch it had no opinion, and people who did watch it found it nice' (Letter 20).

Apparently this letter-writer lives in a cultural milieu in which the ideology of mass culture has little effect on the way in which people judge patterns of cultural consumption. Hating *Dallas* and loving *Dallas* are in this context positions which are relatively free of the associations evoked by the ideology of mass culture. For this letter-writer, who apparently has no idea of the constraint that the ideology of mass culture exercises on so many other lovers of *Dallas* – 'I am curious about your "odd reactions"', she writes – loving *Dallas* is a pretty carefree affair because she does not seem to be surrounded by the taboo which is created by the ideology of mass culture.

A few other letter-writers do seem to be subject to this atmosphere of taboo, but take up an attitude towards it based on deflating the standards of the ideology of mass culture itself.

That can be achieved by simply refusing to let it bother them: 'When I say I like watching *Dallas*, I often get odd reactions too, but I also like eating at MacDonalds and like poetry a lot, things that get just as strange a reaction' (Letter 24). This letter-writer even flirts a bit with her love for 'mass culture' (MacDonalds!), so that a defence against 'odd reactions' is not necessary.

Other letter-writers again try to undermine the ideology of mass culture by not only resisting the negative identity forced on them, but by retaliating to put the position of those who hate *Dallas* in a negative light. Sometimes they do this in a rudimentary way, for example by turning the tables on those who pretend to loathe the programme: 'I have noticed that among people in my milieu they won't honestly admit that they like watching it, but I do, I really like watching it. [. . .] People often find it sugary but they would like to have a taste of that sugariness just as well, wouldn't they?' (Letter 6).

Against the identity that the ideology of mass culture foists on her, the following *Dallas* fan tries herself to construct an elaborate counter-identity:

> There is no time (in this society) for emotions, which is why you and I often get negative reactions when you're talking about *Dallas*. So various people brand *Dallas* as 'childish', 'too sentimental' or 'slimy'. Perhaps it's also because there are also people who only like action and violence. [. . .] I think *Dallas* is a serial for people with feelings, but I could be wrong of course. (Letter 18)

Another lover of *Dallas* goes even further. In her letter she tries to indicate the social origin of the ideology of mass culture, in order then to make her resistance to it known:

> When I ask for an opinion at school I get the same reactions as you. Does it perhaps have something to do with the fact that I am at grammar school and have my final exams this year? I think so. For you 'have to' follow current affairs

programmes and 'good' films, but who decides for me what *I* find good? I myself of course. (Letter 5)

Her use of language ('I myself of course') reveals a certain degree of pugnacity in her resistance to the norms and opinions of the ideology of mass culture. Here she invokes something like an 'individual right of determination' and betrays a certain allergy to aesthetic standards determined from on high. So she speaks from an ideological position which can be aptly summed up in the well-known saying: 'There's no accounting for taste.'

This is the core of what we can call the ideology of populism, an ideology which is completely opposite to the ideology of mass culture: it arrives at its norms and judgements in a radically opposite way. But it is not impossible for the two ideologies to be united in one person. Thus one ironizing lover characterizes *Dallas* on the one hand as a 'hideously cheap serial' (a statement which fits within the discursive repertoire of the ideology of mass culture), while on the other hand she judges those who dislike *Dallas* from a populist perspective: 'I find the people who react oddly rather ludicrous – they can't do anything about someone's taste. And anyway they might find things pleasant that you just can't stand seeing or listening to' (Letter 36).

This statement clearly illustrates how the populist ideology functions. It is, first and foremost, an anti-ideology: it supplies a subject position from which any attempt to pass judgement on people's aesthetic preferences is *a priori* and by definition rejected, because it is regarded as an unjustified attack on freedom. The populist ideology therefore postulates an identity which is characterized by an appeal to total autonomy: 'But there's just one thing I'd like to make quite clear: please don't let yourself be sat on by other people with their own (odd) ideas (like me)' (Letter 36).

Viewed in this way, the populist position must be particularly attractive for lovers of *Dallas*, because it provides an

identity which can be forcefully employed against the codes of the ideology of mass culture. Why is it then that we can trace so little of this position in the letters written by fans?

One explanation lies in the difference in the way both ideologies function. The populist ideology derives its attraction from its direct mode of address, from its ability to produce and ensure immediate certainty.[10] Its discourses are anti-intellectual and consist mainly of no more than short slogans, as the saying 'There's no accounting for taste' makes clear. The populist ideology functions therefore mainly at a *practical* level: it consists of common-sense ideas which are assumed almost 'spontaneously' and unconsciously in people's daily lives. The ideology of mass culture on the other hand is mainly of a *theoretical* nature: its discourses possess great consistency and rationality, they take on the form of more or less elaborate theories. The ideology of mass culture is therefore an intellectual ideology: it tries to win people over by *convincing* them that 'mass culture is bad'.[11]

This difference can explain why in the letters the ideology of mass culture is present in a much more pronounced way than populist ideology. At a theoretical level the latter is the subservient one. It has literally fewer words and less clear-cut 'rational' prescriptions available to defend and legitimize its general attitude that 'there's no accounting for tastes'. For the opposite attitude, namely that 'mass culture is bad', very many arguments lie to hand. So it is not surprising that, if people have to account for taste, for example when they have to give reasons why they like or dislike *Dallas*, they cannot, or only with difficulty, evade the discursive power of the ideology of mass culture. This is why the ideology of mass culture succeeds in ensuring that each category of letter-writers – haters, ironizing lovers, 'real' lovers of *Dallas* – is alive to its norms and judgements and why it seems to brush aside the populist position.

Popular culture, populism and the ideology of mass culture

But the power of the ideology of mass culture is certainly not absolute. Indeed, it is precisely the markedly 'theoretical', discursive nature of this ideology that reveals the limits of its power. Its influence will be mainly restricted to people's opinions and rational consciousness, to the discourses people use when *talking* about culture. These opinions and rationalizations need not, however, necessarily prescribe people's cultural *practices*. It could even be that the dominance of the normative discourses of the ideology of mass culture – as it is expressed in all sorts of social institutions such as education and cultural criticism – has in fact a counter-productive effect on people's practical cultural preferences so that, not through ignorance or lack of knowledge, but out of self-respect they refuse to subject themselves to the prescriptions of the ideology of mass culture or to let their preferences be determined by it.[12] The populist position offers a direct justification for such a refusal, because it rejects altogether any paternalistic distinction between 'good' and 'bad' and dismisses any feeling of guilt or shame over a particular taste. There exists then a cynical dialectic between the intellectual dominance of the ideology of mass culture and the 'spontaneous', practical attraction of the populist ideology. The stricter the standards of the ideology of mass culture are, the more they will be felt as oppressive and the more attractive the populist position will become. This position offers the possibility, contrary to the morals of the ideology of mass culture, of following one's own preferences and enjoying one's own taste.

The commercial culture industry has understood this well. It employs the populist ideology for its own ends by reinforcing the cultural eclecticism underlying it and propagating the idea that indeed there's no accounting for taste, that in other words no objective aesthetic judgements are possible. It sells its products by propagating the idea that everyone has the right to his or her own taste and has the freedom to enjoy pleasure in his

or her own way. Perhaps it's not so surprising that the most striking description of the commercial application of the populist position was recently given by Frankie Goes To Hollywood: 'One of the main jobs of the advertisers [. . .] is not so much to sell the product as to give moral permission to have fun without guilt.'[13]

But the populist ideology is applicable not only for the aims and interests of the commercial culture industry. It also links up with what Bourdieu has called the popular 'aesthetic':[14] an aesthetic which is the exact opposite of the bourgeois aesthetic disposition in which an art object is judged according to extremely formal, universalized criteria which are totally devoid of subjective passions and pleasures. In the popular 'aesthetic' on the other hand, no 'judgements of Solomon' are passed on the quality of cultural artefacts. This aesthetic is of an essentially pluralist and conditional nature because it is based on the premise that the significance of a cultural object can differ from person to person and from situation to situation. It is based on an affirmation of the continuity of cultural forms and daily life, and on a deep-rooted desire for participation, and on emotional involvement. In other words, what matters for the popular aesthetic is the recognition of pleasure, and that pleasure is a personal thing. According to Bourdieu the popular aesthetic is deeply anchored in common sense, in the way in which cultural forms in everyday life are approached by ordinary people.

Pleasure, however, is *the* category that is ignored in the ideology of mass culture. In its discourses pleasure seems to be non-existent. Instead it makes things like responsibility, critical distance or aesthetic purity central – moral categories that make pleasure an irrelevant and illegitimate criterion. In this way the ideology of mass culture places itself totally outside the framework of the popular aesthetic, of the way in which popular cultural practices take shape in the routines of daily life. Thus it remains both literally and figuratively caught in the ivory towers of 'theory'.

4

DALLAS
and feminism

Women and DALLAS

As a prime time TV programme, *Dallas* is aimed at a widely heterogeneous, general TV audience, which cannot be defined in terms of a specific class, sex or age. On the contrary, from the perspective of the programme's producers, it is necessary in order to draw as many viewers as possible to make sure that the interest of all members of the (American) family is aroused. In this sense too *Dallas* differs from the daytime soap operas which *are* made with an eye to a specific social audience, namely housewives. This production context inevitably has repercussions on the general narrative content of *Dallas*, because it has to address different spheres of interest and it cannot be restricted to themes and plots which are only attractive for one section of the general audience.

As a result, male characters occupy a much more important place in the fictional world of *Dallas* than in daytime soaps; themes and plots which are traditionally mainly appreciated by

men, such as the business world, have a much larger part in the narrative.[1] So it is doubtless no accident that the role of the villain in *Dallas* is occupied by a man (J.R.), instead of a woman, as is mostly the case in daytime soaps.[2] (But it is equally striking that in other prime time soap operas, such as *Dynasty* and *Falcon Crest*, female villains do play a main part.) It is therefore not totally justified to regard *Dallas* as a programme primarily aimed at women, whereas the traditional soap operas in general can indeed be regarded as a 'women's genre'.

None the less, there are indications that *Dallas* is in fact watched and appreciated more by women than by men. For example, in March 1982, when the popularity of *Dallas* had more or less reached its peak in the Netherlands, an average of 52 per cent of the Dutch TV public watched *Dallas* weekly, 69 per cent of whom were women.[3] Moreover, data are available which suggest that women watch *Dallas* in a different way from men. Dutch women seem to be most interested in the mutual relations within the Ewing family and in the love complications in *Dallas*, while they respond much less to the business relations and problems, the cowboy elements and the power and wealth represented. It is not really surprising that for male viewers exactly the opposite is the case.[4] In other words, it is clear that *Dallas* in general means something different for women than for men. And it is precisely those themes that are always dealt with in soap operas that seem to make up the pleasure of *Dallas* for women.

The widespread and continuing popularity of soap operas among women has attracted a lot of attention from feminists. How must the fact that so many women obviously get pleasure from watching soap operas be judged politically from a feminist perspective? Is *Dallas* good or bad for women?

Unfortunately, a lot of mainstream feminist criticism seems to be inspired all too easily by the paternalism of the ideology of mass culture. Especially in the case of the mass media, much energy is spent in obsessively stressing how 'stereotyped',

'role-confirming' and 'anti-emancipatory' the images of women in the media are. This is usually as a result of a content analysis that bears all the limitations of empiricist realism, so that the firm conclusion is reached that such images reflect sexist or patriarchal values. Combined with a mechanistic conception of the effect of such representations on the behaviour and attitudes of women, this leads to a total condemnation of soap operas as reinforcers of the patriarchal status quo and the oppression of women. Women are therefore seen as the passive victims of the deceptive message of soap operas, just as the ideology of mass culture sees the audience as unwitting and pathetic victims of the commercial culture industry. In this context an ideological atmosphere arises containing an almost total dismissal of and hostility towards narrative genres which are very popular among women.

Such a 'monstrous alliance' between feminist criticism and the ideology of mass culture has something self-destructive about it. According to the normative parameters of the ideology of mass culture, 'female' forms of 'mass culture' such as soap operas and popular romances are the lowest of the low, while 'male' genres such as detective and science fiction are considered able to rise above the low level of 'mass culture'. A double standard which reveals a sexist inclination in the ideology of mass culture itself!

But feminist criticism operating along these lines also has more serious drawbacks. Not only is the specifically fictional character of soap operas overlooked, and thus the specific meanings produced in soap opera texts; but the pleasure that female viewers get from programmes like *Dallas* is totally disregarded. As Tania Modleski puts it: 'feminist critics seem to be strenuously disassociating themselves from the seductiveness of the feminine texts'.[5]

Fortunately, however, other views have emerged recently too. The idea that the soap opera is an inherently conservative genre that is not only culturally inferior but also harmful for regular viewers, seems to be gradually losing its self-evident

character and its legitimacy. Jane Feuer, for example, in an article in which she analyses the ideological structuring of continuing melodramatic serials like *Dallas* and *Dynasty*,[6] comes to the conclusion that such programmes represent a 'potentially progressive form', precisely because the serial form and the multiple plot structure of these prime time soap operas do not allow for clear-cut ideological positions and constructions. 'Since no action is irreversible, every ideological position may be countered by its opposite. Thus the family dynasty sagas may be read either as critical of the dominant ideology of capitalism or as belonging to it, depending upon the position from which the reader comes at it.'[7] This relative optimism with regard to the possibly progressive effect of prime time soap operas is formulated even more explicitly by Ellen Seiter, who reveals gentle feminist sympathy for the soap opera: 'The importance of small discontinuous narrative units which are never organized by a single patriarchal discourse or main narrative line, which do not build towards an ending or closure of meaning, which in their very complexity cannot give a final ideological word on anything, makes soap opera uniquely "open" to feminist readings.'[8]

Both Feuer and Seiter therefore base their optimism on the relative 'openness' of soap opera narratives, i.e. on the fact that it is impossible to achieve an ideological consensus in soap operas, for the very simple reason that the representation of ambivalence and contradiction forms the very material substance of the genre. This continuing ideological uncertainty creates a certain 'freedom' for viewers to construct their own meanings. It is, then, the viewers and their readings of the text that define the ultimate ideological stance of soap operas. In other words, Feuer and Seiter fasten their hopes on the possibility that viewers will make use of the freedom offered to them, so that the latent progressive potential contained in this narrative form will actually be translated into the manifest production of subversive, feminist meanings.

However, in the absence of any evidence about the way in

which actual readings take place, this reasoning remains abstract. Merely appealing to a progressive potential is a strictly formal matter which is detached from any examination of the concrete social and cultural context in which the programmes function. In this connection it can be relevant to concentrate for a moment on what the letter-writers – mainly women – have told us. As we have seen in previous chapters, the pleasure of *Dallas* for many of them is linked with a tragic structure of feeling that they read from *Dallas*. Such a reading does not seem to be exactly subversive: on the contrary, it fits in totally with the hegemonic consensus constructed in *Dallas* that nothing exists but age-old and eternally insoluble contradiction. Little that is feminist is to be discovered in such an ideological position. If we assume that the tragic structure of feeling is the principal way in which female viewers experience pleasure in *Dallas*, does that mean that Feuer and Seiter's hope is unfounded because any 'feminist potential' of *Dallas* is, alas, not taken up by viewers? Or have we jumped too quickly to this conclusion?

Feminism and the tragic structure of feeling

As a political and cultural movement, feminism is sustained by collective fantasies of a social future in which the oppression of women will have ceased to exist. A future, in other words, in which women's lives will no longer be dominated and hindered by patriarchal structures and sexist practices. All feminist struggles into which women put so much energy in present-day societies are always related in some way or other to this (imaginary) Utopia. Feminist fighting spirit and solidarity today are always motivated by a desire to achieve that distant Utopia, however much that desire is repressed in concrete situations and in the thick of the fight in the deeper layers of day-to-day consciousness.

As a narrative, then, feminist discourse tends to move in the direction of an imagined happy ending. It is the belief in and the

commitment to the necessity for this happy end that keeps feminists going. In this sense feminist discourse bears some similarity to the structure of popular romantic fiction, in which the search for a happy ending – for that orgastic moment of 'and they lived happily ever after' – also forms the motor of the narrative. However, the feminist notion of the happy ending has a totally different content from the happy ending of the popular romantic novel, in which the heterosexual, monogamous couple are eternally united in harmony. More strongly still, the way in which this romantic Utopia is achieved is generally deplored because it is seen to be in conflict with the feminist ideal: the heroine of the popular romantic novel wins happiness only after having given up her striving for independence and her resistance to the arrogance and violence of the male hero, and having subjected herself to his authority and paternalist protection.[9] In this sense the narrative of popular romantic fiction is one which asserts that the utopian situation can be realized within the framework of existing, patriarchal power relations between men and women – an imaginary 'solution' totally at odds with the feminist scenario.

But what about soap operas, with their total lack of any sense of progress, a total absence of an outlook on any kind of happy ending? In soap operas it is by definition impossible for the characters to remain happy. A utopian moment is totally absent in soap opera narratives: circumstances and events continually throw up barriers to prevent the capture of that little scrap of happiness for which all the characters are none the less searching. Life is presented as inherently problematic. Unhappiness is the norm, the rule and not the exception. This is the core of the tragic structure of feeling.

As a consequence, women in soap opera can never be simply happy with the positions they occupy. On the contrary, it is often these positions themselves that give rise to many problems and conflicts. This holds pre-eminently for the traditional positions which are ascribed to women in contemporary society. So although motherhood is presented in soap opera as a

feminine ideal, at the same time it is a source of constant care and worry. And marriage is not shown to be the blissful region of conjugal harmony but as subject to continual conflict. In a certain sense, then, a tense relationship is expressed in soap operas between the traditional destiny imposed on women by patriarchy and the non-viability of that destiny for women themselves. In other words, it would appear that some points made in feminist analysis of women's oppression are recognized in an intuitive way in soap operas: the contradictions which patriarchy generates are expressed time and again.

But it is precisely the lack of a prospect of a happy ending which makes any solution of these contradictions inconceivable. Women in soap opera never rise above their own problematic positions. On the contrary, they completely identify with them. In spite of all the miseries, they continue to believe in the ideals of patriarchal ideology: whatever the cost, the family must be held together (Miss Ellie); if your marriage breaks down you try again with another man or you become cynical (Sue Ellen); your happiness cannot be complete without children (Pamela). Hence the problems in *Dallas* can never be solved and are essentially cyclical: the patriarchal status quo is non-viable but remains intact.

Viewed in this way, the melodramatic sentimentality of *Dallas* is ideologically motivated by a sense of the essential impossibility of a fundamental alteration in the very structures which should be held responsible for all the trouble and unhappiness. This induces feelings of resignation and fatalism – sentiments which are not exactly conducive to resistance to those structures. From a feminist point of view the *Dallas* women therefore represent 'bad' positions: theirs are positions characterized by fatalism and passivity, while 'good' – feminist – positions should be accompanied by a fighting spirit and activity. It would seem, then, that the tragic structure of feeling is incompatible with a feminist sensibility.

Sue Ellen versus Pamela

Two female positions in *Dallas* are particularly interesting in this respect, because they appear at first sight to be mutually conflicting: those occupied by Sue Ellen and Pamela. It is striking in this context that the opinions of the letter-writers are particularly divided over these two characters. Not all the letter-writers speak about their sympathies and antipathies towards the *Dallas* characters, but some letters indicate that whoever likes Pamela doesn't like Sue Ellen, and vice versa.

> Pamela: a nice girl (I find her a woman of character: she can be nice, but nasty too). Sue Ellen: has had bad luck with J.R., but she makes up for it by being a flirt. I don't like her much. And she's too sharp-tongued. (Letter 3)

> Why do I watch *Dallas* every Tuesday? Mainly because of Pamela and that wonderful love between her and Bobby. When I see those two I feel warmth radiating from them. [. . .] I also find the relationship between Miss Ellie and Jock nice, but I'm scarcely interested at all in J.R. and Sue Ellen. (Letter 8)

> Sue Ellen: just *fantastic,* tremendous how that woman acts, the movements of her mouth, hands, etc. That woman really enters into her role, looking for love, snobbish, in short a real woman. Pamela: a Barbie doll with no feelings, comes over as false and unsympathetic (a waxen robot). (Letter 12)

> Sue Ellen is definitely my favourite. She has a psychologically believable character. As she is, I am myself to a lesser degree ('knocking one's head against a wall once too often') and I want to be (attractive). [. . .] Pamela pouts, and is too sweet. (Letter 17)

> My main person is Sue Ellen (I'm in love with Sue Ellen). She is in fact the only normal person around, especially now she's gone mad. Perhaps that's the secret of *Dallas*. You never know exactly whether anyone is good or bad. Sue Ellen, for example, is she really nice but now and then a bit

disturbed so that she sometimes does something rotten? Pamela, she's always so terribly nice and sweet, I wouldn't trust her an inch. (Letter 23, from a man)

The problematic and conflicting character of Sue Ellen's life stands out most. She tries to compensate for her stormy marriage with J.R. mainly by entering into extramarital relations with other men (Cliff Barnes, Dusty Farlow), and when these fail too she reaches for the bottle. The inner conflicts this causes for her are explicitly expressed in the scenes in which she pours out her heart to her psychiatrist, Doctor Ellby. This Doctor Ellby, by the way, disappeared without trace at a certain moment – he seemed simply not to exist any longer from one episode to the next. But during his presence in *Dallas* he functioned as it were as Sue Ellen's alter ego, he kept telling her that she must believe in her own strength and must begin a new independent life, but Sue Ellen herself does not feel up to this and continues to rely on the help and guidance of a man ('Dusty will get me out of here'). Although she certainly is aware of what makes her unhappy – her dependence on J.R. – she finds no possibility of finally freeing herself from him: she remains with J.R. and at South-fork because she can't go anywhere else.

Pamela's position is different. Certainly at the beginning her marriage to Bobby can definitely be called happy: they really love one another and Bobby is a gentle, understanding man. Of course there are problems: the fact that Pamela can't have children puts a damper on their marital bliss (she has a miscarriage), and when both of them put a lot of energy into their work for a while (Pamela in a fashion business, Bobby in Ewing Oil), it threatens to weaken their marriage. But in Pamela's case the hope remains that finally love will conquer all.

Sue Ellen and Pamela are not close friends. They have little to do with each other and don't pay each other much attention: the major part of their emotional energy is bestowed on the men in their lives. Scenes dealing with the relations between the

two women are, true to type, very infrequent in *Dallas*. Yet we do get to see such scenes from time to time. It is, however, striking that the subject of discussion in these scenes is nearly always the same: their common position as Ewing wives.

In one of the scenes the discussion starts because of Miss Ellie's mastectomy. In an earlier scene Sue Ellen has told J.R. that she finds what has happened to Miss Ellie appalling. 'But she will stay alive', J.R. had said to her, as though to reassure her, but she answers: 'Sometimes that is not enough.' In the following dialogue with Pamela it becomes clear exactly what she means by this:

Pamela: You can't handle it, can you?

Sue Ellen: I don't know what you're talking about.

Pamela: I'm talking about Miss Ellie's operation.

Sue Ellen: Can *you*?

Pamela: I don't know, and I hope I don't ever have to know.

Sue Ellen: J.R. fell in love with me because I was a beauty queen . . .

Pamela: There are other things important to a woman besides beauty.

Sue Ellen: What? Brain, charm, personality? You don't believe that for a minute, do you?

Pamela: Yes, I do.

Sue Ellen: Well, I've never met a man yet who thought of brains when he first looked at a woman.

Pamela: Women don't just exist for men, we exist for ourselves first!

Sue Ellen: Not if you're married to a Ewing.

Pamela: Well, I am married to a Ewing.

Sue Ellen: Then open up your eyes! The Ewing men come first, I would have thought you've learned that by now!

Pamela: I think you forget that I'm married to Bobby not J.R.

Sue Ellen: Bobby, J.R., Jock, it doesn't matter. In a couple of years they'll look at you in the same way: as property. And you'd better be wrapped up in a pretty little package!

In another scene in which the two women have a conversation, many months later, they each occupy roughly the same standpoints, although Pamela's marriage at that moment is suffering severely from the fact that Bobby has thrown himself completely into his position as director of Ewing Oil and has therefore alienated himself a little from her. Pamela feels neglected and looks for compensation not only in her own work, but also in a friend, a certain Alex Ward. This Alex makes every attempt to seduce Pamela. Pamela definitely does not appear impassive to this, but as yet she does not want to be unfaithful to Bobby. The discussion with Sue Ellen takes place after Sue Ellen has noticed Pamela in the company of Alex in a restaurant. We are in the living room of Southfork Ranch, where Pamela has just knocked back a stiff drink. At that moment Sue Ellen comes in.

Sue Ellen: It looks like you needed that drink, Pam. I know the difference between problem drinking and drinking for pleasure!

Pamela: Hello, Sue Ellen.

Sue Ellen: Your secret is safe with me, Pam.

Pamela: I see Alex quite often. [. . .] It was a business lunch.

Sue Ellen: Well, I'm not the one to give you advice, but we're both married to Ewing men. It would be easier for you to realize that Ewing women must make their own lives.

Pamela: Well, I've made a life of my own, I work.

Sue Ellen: I'm not talking about work, I'm talking about total lives. The Ewing men are into power first, and affection second.

Pamela: I will never accept the fact that Bobby and J.R. are the same.

Sue Ellen: How can you say that? What was your life like when he was running Ewing Oil?

. . .

Sue Ellen: If J.R. seeks sex and affection somewhere else, so why shouldn't I? And why shouldn't you?

Pamela: Because it's not that way!

Sue Ellen: Pam, I just want you to protect yourself. All Ewing men are the same. [. . .] And for you to survive you have two choices. You can either get out, or you can play by their rules!

At this moment Bobby comes in. He steers towards Pamela and embraces her tenderly. We see a close-up of Pamela, looking over Bobby's shoulder radiantly and triumphantly at Sue Ellen, as though to say: 'You can see we really love one another!' But the last shot of the scene is a lingering close-up of Sue Ellen, looking smilingly after the embracing couple with a look clearly expressing her conviction of the inevitable decline of their love.

Sue Ellen and Pamela share a common social position – that of a (Ewing) wife – but they have very different attitudes towards it. Sue Ellen's cynicism with regard to the male world makes her subject herself recklessly to the norms and rules of that very male world. Pamela on the other hand still believes in the possibility of a harmonious, equal relationship with a man, refuses to acknowledge that there are unbridgeable contradictions and panics when she is actually confronted with them. Sue Ellen's position, then, fits into and expresses to an extreme degree the tragic structure of feeling, while Pamela's position is based on an obstinate denial of it. Indeed, her continuing belief in the Utopia of 'true love' reminds one rather of the structure of feeling borne by the heroine of the popular romantic novel. No wonder that some letter-writers affirm their sympathy for Pamela by projecting on to her the fantasy of the romantic happy ending:

> I really like watching it, and especially Pamela and Bobby because it comes across (in the film) like genuine love, even though it's only a film. (Letter 6)

> If they (the writers) ever write Pamela and Bobby out of the serial then it's over for me. The good relationship between those two is for me the reason for watching. But then, I still firmly believe in 'true love'. (Letter 8)

But within the framework of a melodramatic soap opera like *Dallas* Pamela's position is an impossible one. No happy ending is ever achievable: her hopes will of necessity remain unfulfilled. So it is not surprising that Sue Ellen's certainty over the futility of Pamela's dream appears later to be verified. The estrangement between Pamela and Bobby seems to have been overcome when they adopt a child, Christopher, but not even that can save their marriage. The tensions become so acute that Pamela even decides at a certain moment to leave Bobby and Southfork and live alone. She begins building up a new life: she becomes her brother Cliff's business partner and meets a new man, Mark Graison, whom she does not really love, however. Bobby continues to haunt her thoughts, although a divorce seems inevitable. For Sue Ellen too the situation is changed, although not fundamentally. She does, it is true, succeed in divorcing J.R., goes to live alone, but quickly gives in to J.R.'s skilful attempts to win her back. Against her better judgement she marries him again. This second marriage is an instant fiasco: J.R.'s sole aim in fact is to ensure that he has an heir (their little son John Ross) and he is otherwise completely unchanged. Confronted with this situation, Sue Ellen decides to abandon all attempts to be happy. . . . During a meeting between the two women in a park, with happily playing children in the background, the dilemmas are made clear yet again.

Sue Ellen: I think it depends on what you want. . . .

Pamela: I want to wipe away the last year, and I want things back the way they were.

Sue Ellen: If only we could wipe away the things that change our lives. Of course, things are much simpler for me than they are for you.

Pamela: Why? We're both married to Ewings.

Sue Ellen: The difference is that you're a strong woman, Pam. I used to think I was, but I know differently now. I need Southfork. On my own, I don't amount to much. As

much as I hate J.R., I really need to be Mrs J. R. Ewing.
And I need him to be the father of John Ross. So I guess I
just have to lead a married life without a husband.
Pamela: Sue Ellen, there are other ways.
Sue Ellen: Not for me, but for you. . . . You've made your
own way of life. Now you're part of Wentworth Industries, you're rich in your own right and you've got Mark
Graison out there waiting to marry you. You can never be
happy at Southfork again. . . .
Pamela: Sue Ellen, maybe everything you say is true. But
what do I do about the fact that I still love Bobby?
Sue Ellen: Sometimes love just isn't enough, Pam. I'm living
proof of that.

Sue Ellen is the one who talks most, because she has found a
'solution' to surviving in her terrible situation. She knows that
there is no way out for her and accepts things as they are.
Pamela however still cannot and will not accept, but is powerless before the overwhelming force of circumstances. She just
doesn't know what to do. Which position is more tragic then:
the cynical fatalism of Sue Ellen, who has given up all her
desires, or the false hope of Pamela, who cannot find an outlet
for her desires, no matter how strong they are?

Sue Ellen and Pamela personify two feminine subject-
positions which are the result of being trapped in an all-
embracing patriarchal structure. Despite the apparent
differences between the two, then, in the end both share the
same fate. The contradictions of patriarchy are experienced at
first hand and even diagnosed, but there is no prospect of
change: feminist fantasies are totally absent in *Dallas*.

Pleasure, fantasy and cultural politics

What then about the 'feminist potential' of *Dallas*? What does
it mean to get pleasure from *Dallas* by recognizing and identi-

fying with its tragic structure of feeling, as so many female viewers seem to do?

Pleasure has so far not been discussed in this chapter. Yet pleasure is something that concerns many feminists and that is often seen as a problem for a feminist cultural politics. As part of a broader political issue, two questions can be asked concerning pleasure. First, what is the relevance of pleasure for a political project such as feminism? And secondly: what is the political and cultural meaning of the specific forms of pleasure which women find attractive?

There are no simple answers to these questions, but feminists certainly are convinced of the political importance of seeking satisfactory answers. Thus Michèle Barrett wonders: 'How can we widen the purchase of feminist ideas if we cannot understand why so many women read *Woman* and watch *Crossroads*?'[10] The relevance of pleasure is argued here by Barrett in a quite specific way. The understanding of women's existing pleasures, she appears to assert, can be useful for developing a more effective way of spreading feminist consciousness among the mass of women. Precisely how remains unclear for the present, but one positive point of Barrett's argument is that the enormous popularity among women of certain cultural forms is taken seriously. Thus she continues: 'We need to know why the "women's weepies" have an apparently enduring appeal ... we need to examine much more open-mindedly and sympathetically their basis in our consciousness and subjectivity.'[11]

By presenting the problem in this way, Barrett avoids the moralism of the ideology of mass culture in which pleasure in 'mass culture' is regarded as illicit. Women's weepies and all other forms of popular culture for women (such as fashion, lyrical love songs and soap operas) must no longer be simply condemned: we must recognize that they have a positive value and meaning in women's lives. At the same time, however, Barrett does not attempt to fall into the opposite extreme; she does not endorse the populist position in which any pleasure is

by definition justified and is above all discussion, because for her the understanding of these traditional pleasures of women is explicitly linked with a feminist aim. It is certainly not the aim to simply glorify those pleasures *because* they are popular among women – which would be a form of deceptive, populist solidarity – but to understand more thoroughly what concerns women today, so that feminists can connect up with it more efficiently. Women fortunately no longer need feel ashamed or guilty if they watch *Dallas*, but at the same time feminists must look for a way of making such pleasures politically productive by situating them in a feminist plan of action.

But it remains unclear what conclusion we must draw from Barrett's argument. How, for example, can the fact that so many women feel attracted to *Dallas* be made politically useful? Does it mean that feminists must make 'feminist soap operas' – whatever they might look like? Or is it a matter of creating contexts in which subversive readings of *Dallas* are promoted, so that the hope that Feuer and Seiter nourish in the 'feminist potential' of soap operas is realized after all?

A serious theoretical problem arises here. This has to do with the danger of an overpoliticizing of pleasure. However much Barrett, for example, tries to approach women's weepies in an open-minded and sympathetic way, her basic premise nevertheless remains that its enjoyment is ultimately politically bad for women, because it does not lead to the adoption of feminist ideas. A new antagonism is constructed here: that between the fantasies of powerlessness inscribed in the tragic structure of feeling, and the fantasies of protest and liberation inscribed in the feminist imagination. But what does this antagonism imply? Does experiencing pleasure in fantasies of powerlessness necessarily lead to political passivity, as the antagonism suggests?

What is at stake here is the relationship between fantasy life, pleasure and socio-political practice and consciousness. In this context it is perhaps of less importance to wonder *why* women's weepies have such enduring appeal, as Barrett would

have it, than to ask *what implications* the sentimental pleasure of identification with the tragic structure of feeling has for the way in which women make sense of and evaluate their position in society. And as the enduring popularity of women's weepies even among feminists would indicate, it is very doubtful whether the two are as intimately interrelated as is sometimes assumed. Must we see an imaginary identification with the tragic and masochistic positions of Sue Ellen or Pamela as a form of 'oppression in ourselves', a patriarchal 'remnant' that unfortunately women still have to hark back to because feminism has not yet developed any effective alternatives? Or can such fantasmatic scenarios have a meaning for women which is relatively independent of their political attitudes?

Although political activity certainly comprises a moment of pleasure because it provides one with a sense of positive identity, the project of feminism as a whole is not and never can be based on pleasure alone, because the project itself is impelled by an angry rejection of the existing social order as essentially unpleasurable, and by a projection of pleasure into a (mythical) ideal future. For that reason many feminist fantasies today are not pleasurable, but are linked with feelings of fury, frustration and pain. Political struggle is directed towards removing the distance between an ideal of the future and a given reality, but the harsh conditions in which this struggle must be waged inevitably create tensions in everyday life. Frustrations are always lurking but, from a political perspective, may not lead to giving up that ideal: the struggle must go on. A feeling of discomfort therefore always underlies, and is essential for, any political struggle for a better future, and for two reasons: because of the realization that that future does not yet exist, and because of the realization that a lot of energy has to be invested to bring that future closer.

But it is impossible to live solely with a feeling of discomfort. We cannot wait until the distant Utopia is finally achieved: here and now we must be able to enjoy life – if only to survive. In other words, any uneasiness with the present, with the social

situation in which we now find ourselves, must be coupled with an (at least partial) positive acceptance and affirmation of the present. Life must be experienced as being worth the effort, not just because a prospect exists for a better future, but also because the present itself is a potential source of pleasure.

One dimension of life in which the distance between a (pleasurable) absent and an (unpleasurable) present can be eradicated is that of fantasy. Fantasies of the feminist Utopia, for example, can remove the feeling of unease by making the absent ideal present – in the imagination. Here it is not primarily a matter of the content of the fantasy, but mainly of the fact of fantasizing itself: producing and consuming fantasies allows for a play with reality, which can be felt as 'liberating' because it is fictional, not real. In the play of fantasy we can adopt positions and 'try out' those positions, without having to worry about their 'reality value'. In this sense then it is also little to the point to assume that imaginary identifications with the positions of 'cynical fatalism' (Sue Ellen) or 'false hope' (Pamela) would be politically bad because they would lead to pessimism and resignation in real social life. At the level of fantasy we can occupy those positions without having to experience their actual consequences. It may well be, then, that these identifications can be pleasurable, not because they imagine the Utopia to be present, but precisely because they create the possibility of being pessimistic, sentimental or despairing with impunity – feelings which we can scarcely allow ourselves in the battlefield of actual social, political and personal struggles, but which can offer a certain comfort if we are confronted by the contradictions we are living in. It is in this sense that we can interpret Terry Lovell's assertion that 'Soap opera may be [. . .] a context in which women can ambiguously express *both* goodhumoured acceptance of their oppression *and* recognition of that oppression, and some equally goodhumoured protest against it.'[12] But, we must add, this acceptance (just like protest) takes place within the world of fantasy, not outside it. It says nothing about the positions and standpoints that the

same women occupy in 'real life'. After all, watching soap operas is never the only thing they do. In other activities, other positions will be (or have to be) assumed.

Fantasy is therefore a fictional area which is relatively cut off and independent. It does not function in place of, but beside, other dimensions of life (social practice, moral or political consciousness). It is a dimension of subjectivity which is a source of pleasure *because* it puts 'reality' in parentheses, because it constructs imaginary solutions for real contradictions which in their fictional simplicity and their simple fictionality step outside the tedious complexity of the existing social relations of dominance and subordination.

It seems therefore impossible to ascertain whether the pleasure of *Dallas* that is based on a recognition of and identification with the tragic structure of feeling is intrinsically progressive or conservative, and therefore politically good or bad – such a question would moreover contain an instrumentalist conception of pleasure, as though pleasure itself doesn't much matter – because that pleasure is first and foremost connected with the *fictional* nature of the positions and solutions which the tragic structure of feeling constructs, not with their ideological content. In terms of *content* the fantasy positions and solutions brought about by the tragic structure of feeling and the melodramatic imagination do seem indeed to incline to conservativism, and of course they can and must also be criticized for this – i.e. in so far as they are conservative representations. The politics of representation does matter. But the fact that we can identify with these positions and solutions when we watch *Dallas* or women's weepies and experience pleasure from them is a completely different issue: it need not imply that we are also bound to take up these positions and solutions in our relations to our loved ones and friends, our work, our political ideals, and so on.

Fiction and fantasy, then, function by making life in the present pleasurable, or at least livable, but this does not by any means exclude radical political activity or consciousness. It

does not follow that feminists must not persevere in trying to produce new fantasies and fight for a place for them; at the level of cultural production the main issue of struggle is clear, as many feminist filmmakers, writers and artists have shown. It does, however, mean that, where cultural consumption is concerned, no fixed standard exists for gauging the 'progressiveness' of a fantasy. The personal may be political, but the personal and the political do not always go hand in hand.

Notes

Introduction

1 R. Corliss, 'TV's *Dallas*: Whodunnit?', *Time*, 11 August 1980, p. 63.
2 A. Mattelart, X. Delcourt, M. Mattelart, *International Image Markets*, Comedia, London, 1984, p. 90.
3 ibid., pp. 17–18.
4 Pierre Juneau, 'Audience fragmentation and cultural erosion: a Canadian perspective on the challenge for public broadcasting', *EBU Review*, vol. XXXV, no. 2, March 1984, p. 20.
5 H. Newcomb, 'Texas: A giant state of mind', *Channels of Communication*, April/May 1981, pp. 40–1.
6 I. Ang and M. Simons, Interview with Stuart Hall, *Skrien*, no. 116, March 1982, p. 14.

Chapter 1

1 See also chapter 3 for the function of what I call 'the ideology of mass culture'.
2 Here some titles of the Dutch gossip magazines are listed.
3 It also appears, according to an enquiry carried out by the

Department for Viewing and Listening Research of the Dutch Broadcasting Foundation (May 1982), that only 12 per cent of Dutch adults who regularly watch *Dallas* frequently read something about *Dallas* in a newspaper or magazine; 49 per cent do not do so, 18 per cent seldom and 21 per cent only now and again. This means that only a small overlap exists between watching *Dallas* and reading about things to do with the programme.

4 D. Prokop, *Faszination und Langeweile. Die populären Medien.* Ferd. Enke Verlag, Stuttgart, 1979, p. 1.

5 S. Frith, *Sound Effects. Youth, Leisure and the Politics of Rock 'n' Roll*, Pantheon, New York, 1982, p. 284.

6 Quoted in Ang and Simons, Interview with Stuart Hall, p. 13.

7 Karl Marx (trans. M. Nicolaus) *The Foundations of the Critique of Political Economy*, Penguin, Harmondsworth, 1973.

8 T. Lovell, *Pictures of Reality. Aesthetics, Politics and Pleasure*, BFI, London, 1980, p. 60.

9 P. Bourdieu, 'The aristocracy of culture', *Media, Culture and Society*, vol. 2, no. 3, 1980, pp. 225–54.

10 This is, for example, the main issue for Elihu Katz and Tamar Liebes in their enquiry into the reception of *Dallas* by different sections of the public in Israel. See E. Katz and T. Liebes, 'Once upon a time, in Dallas', *Intermedia*, vol. 12, no. 3, May 1984.

11 Some sociologists emphasize that what we call leisure time is not in fact *free* time at all because the way we spend it (what, when, how) is determined by all sorts of institutions which have pounced on the organization of leisure. This is correct, but it should be added that leisure is in fact really *experienced* as free time: as the opposite of work time. And it cannot be denied that the possibilities of filling leisure time according to one's own ideas, although institutionally limited, are in general greater than at the workplace or at school, where the rules one is subjected to are much more rigid than the 'invisible' rules of how one spends one's leisure time.

12 Except of course for the professional television watchers, the critics, who generally can only grumble about television.

13 There are two television channels in the Netherlands. Research has revealed that only very few viewers – at most around 10 per cent – occasionally watch foreign (German or Belgian) broadcasts. Most viewers have a pronounced preference for the domestic channels.

14 R. Williams, *Television, Technology and Cultural Form*, Fontana, London, 1974, p. 94.

15 Of course this idea is often ideologically misused to justify broad-

casting policy in an easy way and to shrug off appeals to cultural responsibility. But that is beside the point here.

16 Frith, *Sound Effects* . . ., p. 92.

17 For a foundation of this semiological approach to television programmes, see *inter al.* U. Eco, 'Towards a semiotic inquiry into the television message', *Working Papers in Cultural Studies*, no. 2, 1972; and S. Hall, 'Encoding and decoding in the television discourse', CCCS Occasional Stencilled Papers, Birmingham, 1973.

18 See also R. C. Allen, 'On reading soaps: a semiotic primer', in E. Ann Kaplan (ed.), *Regarding Television*, American Film Institute, Los Angeles, 1983.

19 D. Morley, *The 'Nationwide' Audience*, BFI, London, 1980, p. 10.

20 J.-M. Piemme, *La Propagande inavoué*, Union Générale d'Editions, Paris, 1975.

21 ibid., p. 176.

22 ibid., p. 114.

23 'Empiricist' because the basic premise is used that reality can be gathered from the manifestation of the world. Cf. C. MacCabe, 'Theory and film: principles of realism and pleasure', *Screen*, vol. 17, no. 3, 1976, pp. 9–11.

24 R. Williams, *Marxism and Literature*, OUP, Oxford, 1977, p. 97.

25 Piemme, *La Propagande inavoué*, pp. 120–1.

26 C. MacCabe, 'Realism and the cinema: notes on some Brechtian theses', *Screen*, vol. 15, no. 2, 1974; reprinted in part in T. Bennett, S. Boyd-Bowman, C. Mercer, J. Woollacott (eds), *Popular Television and Film*, BFI, London, 1981, pp. 216–35.

27 'While traditional debates about realism have centred on the content and the ability to reflect reality, classic realism should be considered as centrally defined by a certain formal organization of discourses whereby the narrative discourse is placed in a situation of dominance with regard to the other discourses.' C. MacCabe, '*Days of Hope*. A response to Colin MacArthur', in Bennett *et al.* (eds), *Popular Television and Film*, p. 310.

28 MacCabe, 'Theory and film: principles of realism and pleasure', p. 17.

29 I can only deal very briefly here with the Hollywood film conventions. See further D. Bordwell and K. Thompson, *Film Art. An Introduction*, Addison Wesley, Reading, 1980. Also useful is J. Monaco, *How to Read a Film*, OUP, New York/Oxford, 1981 (rev. edn).

30 See also Piemme, *La Propagande inavoué*, 170–1.

31 For a critique of the theory of the classic-realist text, see *inter al.* T. Lovell, *Pictures of Reality*, pp. 84–7; also D. Morley, 'Texts, readers, subjects', in S. Hall, D. Hobson, A. Lowe, P. Willis (eds), *Culture, Media, Language*, Hutchinson, London, 1980, pp. 163–73.

32 The distinction between denotation and connotation is made among others by Roland Barthes in his *Elements of Semiology*, Jonathan Cape, London, 1967. Subsequently various semiologists have contested this distinction, because it suggests a hierarchy between 'literal' and 'figurative' meaning, which does not in fact exist. However, in his *S/Z*, Hill & Wang, New York, 1974/ Jonathan Cape, London, 1975, Barthes defends this distinction if it is a matter of the analysis of what he calls 'the classical text' (as opposed to the 'modern text'). It is in any case important to regard the distinction between denotation and connotation as an analytical difference. See also S. Hall, 'Encoding/Decoding', in Hall *et al.* (eds), *Culture, Media, Language*.

33 R. Barthes, *The Pleasure of the Text*, Hill & Wang, New York, 1975/Jonathan Cape, London, 1976, pp. 11–12.

34 This supposition is not completely correct. There will also be things in *Dallas* the importance of which is so self-evident for faithful viewers that they are no longer aware of it. Thus what is *not* said also plays a role. Here lies one of the limitations adhering to research that uses people's statements as the empirical point of departure.

35 The concept 'structure of feeling' comes from Raymond Williams. See for example his *Marxism and Literature*, pp. 128–35.

36 For a fundamental critique of the way in which the concept 'escape' is used in mass communications theory, see J.-M. Piemme, *La Télévision comme on la parle*, Labor, Brussels, 1978, chapter 4.

Chapter 2

1 For the theoretical problems and consequences of the use of the concept of genre in film theory, see S. Neale, *Genre*, BFI, London, 1980.

2 C. Geraghty, 'The continuous serial: a definition', in R. Dyer (ed.), *Coronation Street*, BFI, London, 1980, p. 10.

3 ibid., pp. 14–15.

4 Todorov, quoted in Geraghty, 'The continuous serial . . .', p. 13.

5 For a history of soap opera, see M. Edmonson and D. Rounds,

The Soaps, Stein & Day, New York, 1973; M. G. Cantor and S. Pingree, *The Soap Opera*, Sage, Beverley Hills, 1983.

6 For the function of soap operas for housewives, see H. Herzog, 'What do we really know about daytime serial listeners?' in P. F. Lazarsfeld and F. N. Stanton (eds), *Radio Research*, Duel, Sloan & Pearce, New York, 1944; D. Hobson, *Crossroads. The Drama of a Soap Opera*, Methuen, London, 1982, chapter 6.

7 Frith, *Sound Effects . . .*, p. 46.

8 See also E. Seiter, 'Men, sex and money in recent family melodramas', *Journal of the University Film and Video Association*, vol. XXXV, no. 1, winter 1983.

9 T. Brooks and E. Marsh, *The Complete Directory to Prime Time TV Shows*, Ballantine, New York, 1981, p. 178.

10 T. Modleski, 'The search for tomorrow in today's soap operas', *Film Quarterly*, fall 1979, p. 12.

11 S. Johnston, 'Crossroads: approaches to popular television fiction', paper read at BFI Summer School 1981, p. 10.

12 G. Swanson, '*Dallas*, part 1', *Framework*, no. 14, spring 1981, p. 62.

13 C. Brunsdon, 'Crossroads: notes on soap opera', *Screen*, vol. 22, no. 4, 1981, p. 34.

14 ibid., p. 34.

15 W. Brakman, in a radio interview, 9 January 1982.

16 D. Thornburn, 'Television melodrama', in R. Adler and D. Cater (eds), *Television as a Cultural Force*, Praeger, New York, 1976, p. 78.

17 See M. Jordan, 'Convention and realism', in Dyer (ed.), *Coronation Street*.

18 H. Newcomb, *TV: The Most Popular Art*, Anchor Books, New York, 1974, p. 137.

19 ibid.

20 T. Elsaesser, 'Tales of sound and fury', *Monogram*, no. 4, 1972, p. 2.

21 ibid., p. 14.

22 S. Sontag, *Illness as Metaphor*, Vintage Books, New York, 1979.

23 M. B. Cassata *et al.*, 'In sickness and in health', *Journal of Communication*, vol. 29, no. 4, autumn 1979, pp. 73–80.

24 Thornburn, 'Television melodrama', p. 83.

25 L. Mulvey, 'Notes on Sirk and melodrama', *Movie*, no. 25, winter 1978, p. 53.

26 Swanson, '*Dallas*, part 1'.

27 See E. Tee, 'Dallas: het gezin van de week', *Skrien*, no. 118, May/June 1982.

28 Swanson, '*Dallas*, part 1'.
29 L. Mulvey, 'Sirk and melodrama', *Australian Journal for Screen Theory*, no. 4, 1978, p. 30.
30 Mulvey, 'Notes on Sirk and melodrama', p. 54.
31 ibid.
32 See also J. Feuer, 'Melodrama, serial form and television today', *Screen*, vol. 25, no. 1, 1984, p. 11.
33 Mulvey, 'Notes on Sirk and melodrama', p. 54.
34 When a soap opera is terminated it is not because the narrative has run out, but mostly for external, commercial or organizational reasons. The narrative must then be turned off in an arbitrary way, which is usually very unsatisfactory for viewers: questions always remain open, narrative lines broken off.
35 Modleski, 'The search for tomorrow . . .', p. 12.
36 Barthes, *S/Z*, p. 76.
37 E. Seiter, 'Promise and contradiction: the daytime television serials', in *Filmreader 5*, Evanston, 1982, p. 158.
38 Modleski, 'The search for tomorrow . . .', p. 14.
39 M. J. Arlen, 'Smooth pebbles at Southfork', in M. J. Arlen (ed.), *The Camera Age*, Farrar, Straus & Giroux, New York, 1981.
40 Johnston, 'Crossroads . . .', p. 11.
41 Modleski, 'The search for tomorrow . . .', p. 14.
42 H. Newcomb, 'Texas: a giant state of mind', *Channels of Communication*, April/May, 1981, p. 41.
43 Newcomb, *TV: The Most Popular Art*, p. 178.
44 Brunsdon, 'Crossroads . . .', p. 36. The concepts cultural competence and cultural capital are borrowed from Pierre Bourdieu.
45 P. Brooks, 'The melodramatic imagination. The example of Balzac and James', in D. Thornburn and G. Hartman (eds), *Romanticism. Vistas, Instances, Continuities*, Cornell University Press, Ithaca/London, 1973, p. 218.
   See also P. Brooks, *The Melodramatic Imagination*, Yale University Press, New Haven, 1976.
46 Brooks, 'The melodramatic imagination', p. 219.
47 ibid., p. 211.
48 V. Morin, 'The television serial: life in slow motion', in *Il Feuilleton in Televisione*, RAI, Venice, 1977, p. 48.
49 Cf. Brunsdon, 'Crossroads . . .'; according to Brunsdon soap opera demands cultural competences which in our culture are mainly possessed by women.
50 But each person acquires so many divergent experiences and impressions that it is impossible to process them all in a theoretically consistent and logical system. On the contrary, the daily

consciousness does not concern itself with (rational) logic. Antonio Gramsci pointed this out in his notes on 'common sense': A. Gramsci, *Selections from the Prison Notebooks*, Lawrence & Wishart, London, 1973.

51 Barthes, *The Pleasure of the Text*, p. 52.
52 ibid., p. 61.

Chapter 3

1 For a more general view of the negative reception by European intellectuals of the rise of American popular culture after the Second World War, see D. Hebdige, 'Towards a cartography of taste, 1935–1962', *Block*, no. 4, 1981, pp. 39–56.
2 J. Bardoel, J. Bierhoff, B. Manschot, P. Vasterman, *Marges in de media*, Het Wereldvenster, Baarn, 1975, pp. 58–9.
3 T. Eagleton, 'Ideology, fiction, narrative', *Social Text*, no. 2, 1979, p. 64.
4 For an evaluation of mass culture theories, see A. Swingewood, *The Myth of Mass Culture*, Macmillan, Basingstoke, 1977.
5 In *De Volkskrant*, 14 November 1981 (my italics).
6 M. Foucault, *L'Ordre du discours*, Gallimard, Paris, 1971.
7 S. Freud, *Jokes and the Relationship to the Unconscious*, Penguin, Harmondsworth, 1976, p. 232.
8 G. Therborn, *The Ideology of Power and the Power of Ideology*, Verso, London, 1980, p. 27.
9 ibid., p. 28.
10 For a more general survey of populism see E. Laclau, *Politics and Ideology in Marxist Theory*, Verso, London, 1977, chapter 4.
11 The difference between practical ideology and theoretical ideology is made *inter al.* by L. Althusser in *Philosophie et philosophie spontanée des savants*, Maspero, Paris, 1974. The Gramscian distinction between 'philosophy' and 'common sense' also links up with this.
12 Compare Bourdieu, 'The aristocracy of culture', pp. 243–4.
13 Frankie Goes To Hollywood, *Welcome to the Pleasure Dome*, Island, 1984.
14 Bourdieu, 'The aristocracy of culture', p. 237.

Chapter 4

1 See Seiter, 'Men, sex and money in recent family melodrama'.
2 See Modleski, 'The search for tomorrow . . .'.

3 These figures come from an enquiry by the Department for Viewing and Listening Research of the Dutch Broadcasting Foundation (May 1982).

4 ibid.

5 T. Modleski, *Loving with a Vengeance. Mass-Produced Fantasies for Women*, Shoe String Press, Hamden, 1982,/Methuen, London, 1984, p. 14.

6 Feuer, 'Melodrama, serial form and television today'.

7 ibid., p. 15.

8 E. Seiter, 'Eco's TV guide – the soaps', *Tabloid*, no. 5, winter 1982, p. 4.

9 For an analysis of the narrative strategies of the popular romantic novel, see Modleski, *Loving with a Vengeance*, chapter 2.

10 M. Barrett, 'Feminism and the definition of cultural politics', in R. Brunt and C. Rowan (eds), *Feminism, Culture and Politics*, Lawrence & Wishart, London, 1982, p. 56.

11 ibid., p. 57.

12 T. Lovell, 'Ideology and Coronation Street', in Dyer *et al.*, *Coronation Street*, p. 51.

Index

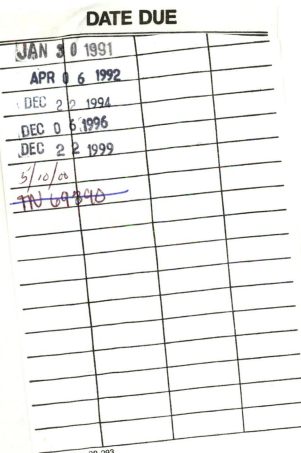